LOCOMOTIVE
· PORTFOLIOS ·

THE

TURBOMOTIVE STANIERS ADVANCED PACIFIC

THE
TURBOMOTIVE STANIERS ADVANCED PACIFIC

TIM HILLIER-GRAVES

PEN & SWORD
TRANSPORT

For my father and uncle, without whom this book would not have been written.

Their influence on my life has been immense.

Ronald Hillier (1922–1984).　　　Bernard Graves (1926–1993).

Pictures taken in the 1940s when they both came into contact with Turbomotive

First published in Great Britain in 2017 by
Pen & Sword Transport

An imprint of Pen & Sword Books Ltd
47 Church Street, Barnsley, South Yorkshire S70 2AS

ISBN 978 1 47388 574 5

Pen & Sword Books Ltd incorporates the imprints of Pen & Sword
Archaeology, Atlas, Aviation, Battleground, Discovery, Family History,
History, Maritime, Military, Naval, Politics, Railways, Select, Social History,
Transport, True Crime, and Claymore Press, Frontline Books, Leo Cooper,
Praetorian Press, Remember When, Seaforth Publishing and Wharncliffe.

For a complete list of Pen & Sword titles please contact
Pen & Sword Books Limited
47 Church Street, Barnsley, South Yorkshire S70 2AS England
E-mail: enquiries@pen-and-sword.co.uk
Website: www.pen-and-sword.co.uk

Design and typesetting
by Juliet Arthur, www.stimula.co.uk

Printed and bound by Replika Press Pvt. Ltd.

CONTENTS

COVER PHOTO:
Turbomotive at speed. (RO)

BACK COVER TOP:
Gleaming and ready for her first day of service. Euston –
June 1935. (LMS/AE)

BACK COVER LOWER:
6202 modified, gets right of way and moves off, her
fireman getting ready for more hard work. (AE/RH)

ACKNOWLEDGEMENTS

This story is as much the product of my late father and uncle's research as mine. It would be wonderful if they were still here to enjoy the fruits of this work. I hope they would think I have brought Turbomotive to life, albeit in spirit only. This book is dedicated to them and all the people who brought this locomotive alive, in reality, and contributed to this story, some of whom I was privileged to meet, though often too young to question them on so many subjects in which they were experts. They are: Roland Bond, H.A.V. Bulleid, Ernest Cox, George Cowper, Bill Darton, George Dowler, Laurie Earl, Alfred Ewer, Sir Harold Hartley, John Hughes, Dr Frederick Johansen, Eric Langridge, Ossie Nock, Robert Riddles, Arthur Roberts, Sir William Stanier, Bill Starvis and Bishop Eric Treacy. Permission to use material they hold and their memories of Turbomotive and their friends and colleagues is greatly appreciated.

I thank the staff at the National Railway Museum and the Institution of Mechanical Engineers for their help in finding material relating to the development of steam turbines and 6202 specifically. The National Archives, through their marvellous and growing online 'Discovery' programme, also illuminated many aspects of turbine development. These three institutions supplemented or confirmed the accuracy of the considerable amount of papers, correspondence and photographs my uncle and Alfred Ewer, late Locomotive Superintendent for Camden and Willesden from 1935–1947, had collected over many decades. In due course these collections will be donated to Search Engine at the NRM for the benefit of future generations.

The photographs in this book come from many sources. They are credited as follows: Ronald Hillier (RH), Bernard Graves (BG), Alfred Ewer (AE), Laurie Earl (LE), Sir William Stanier (WS), Frederick Johansen (FJ), Bishop Eric Treacy (ET), Metropolitan Vickers (MV), BR LM (BR), PR Dep't of the London, Midland and Scottish Railway (LMS), Rail Photo Prints (RP), Rail Online (RO), Roland Bond (RB), Robert Riddles (RR), Sir Harold Hartley (HH) and the author.

Copyright is a complex issue and often difficult to establish, especially when the same photos exist in a number of collections, both public and private. Strenuous checks have been made to ensure each picture has been correctly attributed, but no process is flawless, particularly when most of the pictures are more than 70 years old and the photographers long gone. If an error has been made, it is unintentional. If any reader wishes to affirm copyright, please contact the publisher and an acknowledgement will be made in any future edition of the book, should a claim be proven. We apologise in advance if a mistake has been made.

A number of official documents are quoted in this book. My thanks to the National Archives and the National Railway Museum for giving me permission to include this material.

It is a fact that historians will sift through many items from many sources in an effort to present an honest and accurate account. But sometimes 'evidence' can be misleading or contradict other sources of information. All a writer can do is try to reach an unbiased view of all this material and present a picture and an interpretation that, on the balance of probability, best reflects what really happened. One thing is certain – there will always be gaps in any story and there will always be disagreements over interpretations or technical assessments. I hope false trails have not led me from a truthful path and that I have told Turbomotive's story as accurately as possible.

INTRODUCTION

Turbomotive in her prime. (AE/RH)

I was born in my grandfather's house to the sounds of steam engines passing by. I grew up in a household where trains were part of life – for work, for holidays and the sense of history they provoked. There were cars and buses, but the world still moved to the rhythm of steam power, arousing the passions and sensibilities of those who had the eye to see and the wisdom to understand this heartbeat of life.

Three generations lived in my grandfather's house and each life had been affected by steam locomotives. They had taken my grandfather to the trenches and brought him home again a badly damaged man. They had taken my father, mother and uncle to another war. Each witnessed horrors, but each returned safely. They took them to work, to the shops and to the seaside, and now they took me.

My father and my uncle were children of the 1920s and grew to be enquiring schoolboys in the 1930s when the press saw and recorded tantalising new inventions. Sleek monoplane aircraft flew, prestigious new ships appeared in Britain's shipyards, Malcom Campbell broke speed records, Alan Cobham's 'Flying Circus' thrilled crowds around the country and modern, streamlined locomotives set in motion an exhilarating competition between railway companies. Young and old alike were captivated. Newspapers headlined the advances, and the *Meccano Magazine, Wonders of Science, Railway Wonders of the World* and many more periodicals gave wonderful insights into these changes. Pictures, articles and cigarette cards were collected and scrapbooks assembled by both boys. One favoured the London Midland Scottish Railway, the other the London North Eastern Railway. Just as one favoured Derby County and aeroplanes, the other fancied Tottenham Hotspur and tanks. In the war that followed one flew fighters with the Royal Navy and the other drove tanks.

When the war ended their interest remained, and when Hornby Dublo produced locomotives again in 1947, they were first to their local train shop to buy models – a red *Duchess of Atholl* and a blue *Sir Nigel Gresley*. When they both died, one in 1984 and the other in 1993, these locos and

their other boyhood collections came to me, but so did much more.

My grandfather's house backed onto a section of the old Great Eastern Line, as it wound through North London. N7 tank engines pulled commuter traffic back and forth to Liverpool Street Station day and night, with freight trains filling in gaps. As I learnt to walk my unsteady legs carried me to the back fence, full of wonder each time I heard a train approaching. In the summer, as children enjoyed the long holiday, a grimy old freight locomotive would often stop at signals right behind my house and the driver or fireman slip down from the cab and place warning detonators under the wheels to amuse their young audience. The children loved the explosions and ran shouting to their homes excited by this unexpected entertainment.

My uncle often took me on trips to Liverpool Street Station, King's Cross and Euston to watch the trains and share our joint passion. My memories of this are hazy, but strong impressions of smoke, noise, steam and the bustle of a busy station remain.

A move to Surrey and the land of electric trains did not break my fascination with railways. Hamleys in Oxford Street on my fifth birthday, in 1956, gave me my first train set and even the sight of Marilyn Monroe, who was in London filming *The Prince and the Showgirl* and attending a Royal Premier that evening, did not distract me.

Living close to Nine Elms, which my father and I often visited, a

work friend and keen amateur photographer having an open pass to visit the sheds, brought me in contact with Oliver Bulleid's Pacific locomotives and a new passion began. But by now steam locomotives were giving way to diesel and electric traction and my life up to the age of 17 witnessed their slow death. In these years I often visited sheds across London, down as far as Bath and Bristol, stood on draughty platforms at Wimbledon, Salisbury, Harrow, Finsbury Park and Hadley Wood with my camera, and saw these wonderful machines streak by. Their absence has not reduced my fascination.

Contact with my uncle was important. We were similar in many ways and since he didn't have children of his own, we formed a strong bond and locomotives were one strand. He understood my interests and helped sustain them. Our conversations and visits, books, documents, photographs arriving by post at regular intervals and contact with those who worked on footplates or in running sheds became a feature of our relationship. And when he died all his model locomotives, albums, paperwork and souvenirs came to me.

My father also played a crucial part in developing my love of engineering, railways and flying. He was a naval aviator who became a mechanical engineer, in peacetime. His career, designing complex machines for the printing industry around the world, meant that signs of his work were around me as I grew up. Even during his rare

6202 slightly modified and at full speed. (AE/RH)

periods of sick leave he would be found turning a Meccano set from a box of parts into a replica of a printing press and then running paper through its rollers. His knowledge and skill fascinated me. Sadly, these abilities were not passed on, but he understood and always tried to explain complex engineering ideas. In the same way, he instilled a love of history in me.

In 1944 he travelled to Canada by convoy from Liverpool, on board the converted liner *Ille de France*. His journey, as a young Fleet Air Arm officer, began at Euston and the boyhood interest in trains returned briefly as he walked along the carriages to see which locomotive would be leading him. Later in his first-class seat he recorded, '15 carriages, all packed, pulled by 6202 Turbomotive'.

Three years later, as his naval career ended, he was again pulled by 6202 on a journey north, now in peacetime with many services lost in the war restored: the luxury of dining cars, white tablecloths and menus to be enjoyed before a return to civilian life and the loss of officer status. He kept the menu as a souvenir, scribbling along the top 'Pulled by Turbomotive.'

When my father died in 1993 I found the menu, his letters and childhood collection of cigarette cards and newspaper cuttings. Turbomotive featured large and I realised how strongly his Hornby Dublo model of *Duchess of Atholl* resembled 6202. His love of engineering and sense of mechanical aesthetics seemed aroused by this experimental and unique engine and among his possessions this theme was clear.

Nine years earlier my uncle had died, still living in the house in which I was born. The trains passing by were now electric. A few weeks after the funeral his widow, a sad ill-balanced soul, asked me if I would like my uncle and my grandfather's 'things`. When I arrived she had set them up around the living room as though in a shop, with prices scribbled on poorly cut pieces of paper. It was a very sad scene as she showed me round, occasionally stopping to encourage me to buy something. Of course, I bought everything and paid the 'correct amount'. Ten box-loads of books, photographs, documents, magazines, newspapers and other material were packed into my car. I was too sad to do anything but store the boxes safely in my parents' attic until able to sort through them.

Pressures of life and family meant that this did not happen for more than twenty years. It was only

tackled because of my mother`s move to a nursing home in 2005 and the impending sale of her house. What I found surprised me and, strangely, some things were tied closely to the few possessions that came to me after my father`s death. Locomotives were a common thread, but so was Turbomotive. Although they had grown up in different parts of London and did not know each other until 1947, they had both followed the development and service of this engine in the 1930s – the same press cuttings, cigarette cards and photographs. My uncle had added much more, some collected during his many trips to engine sheds and works. With no family he had had the time, energy and finances to follow his interests and here were the fruits of his work. Last, but not least, he had documented the Harrow rail disaster of 1952, where Turbomotive`s operational life ended.

They left me a rich legacy: a love of locomotives and engineering and a sense of history. When writing the story of this engine I sensed their hands guiding me.

There have been many references to 6202 since construction in 1935 and many renowned engineers and railway historians have analysed her development and operational performance. However, these are often academic accounts and do not place the loco`s history in the broader context of time and place. Engineers have concentrated on the complexities of design and construction; historians on timings and performance. Between the two

we have many more areas to understand. The lives of the men who built her and those who rode on her footplate. The conflicting economics of business and scientific advance. The work of the LMS Publicity Department, which took such pains to make sure that 6202 remained in the public eye for so long. The decision to rebuild the loco to a more traditional form. The Harrow disaster, its aftermath and much more.

There are many threads, and when drawn together they pay tribute to the efforts of so many people of different skills, backgrounds and responsibilities. This gives a clearer understanding of their efforts and the problems they faced in making sure one locomotive and a whole diverse network ran successfully.

One image of Turbomotive has stayed with me for most of my life. As a small child struggling with reading in a typical 1950s primary school class of nearly fifty children and failing badly, I looked for any encouragement I could find. *Janet and John* books were our staple reading diet and my classmates seemed to leap ahead of me in comprehending their words. In my confusion I tended to focus on the pictures, passing the interminable hours imagining a life outside the drab interior of the classroom. In one book I was delighted to find a painting of Janet and John looking up and admiring a blue Turbomotive passing across a nearby bridge. This picture sits with me now.

CHAPTER 1

CENTRAL HALL EUSTON
(6 NOVEMBER 1952)

t had been nearly a month since the rail disaster at Harrow, but the horror of that day had not diminished. Physical wounds had begun to heal, but the mental anguish remained. Each morning would bring constant reminders of what had happened, the terrible sights witnessed and the loss of 112 lives. And, for many, the nights brought little relief.

The investigation had begun within hours of the crash on 8 October. A necessary ritual required by law, but also common humanity. No life should be lost without an understanding of events, an explanation and change, where necessary. Lieutenant Colonel George Wilson, a man of great understanding of railway matters, had been assigned the sensitive and unpleasant task of investigating the accident and had witnessed the human cost of the tragedy, crawling among the wreckage within a few hours of the crash.

As a Chief Railway Inspector with the Ministry of Transport since 1949, he had become used to such horrors, but even he was shocked by the result of three trains colliding in the heart of Harrow and Wealdstone

Station in the space of a few minutes. Even for a veteran of the two world wars this was too much, but he had a job to do and his strong sense of duty and professionalism kept him going.

In the days that followed the accident Wilson, British Rail, the Metropolitan Police and the

Coroner's Office slowly gathered evidence and began the process of evaluation. But there was so much to do. The survivors and relatives of the dead took priority and their predicament demanded time and space to recover. Yet it was among this huge number that the full story

Harrow, 8 October 1952. The scene two hours after the devastating crash. (RH/BR)

The scene of unimagined carnage. (RH/BR)

of what had happened that day lay. Only time and gentle urging would unlock these shocked, uncomprehending minds.

For the moment, Wilson could only cast an experienced eye over physical evidence and draw broad conclusions, hoping that these thoughts would be confirmed when witnesses could be questioned later.

Some facts were quickly uncovered and Wilson wrote a short summary for the Minister of Transport, Alan Lennox-Boyd MP, so that any questions that arose in the House of Commons could be answered:

'Two trains were concerned in the first collision at 8.19 am. The 7.31am local passenger train from Tring to Euston with 9 coaches, hauled by a 2-6-4 tank engine [42389] and the 8.15 pm 11 coach express from Perth to Euston, hauled by a 4-6-2 tender engine [46242 – City of Glasgow]. The third train which ran into the wreckage of the first collision was the 8.0 am from Euston to Liverpool and Manchester; this train was double-headed with a 4-6-0 type engine [45637 – Windward Islands] in front leading a 4-6-2 type engine [46202 – Princess Anne, recently converted from a turbine design] attached to the 15 coaches.

'The local train had crossed from the Up Slow to the Up Fast line at the *country end of the station and had stopped, as booked, at the Up Fast [No 4 Platform]. It had been standing there for about one and a half minutes and the brakes had been released when it was struck heavily at the rear by the Perth Express which had passed the colour light distant signal at caution and two semaphore signals at danger in patchy fog and was travelling at 50-60mph on the Fast Up line.*

'*The resulting wreckage was spread across the adjacent Down Fast line on which the Liverpool express was approaching and the leading engine struck the derailed engine of the Perth train shortly after the first collision. Both the Liverpool train engines were diverted to the left across one of the platforms.*

'*The damage to the three express engines and the local train was exceptional resulting in a casualty list that has only once been exceeded on British railways.*'

A more complete examination had to wait until a full Board of Inquiry could be convened and witnesses sufficiently recovered to face questioning. The earliest this could be achieved was on 15 October and only then with some of the survivors present; others were still hospitalised.

After two days of questioning witnesses and sifting evidence, Wilson felt able to temporarily halt proceedings. There were others to be questioned but they were still too ill to attend. He felt that their statements would not alter the key facts, only add to them. In closing, he took the unusual step of publicly stating that the primary cause of the accident lay in the Perth Express

running past two stop signals at danger. The needs of his political masters, and the clamour of reporters seeking cause and reassurance, meant that he had to offer an explanation and apportion blame as soon as possible.

In the week that followed the accident, the slow process of clearing wreckage went on. All three express locomotives were severely damaged, but until they were free of debris their condition could not truly be assessed. Only three of the six enginemen had survived and two of them were still in hospital. Seeing the condition of all three cabs, it was a wonder that any of them had survived. Even without collision damage, safety on the footplate was easily compromised. Superheated steam, the boiler, many protruding obstacles and the weight of loose coal in the tender made accidents only too frequent.

Of the three locomotives, 46202, *Princess Anne*, seemed the least

damaged, having been protected from the worst of the crash by the leading engine, the Jubilee class *Windward Islands*. She was lifted, set down on the track and then moved to a nearby siding to await assessment. Maintenance crew from nearby Camden Shed, where 46202 was based, thought she might be quickly repaired and returned to traffic. She had, after all, just completed an expensive rebuild and was thought of as a prestigious, even famous locomotive. From her construction in 1935, as an experimental turbine-driven engine, she had attracted a great deal of attention within the railway world and outside it. Few, if any, thought she would be scrapped.

As she languished in a siding awaiting her fate, the public inquiry reconvened at Euston on 6 November, a week after the coroner's inquest had ruled that all the deaths had been accidental. Only one day was set aside to hear the evidence of the

The rail accident inquiry gets underway at Euston. (RH/BR)

Lieutenant Colonel G Wilson (right) questions witnesses and sifts evidence. (RH)

few remaining witnesses Wilson felt could be of use – including two of the surviving engine crew: William Darton, 46202's Driver, and George Cowper, the Fireman on *Windward Islands*.

Both men had travelled to London the day before, Darton from his home in Liverpool and Cowper from a nursing home in Dawlish, and spent the night together at the Royal Hotel near Euston. After release from hospital, each man had been on sick leave due to their injuries and

anxiety caused by the accident, probably not helped by time to think about these events. Their thoughts, as they waited to be interviewed, are not recorded, but one can assume they both felt nervous about facing the inquiry. Across the table in Central Hall they would see a panel of eleven senior managers from the Inspectorate and British Rail, but they did have the support of their Trade Union representatives.

Wilson was expert in dealing with people in stressful situations

and guided each man through their testimony. In the words, recorded by a stenographer, the calmness of his questioning coaxed out the horror of that day's events, but also recorded a reticence very common in those days. William Darton gave evidence first:

Lieutenant Colonel George Wilson – 'Before I ask you how you are feeling I must give you my congratulations on your escape. How are you getting on?'

William Darton – 'Pretty well sir, but my hand is very sore.'

GW – 'You had your thumb badly torn I think?'

WD – 'Yes.'

GW – 'How are you feeling generally?'

WD – 'Pretty fair, sir, under the circumstances.'

GW – 'Have you a lot of pain?'

WD – 'Just the soreness, but apart from that I'm not doing too badly.'

GW – 'Are you still in hospital?'

WD – 'I am on leave for a fortnight, but I have to return for further treatment.'

GW – 'Did you work a train up to London on the day before the accident?'

WD – 'Yes the 2.0pm from Lime Street.' [and lodged in London overnight].

GW – 'I know there's not much you can tell me about this accident, but did you see anything in front of you as ran through Harrow?'

WD – 'Nothing whatever. The engine was taken completely out of my hands.'

GW – 'Were you looking out?'

WD – 'Yes, on the left hand side.'

[On the opposite side of the loco from the point of contact, where the long boiler, the leading engine and the gentle curve of the track into the station obscured his view ahead.]

GW – 'You did not see anything ahead of you for a second?'

WD – 'No, everything was going very smoothly, I thought we were in for a nice trip.'

GW – 'At what pace were you going?'

WD – 'About 50mph, I should think.'

GW – 'Might it have been a little more?'

WD – 'It might have been at that point.'

GW – 'You had a big train with two engines?'

WD – 'We would not have been overloaded by ourselves.'

Darton could not hide his sense of pride in driving 46202. As a 52-year-old driver he had progressed through cleaning and firing engines since the 1920s and he valued the qualities of this magnificent loco and appreciated its status.

GW – 'Yes, I understand; the other engine was "assisting, not required". So you had plenty of power in front of that train? And you had a little bit of a late start owing to some vacuum trouble?'

At this point Mr J. Knight, the Carriage and Wagon (C&W) Engineer, interjected: 'The hosepipe at the rear of the train was not properly seated on the plug, and it had to be held down whilst a vacuum was created.'

GW – 'I suppose you were trying to recover a bit of time?'

WD – 'I made it a 4 minute late start. I opened the regulator and said to my mate 8.4am. It was 8.13 when we passed Willesden and we had picked up a minute and another minute when we had passed Sudbury. We could not help picking up time with the power we had.'

GW – 'What was the visibility like that morning?'

WD – 'When we left the shed and were on our way to Euston station we were stopped by signals for 5 minutes approaching the station, and then I got the main signal. I judged the visibility at the time to be 500 or 600 yards. I could see right down that engine line and did not think it that bad.'

Frequent heavy, often impenetrable fogs were a very common feature of life then. Coal was the main fuel and its effect could be devastating during the autumn and winter months. Within a few days of this Inquiry being held, London and the Home Counties were hit by a smog that lasted days and brought the city to a virtual standstill. Small wonder that the railways were so badly affected.

GW – 'What was it like near Harrow?'

WD – 'The sun was coming through and I remarked to my fireman it was going to be a nice day, but I did not see much of it unfortunately.'

GW – 'The fog didn't cause you any trouble in seeing the signals? By all accounts it was clearing at Willesden. There was a patch of fog or mist around Hatch End and Harrow. You never saw anything in front of you, running into Harrow?'

WD – 'None whatever (in both cases)'

GW – 'Were you knocked unconscious?'

WD – 'No sir.'

GW – 'How long were you there before they got you out?'

WD – 'Not many minutes. I got myself out, then a policeman took charge of me. The first thing I said was, "Is anybody protecting the opposite running line?" There was a chap there, I think he was a Booking Clerk and he said everything was alright and told me to come with him. I didn't know where the other driver was although I asked after him.

George Dowler, 46202's fireman on 8 October caught in the full glare of publicity during the first phase of the inquiry. (RH)

[Driver Albert Perkins, who was in charge of *Windward Islands*, had been killed when the collision took place].

GW – 'Did the coal come down on top of you?'

WD – 'Yes, we had a good load of coal on, and that is what injured my hand when I put it over my head.'

GW – 'Are you in the usual express link from Liverpool to London and how often do you get to London with fast trains?'

WD – 'No I am a spare driver, but I have had pretty good experience for the last 8 or 9 years with fast trains.'

GW – 'If you are driving on the Up Main running down from Watford through Harrow and Wealdstone, what sort of regulator opening do you generally keep?'

WD – 'I nearly always work on the first regulator if possible.'

GW – 'And your gear?'

WD – 'According to speed.'

Wilson, with an experienced driver before him, was drawing on his knowledge to see if custom and practice of express crews dictated a particular approach to this length of line by trains from the North. Wilson was trying to get into the mind of the deceased driver on the Perth to Euston Express to understand his actions. He went on:

GW – 'Do you often coast down from taking water at Bushey?'

WD – 'It is according to the time. If we are running to time and doing alright, then I can let the engine run itself. If we are behind time we endeavour to keep a bit of speed up.'

A few more questions followed, but it was clear that Darton could add little more to the discussion, although he did confirm that he saw the signals clearly as he approached Harrow from Euston. He also confirmed that he was not working 46202 very hard and she was running well.

George Cowper, the Fireman on *Windward Islands*, could add very little when questioned, having been knocked unconscious when the trains collided. When he came to he found that he had been thrown from the engine's cab and was lying on *Princess Anne's* nameplate, badly cut about the head and in deep shock.

As the day drew to a close the remaining witnesses gave their evidence and quietly withdrew. There was little doubt now that the driver of the Perth express had lost concentration, missed crucial signals and had no time to slow his engine before the collision, although when his body was found his hand was on the vacuum brake suggesting he had tried to bring the train to a halt. With the driver and fireman dead the reason for this mistake could not be assessed with any accuracy and some of the Inquiry's findings had to be speculative.

So the Inquiry ended and Wilson was left with the task of considering all he had seen and heard and writing his report. Draft versions circulated early in 1953 and the final version was published later that year.

Darton returned to work before Christmas and often wondered about the accident at Harrow. His last sight of engine 46202 on 8 October was a sad, fleeting one as he was taken to hospital for treatment. He felt he was leaving part of himself behind. But like the men who had lifted the wreck, he thought that she should be repaired and was surprised when the recently rebuilt locomotive did not return to traffic. As her last driver he felt some responsibility for the locomotive and a paternal interest in her remained until his death in 1981.

So the wreckage was cleared, the dead were buried, the accident investigated and the survivors returned to their lives, scarred but thankful that the worst was behind them. The three seriously damaged locomotives were transported in pieces to Crewe engine works. *Windward Islands* was quickly deemed beyond repair and soon scrapped, *City of Glasgow* was eventually repaired and returned to service in 1953, but *Princess Anne* languished in the works yard for many months. Repair was possible and many speculated on her future. There was hope that this unique locomotive would be restored to working order and again be seen on her regular run to Liverpool, but this was not to be and she was scrapped in 1954, only her boiler and tender surviving to be used on other locomotives.

A sad end to a life that started in 1935, at Crewe, as an experiment.

CHAPTER 2

SEARCHING FOR THE FUTURE

From 1902 to his retirement in 1922, George Churchward, Chief Mechanical Engineer (CME) of the Great Western Railway Company, had shone a light on the way railways should be run. Innovation and modernisation, matched with common sense and an understanding of business needs, had been his primary aims and the company had benefited greatly from his work. The rest of the railway industry cast envious eyes at the GWR and sought to follow its example.

Even in retirement Churchward took a profound interest in all railway matters and often visited the works at Swindon to see how ideas he had set in motion were progressing. His home became something of a Mecca for his 'old boys', who delighted in his company and sought him out to discuss ideas forming in their own minds. Even in old age, and a decade after his retirement, Churchward's opinions and advice were greatly valued. But all this came to an end suddenly and very violently on a foggy December morning in 1933, in his 77th year. As was his habit, he took a shortcut to the Swindon Works nearby, from his GWR-owned home, along the main line, did not hear an approaching train and was struck by the late running 08.55 Paddington to Fishguard express.

Three days later, on 22 December, his coffin was drawn along Swindon's streets before a crowd of thousands to Christ Church where the Bishop of Barking performed the committal:

'So we take leave of George Jackson Churchward. His influence will still live amongst us. You are the richer for having had him amongst you for nearly 60 years. You cannot all emulate his achievement, for there are diversities in human life, but you can all emulate his sense of duty and his interest in the service of his fellow men.'

Such was his reputation and influence that the funeral was attended by GWR's senior managers and many other noteworthy people. But two of the principal mourners were William Stanier and Nigel Gresley, men who were disciples of Churchward and now had the power to continue his work, as CMEs of the London, Midland and Scottish Railway (LMS) and London and North Eastern Railway (LNER) respectively. On such a sad occasion

George Jackson Churchward. (WS)

their thoughts must have turned to the part Churchward had played in their industry, but also their memories of such an influential man. Some considered his time as the GWR's CME had been a golden age for that company and, by association, railway development across the country. Stanier and Gresley recognised this and were themselves ushering in a new golden age for steam locomotion. Funerals are about the past and celebrating

William Stanier. (HH)

Josiah Stamp. (HH)

the lives of those who have died, but the future will always loom large and the conversations of these two men, on that cold December day in Swindon, would have been fascinating to hear.

Although each of the four railway companies formed in 1922/23, from a plethora of smaller businesses, were in competition and loath to share anything that might give the other an advantage, their designers belonged to a much bigger world. Some described this as a brotherhood of engineers, where knowledge was pooled for the common good of science. Competition existed and each tried to be the first to develop and initiate new ideas, then publish the results in learned journals, but each was aware that invention and improvement were often collective in nature. Science is full of examples of unrelated inventions that might lay dormant for years suddenly being brought into focus by a seemingly unrelated development; locomotive design benefited greatly from this collective approach.

Engineers from all industries around the world had the focal point of the Institution of Mechanical Engineers, based in London, to develop their ideas and make them public. Also, locomotive designers had the Institution of Locomotive Engineers to meet their more specific needs. Stanier and Gresley, as did most engineers in their industry, belonged to both and became leading lights in each institution.

After long apprenticeships at increasingly senior levels in the GWR and Great Northern Railway (GNR), each man had risen to greater prominence in the years after the First World War, a time of austerity and gloom as most families recovered from the deepest of traumas. The railways had been heavily used in the war and were in a dilapidated state, but the level of investment needed to restore the system to pre-war standards was not forthcoming as the country struggled to meet its debts. In many ways its condition matched the war-weary population and its returning soldiers. But as the 1920s passed and gave way to the 1930s, the effects of the war lessened, some optimism returned and, helped by low interest rates and negative inflation, there was an easing of financial pressures. Even though unemployment hovered about 20 per cent and the economy was not booming, businesses and those in work felt they had more money to spend. But more importantly, confidence in society and the future was returning after years of suffering and depression. As the 1930s progressed this hope translated itself in many ways and through many levels of society, not least of all on railways where passenger numbers and the volume of freight traffic increased.

With the grouping of railway companies had come a realisation that much of the rolling stock, particularly locomotives, barely met current needs let alone future demand, except the GWR, where Churchward's influence had forced change decades earlier. The LMS, the largest of the four new companies, was, probably, in the worst condition. The LMS had inherited more than 10,300 engines from its many constituent companies. Many were elderly and inefficient and badly in need of replacement. There was also a huge variety of types and power output, reflecting the needs of individual businesses. Also, there was little commonality of spares, maintenance programmes or running practices.

Change was inevitable, but with limited funds and many complex problems to solve the company looked for strong, modernising leadership. The LNER appointed Gresley as their first CME in 1923. He quickly put together a formidable team of engineers and soon began the process of shaping the LNER into a modern, commercially viable railway. The LMS, as the decade ended, was still struggling to make progress and looked for leaders of vision and determination.

In 1926 the company found the first of these leaders, when Josiah Stamp was recruited as President. It was an unusual appointment for the time. He had no railway background, but was an economist of great repute, a tax expert and a director of Nobel Industries, which gave him experience of industry and its needs. A year later he was also appointed Chairman and stepped up the speed of the LMS's transition, importing many new business practices into an often archaic organisation. He also made many staff changes and recruited people he thought better able to manage business needs more successfully. In

1930 he engaged Sir Harold Hartley, an eminent physical chemist and Fellow of the Royal Society, as Vice President and Director in charge of scientific research. Both men appreciated that the company needed a railway expert to supplement their own skills and looked for a suitable candidate to appoint as CME, the pivotal post in modernisation. They inherited many highly qualified engineers from the constituent companies, but they feared that they might be tainted by past allegiances. An external search brought William Stanier's name to the fore.

Stanier was a Swindon man in all respects. He was born in the city, and his father was a lifetime employee of the GWR. He himself joined the company in 1892, aged 15, as an office boy before taking up an apprenticeship in the works shortly after his 16th birthday, which he completed in 1897. Rapid promotion followed, guided by Churchward, and by 1906 he was Divisional Locomotive Superintendent at Swindon. On his mentor's retirement, and following grouping, he became Principal Assistant to the CME, C.B. Collett, Churchward's replacement, who was only slightly older than Stanier so was unlikely to relinquish the post in his favour before the younger man's own retirement. At this point Stamp and Hartley entered Stanier's life.

Lunch at the Athenaeum Club in London with Hartley, and Ernest Lemon, the LMS's current CME, followed in October 1931, at which Stanier was interrogated about

Harold Hartley. (HH)

locomotive design. Clearly impressed by what he heard and already knew, Hartley, with Stamp and Collett's approval, met Stanier for lunch again, this time at the Travellers Club, and offered him the post of CME, succeeding Lemon who would become a company vice president. For many men this task would have seemed an impossible one and, before accepting, Stanier closely questioned both Stamp and Hartley about their expectations and the targets they had set, principally the standardisation of locomotives and production of more powerful

Ernest Lemon. (HH)

his work at Swindon, with Collett's approval, such was the strength of professional bonds that existed between these engineers. The GWR influence would soon be felt at all the establishments Stanier managed.

Time was pressing and in the months that followed his appointment Stanier had quickly to introduce new working practices and fashion a design team capable of meeting the company's needs. But he was not oblivious to the history of the LMS and its many constituent parts and submerged himself in the culture of all he saw at the main centres of work: Euston, Crewe and Derby. He wanted to merge the best of what the company could offer with the new. Among all these important tasks one primary need stood out: to build a new class of express locomotive capable of pulling 500 ton loads unassisted on nonstop runs of 400 miles or more. His and Lemon's predecessor, Henry Fowler, had seen 4-6-0 type engines as the solution and work had commenced building the Royal Scot and Patriot Classes. Stanier believed that they would not have the power or endurance required and proposed a 4-6-2 design instead, mirroring the LNER in its development of Pacific Class locomotives through the 1920s into the new decade, to pull express trains along its East Coast route to Scotland.

His own experience of the type was limited. In 1908 Churchward and the GWR developed a single Pacific Class locomotive as an experiment. It was a wholly new concept in Britain, although quite common overseas, and the GWR produced a sound design, but later rejected it in favour of 4-6-0 classes, as these met the company's needs more effectively. *The Great Bear*, as the loco was named, ran until 1924, when it was converted to 4-6-0 form. Stanier had been part of its development and had been impressed by its potential and now saw this type of locomotive as the answer to the LMS's shortage of motive power.

A design was produced and Board approval to build a batch of three engines was given. Churchward's influence was clear from the start, with four cylinders, a wide firebox and a large tapered boiler incorporated in the design, but, in reality, it was a new engine that had benefited from lessons learnt elsewhere, not a copy.

In the months after his departure Stanier kept in close contact with his mentor in Swindon and often visited Churchward at his home. Although ageing rapidly, hard of hearing and with deteriorating eyesight, Churchward maintained an active interest in locomotive design. He liked nothing more than to discuss new developments and the two men spent many hours lost in deep conversation about the past and future. Undoubtedly Stanier would have mentioned his new locomotive and sought the older man's views on this design and his recollections of his own work in this field. These regular visits went on until Churchward's death. His pride in the younger man's achievements was often expressed, as was the

engines. The great progress made by the GWR in these areas was clearly not lost on either of them and they saw Stanier, one architect of Swindon's success, as being the man to achieve these goals for the LMS.

He accepted their offer and began work at Euston on 1 January 1932, quickly immersing himself in the many issues facing this awakening giant. He seems to have been undaunted by the challenge and arrived bearing many plans and documents that had been central to

GWR influence that was directing so much of what the LMS was achieving.

While being built, the editor of the *Railway Gazette* was allowed by Stanier to view all stages of its development at Crewe. His thoughts were recorded in the Gazette on 30 June and must have made satisfying reading for the new CME:

'The engine, in our view, is a credit to everyone concerned in its design and construction…it scores very high marks indeed, and adds something of a definitely outstanding character to the status of modern locomotive practice.

'In the first place it was desired to provide a really large boiler having a wide firebox, affording a grate area of 45 sq ft, a figure not hitherto reached in any British locomotive employed in passenger service. Thus uncoupling trailing wheels become necessary…. The engine is designed to use steam at a high pressure, in four single-expansion cylinders with divided drive, each cylinder having its own independent set of valve motion of the Walschaerts pattern and an 8 inch diameter piston valve with the unusually long travel of 7¼ in.

'The cylinders are exceptionally well designed and particularly so in respect of the steam and exhaust passages… which may be expected to improve still further the cylinder performance. The adoption of four sets of valve gear (one to each cylinder) is another good point, favourably affecting the distribution of steam to the cylinders

'When we turn to the boiler we find much to admire…. Our close inspection during construction left us in admiration of the general excellence of design…. Both the welding and riveting

work are beyond reproach, the type of firebox has everything to commend it, and we expect the boiler to achieve a really high evaporation.

'The tractive effort that the engine will be capable of exerting, namely 40,300 lb at 85% boiler pressure, will serve in good stead in meeting difficult conditions at starting and when moving heavy trains on upgrades, and especially when accelerating to normal speed after being checked or stopped…. It will be noted that each coupled axle carries a load of 22 ½ tons, giving a total adhesion of 67 ½, which should be fully adequate for all requirements.

'We should draw our readers' attention to the design of the coupled wheels, and particularly the liberally proportioned vee-shaped rims, which combined with the fact that the rims and tyres have a width of 5 ¾ in, provide not only increased strength but an excellent bearing surface between the wheel rim and the tyre, increased fastening area, and greater security at a vital point.

'A wise feature in the design is the excellent bracing of the frame plates, particularly in the area covering the grouping of the coupled wheels. Nothing is more likely to set up abnormal wear in the axle boxes or cause them to run hot than whip in the frames at these points. There is little or no chance of this occurring in this new locomotive.

'To sum up, we regard this engine as something of which not only Mr Stanier and his staffs at Derby and Crewe, but also the railway company and directors, may be justly proud.'

A 'good press' was essential. Although CMEs and their staff may have fostered good relations and shared ideas with one another, these

were commercial concerns and a strong business rivalry existed, especially where the companies were in direct competition for trade. The Southern Railway and GWR competed on the lucrative London to West Country lines, and the LNER and LMS went head to head between London, the North and Scotland. So each sought new ways of exploiting their markets. Reliability, convenience and low cost will always be central to passenger needs, but speed and comfort also feature and become compelling selling points, especially in such austere times when aspirations were strong and glamour was at a premium.

The launch of such a powerful locomotive, with the promise of great speed and many benefits for customers, was a public relations opportunity too good to miss. The customers of the 1930s needed more than a basic service and the LNER and LMS took advantage of these ambitions. But Gresley, on the East Coast route, had stolen a march with his new, high-powered Pacifics and planned many more new developments with locomotives and rolling stock. The LMS was catching up, but Stanier and his Board knew they had to exploit each opportunity, and so a race began that only the coming of war in 1939 would end. While it lasted, the rivalry, although seemingly friendly, was intense and pushed design and image to the limit.

In giving the LMS a range of new, more powerful engines, and getting the best from those he had inherited, Stanier and his team drew upon what was best in locomotive design

Henry Guy. (BG)

wheels on curves and prevented oscillation on straight track.

'Then followed a description of his axle-boxes and their lubrication that had done so much to reduce hot boxes on the LMS. He then emphasized the importance of streamlining the steam passages in order to reduce pressure losses to a minimum and to obtain the necessary draught from the blast-pipe with the least loss of energy. This brought him to the front-end design and the need for a testing station in which various combinations of the variable elements in design of boilers, grates and blast pipes could be tested to determine the optimum combination for good steaming and fuel efficiency.'

Hartley knew that the LMS, at that stage, needed someone with these engineering and production skills, not a designer who might lose sight of the company's needs in pursuit of esoteric or unconventional ideas. Let others do this where costly flights of scientific fancy could be absorbed. But Stanier, for all his practical approach to design and construction, was intrigued by the search for new ideas and through his membership of engineering institutions kept in close touch with developments, identifying those that might be of use in his field. His openness to new ideas would soon lead him down an unconventional route.

He relished the contacts he made through these institutions, many leading to lifetime friendships. One of these was Henry Guy, who Stanier met while with the GWR. If Stanier was a practical user of science, Guy was an innovator and inventor.

Born in Penarth in 1887, at 16 years old Guy joined the Taff Vale Railway Company as a pupil to its CME, T. Hurry Riches. After technical college he obtained a scholarship to the University of Wales to study Mechanical, Electrical and Civil Engineering, gaining diplomas in all three subjects. He qualified as a Doctor of Science three years later, being recognised as one of the finest engineering students of his generation, but there was more to him than this, as one contemporary later wrote:

'His ready help to all newcomers was typical of his attitude to young engineers. In fact for a young man he possessed extraordinary vision which made all his colleagues, both young and old, look up to him with something akin to awe.'

Guy was attracted to locomotive engineering but realised that this competitive field did not offer good opportunities for more than a small number of engineers. Instead he believed that steam turbines were the prime mover of the future and specialised in this area of design, in the years leading up to the First World War. His studies soon revealed that success in developing strong, reliable turbines depended on advances in metallurgical science and improvement of ancillary equipment.

In 1910 Guy felt that his academic work would benefit from the experience of industry and he joined the British Westinghouse Company, in Manchester, to continue his research into turbines and develop practical solutions to customer needs. In 1918 he was appointed as Chief Engineer to this company's

worldwide, adapting it to suit the company's specific needs. His skills are best described by Harold Hartley, writing shortly after Stanier's death in 1965:

'He was a devoted, intuitive engineer whose strength lay in his lifelong study and practice of production techniques rather than in outstanding originality or scientific approach.... In 1939, during an address to the Institution of Mechanical Engineers, he revealed something of his design philosophy. Starting with the locomotive as a vehicle he described his design for the leading bogie or pony truck that reduced the flange forces exerted by the coupled

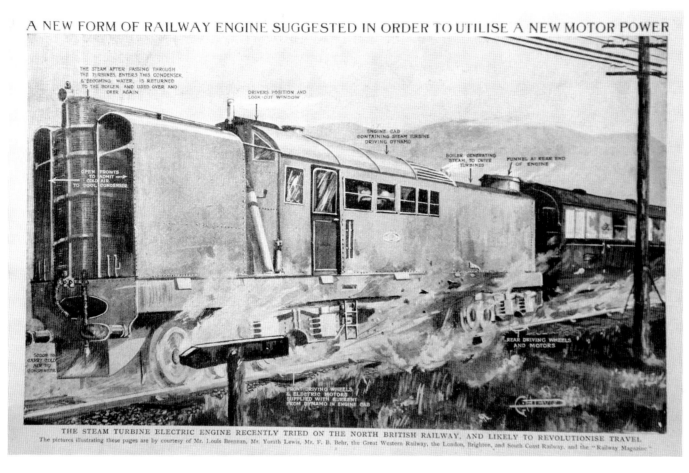

A NEW FORM OF RAILWAY ENGINE SUGGESTED IN ORDER TO UTILISE A NEW MOTOR POWER

THE STEAM AFTER PASSING THROUGH THE TURBINES, ENTERS THIS CONDENSER, & BECOMING WATER, IS RETURNED TO THE BOILER AND USED OVER AND OVER AGAIN

DRIVER'S POSITION AND LOOK-OUT WINDOW

ENGINE CAB CONTAINING STEAM TURBINE DRIVING DYNAMO

BOILER GENERATING STEAM, TO DRIVE TURBINES

FUNNEL AT REAR END OF ENGINE

OPEN FRONTS TO ADMIT COLD AIR TO COOL CONDENSER

REAR DRIVING WHEELS AND MOTORS

DOOR TO CARRY COLD AIR TO CONDENSER

FRONT DRIVING WHEELS & ELECTRIC MOTORS SUPPLIED WITH CURRENT FROM DYNAMO IN ENGINE CAB

THE STEAM TURBINE ELECTRIC ENGINE RECENTLY TRIED ON THE NORTH BRITISH RAILWAY, AND LIKELY TO REVOLUTIONISE TRAVEL
The pictures illustrating these pages are by courtesy of Mr. Louis Brennan, Mr. Yorath Lewis, Mr. F. B. Behr, the Great Western Railway, the London, Brighton, and South Coast Railway, and the "Railway Magazine"

Turbine drive as the future – optimism in the face of escalating costs and mediocre performance. (RH)

successor, the Metropolitan-Vickers Electrical Company. He remained in this post until 1941.

Early in his career Guy became a member of the Institution of Mechanical Engineers and here became acquainted with many railway engineers, including Stanier and Gresley. He later recalled meeting Stanier on many occasions and finding his company both stimulating and challenging. Although his time with the Taff Vale Railway had been brief, he felt a strong link to locomotive

development and in Stanier he found a man with skills and vision similar to his own. A strong bond developed between them and their discussions covered a broad range of scientific subjects. There was a meeting of minds during which Guy explained the potential of his work and impressed Stanier with the depth of his knowledge.

Both men knew that there had been many efforts to build a turbine-powered railway engine, but each had been unable to improve on the performance of more conventional

designs. The first example was designed by Guiseppe Belluzzo in Italy during 1908, his turbine system being grafted onto an old shunting engine. This locomotive had two axles that were not coupled together and each axle was driven through a single mechanical reduction gear by two turbines. Even with uncoupled wheels the behaviour and grip of the locomotive were thought excellent. The coming of war in 1914 brought this research to an end.

In England, during 1910, Hugh Reid and D.M. Ramsey developed a turbo-electric design locomotive, of 4-4-0 + 4-4-0 configuration, weighing 132 tons, for the North British Railway Company. It received little attention and trials proved inconclusive. In 1922 a second turbo-electric locomotive appeared, designed by Ramsey for Armstrong Whitworth. It was tested for eighteen months between Bolton and Southport primarily, pulling empty rolling stock. Its performance was poor with consumption of fuel and water way below expectations. Testing continued into 1923, but despite modifications it did not improve and was withdrawn and written off.

The next experiment, a geared turbine steam locomotive, was designed by Hugh Reid and James Macleod, a turbine expert and friend of Guy, again for the North British Railway. On paper *Challenger*, as the loco became known, seemed to hold out the hope of success and the prototype was completed in time for the 1924 British Empire Exhibition at Wembley, sitting alongside the recently completed LNER Pacific *Flying Scotsman*.

The engine was built on continuous girder frames carrying a boiler, coal bunkers, water tanks, cab, condenser and auxiliary equipment all supported on two 4-4-0 bogies. Many parts came from the company's 1910 experiment. Mainline trials did not start until 1926 and continued up until April 1927, when it suffered axle box problems and then a serious turbine failure. It never ran again and trials by North British ended. One can only assume that the expected benefits did not materialise.

Many engineers felt that the development of steam locomotives had gone as far as it could and all that was left was a series of refinements to known designs and then a mass movement to diesel and electric locomotion would soon follow. But others believed there was more to come and sought new ideas that would evolve steam locomotives still further. Perhaps they were being unrealistic and taking too blinkered a view of steam traction. If so, they could point to the economics of the time as reason for their actions: coal was cheap and plentiful, oil was not; the railway infrastructure was geared to steam and money for new investment was hard to find in a time of austerity. Stanier, ever the realist, saw the future but knew that change would only happen slowly and steam power still had a long way to run before giving way to other forms of power. His conversations with Guy and knowledge of experiments overseas convinced him that steam turbines might increase efficiency still further and this most conventional of engineers considered an unconventional and largely untried concept.

The turbine certainly offered many potential advantages over traditional reciprocating engines. Engineers believed that a steam turbine locomotive would be more efficient pulling heavy loads and burn less coal and use less water. Mechanical simplicity would make maintenance easier and improve reliability. Reciprocating engines exerted far more force or hammer blows down to the track, increasing wear to wheels and shortening the life of the track. The smoother take-up of turbine drive could reduce wheel slip considerably and make the ride on the footplate much more comfortable.

Even very early in development engineers foresaw some problems. They felt that greatest efficiency might only be achieved when pulling heavy loads and with the addition of condensers, which generated a vacuum to absorb the exhaust, but would add too much weight and significantly retard performance. Finally, it was believed that a single turbine could not be designed to run forwards and backwards, so a second unit was needed to make sure that an engine could reverse. Guy, Stanier and engineers in other countries believed these shortcomings could be solved and development work continued, principally in Sweden by the Ljungstrom Company where new steam turbine locomotives evolved.

In 1926 a paper was presented to the Institution of Locomotive Engineers by J.G. Handley, Head of the Mechanical Department of the Argentine State Railway, in which he described a turbine locomotive bought by them to pull very challenging loads:

'The locomotive is designed to haul trains with a maximum wagon load of 700 tons at a speed of 25kph on long gradients of 1%, and the same load at a speed of 65kph if the gradient is only 0.4%. The locomotive is designed for

The Argentine State Railway's foray into turbine development. (RH)

running 800 kilometres without any re-newal of its water or fuel, heavy duty oil.

'The whole performance of the engine may be considered satisfactory, apart from slight difficulties which were encountered.'

In reality the loco offered few advantages over more traditional designs, but engineers in Britain took note of the latest advance and watched developments at Ljungstrom, none more so than at the locomotive firm Beyer, Peacock and Co Ltd. In 1926 a collaborative effort between both companies resulted in another experimental locomotive being built, at a cost of £37,000. This engine ran for the first time in July of that year, followed by trials on the main line from St Pancras to Manchester and Leeds to London. In May 1928 the LMS Drawing Office published the results for two of the Leeds tests:

'On the whole the trains ran well to time. The principal loss of time which can be debited to the engine was due to two stops, totalling 27 minutes, made on 28th March on the 1 in 100 bank out of Sheffield due to a shortage of steam. This was caused by a damper having fallen shut in the air duct connecting the preheater with the ashpan resulting in defective combustion throughout the run. Coal consumption was considerably higher on the return run than on the outward trip and there is no apparent reason for this.

'When in good order the engine showed itself able to keep booked time in all sections. During the tests the engine developed a number of small defects and these affected the fuel consumption and on some occasions the timekeeping.

'In comparison with a 2-6-0 engine, over the same route, the turbine engine used 4% more coal. In water consumption, the saving over the standard engine was considerable, being 83.9% on average.'

Once again the tests showed that turbine engines ran relatively smoothly, but offered no great advantage over more traditional locomotives. But on this occasion the trials were spread over a long period and gave the railways a chance to test the design fully before rejecting it. In reality these engines suffered from two handicaps that were hard to overcome: the need to incorporate a condenser, which was substantial in size and weight and expensive to build and maintain, plus a natural bias against new, unconventional designs among running shed and works staff. On the plus side, this design did add considerably to the ever increasing knowledge of turbines in locomotives and pointed the way for future developments, with Ljungstrom continuing to take the lead.

Meanwhile in Germany, engineers, observing developments elsewhere, also experimented with turbine-driven locomotives. Between 1927 and 1929 Krupp-Zoelly, Maffei and

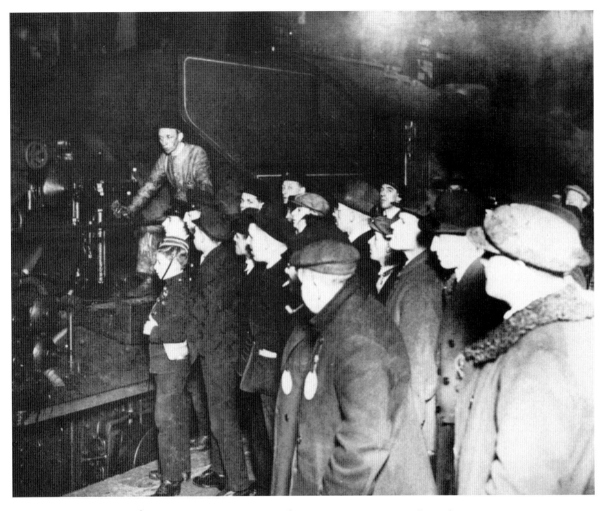

The Beyer Ljungstrom Turbine locomotive draws an interested crowd eager to view this latest development. The young bellboy has achieved pride of place at the front. (AE/RH)

Henschel all produced their own models, but achieved only limited success, with two lasting until 1940 and 1943 respectively, when damaged by bombing, and the third experiment being discarded in 1937.

Ljungstom's designers focused on creating a non-condensing turbine locomotive and during 1931 came up with a workable solution. With Nydquist and Holm of Trollhattan they produced a 2-8-0 turbine locomotive to run alongside a number of 2-8-0 reciprocating engines operated by the Grangesborg-Oxelosund Railway. Stripped of the need to incorporate a condenser, this new locomotive had a balanced, more traditional look. It also weighed substantially less, allowing more generated power to be absorbed in pulling rolling stock, rather than wasted in coping with its own excessive weight.

The engine proved a great success and three were built, remaining in service into the 1950s. They were seen as goods engines primarily, their usual and heaviest work hauling iron-ore trains of 1,750 tons up long inclines of 1 in 100. In service they ran more than 70,000 miles before needing a general repair, compared to the 36,000 miles achieved by the reciprocating 2-8-0s, with a 23.8 per cent fuel saving. With three available, there was an economy of scale in procuring spare parts for the turbines and their ancillary equipment, the rest being shared with the conventional 2-8-0s. So in service they proved very effective and economical to run and were only replaced when diesel locomotives were introduced. All three have been preserved.

The success of these engines was not lost on Henry Guy, who had advised Ljungstrom on turbine development for many years and how they might simplify the design to make it more practical and cost effective. His enthusiasm was infectious and in Stanier he had a willing listener and a man of great practical ability, who had the power to push through new developments. With the LMS committed to designing and building a new fleet of standard locomotives, there was the potential for incorporating new ideas into this substantial building programme. The recent success in Sweden gave fresh impetus to try steam turbines again in Britain, but first the LMS and Stanier had to be convinced of the benefits. So Guy began a campaign of gentle persuasion, at the same time as convincing his own Board of the scheme's potential and the part they might play in a project.

In late 1931 Ljungstrom gave Guy test data and specifications and he did preliminary work on grafting their design onto a suitable British-built locomotive. He was aware, from their discussions, that Stanier was leading his team in designing a new class of Pacific engine and had seen the plans. Modifying an already established type of locomotive presented many difficulties, not least of which was the extent of rebuilding necessary to incorporate a turbine. Taking a loco still on the drawing board, so capable of a redesign without a substantial investment in new equipment and rebuilding, especially one with so much potential as the new Pacific, was attractive.

A man of Guy's influence and experience would not tackle such a project without considering all aspects of design and cost. So when he approached Stanier in 1932 his proposals and analysis quickly bore fruit. The matching of a good idea to chance circumstances has often allowed scientists to make undreamt leaps forward and it seemed that the work of Ljungstrom and Stanier had this potential. No wonder the normally conventional LMS man found the idea attractive. But much remained to be done before either company would approve this new development. Early discussions with their presidents and directors were positive and the project moved into a data-gathering stage, where viability could be gauged. As part of this, Stanier and Guy, on a trip sponsored by Harold Hartley, visited Ljungstrom to see their new locomotives in operation and discuss the design and its potential.

Stanier and Guy were accompanied to Sweden by Herbert Chambers, Stanier's Chief Draughtsman, and Richard Bailey, from Metrovick. Bailey, a locomotive engineer who had specialised in turbine design, had been recruited by the Manchester company shortly after the First World War. In the years that followed he researched the way metals deform over time when under load, especially at very high temperatures. In 1924 the significance of this effect, known as 'creep', on steam turbines was recognised and Bailey's research was directed towards solutions. He realised that creep was not an isolated phenomenon, but had to be linked to other changes in the structure and properties of material. This led to the development and use of improved materials, such as Nickel-chromium-molybdenum, which in turn led to the development of molybdenum-vanadium steel. This material had remarkable creep qualities and greatly enhanced the performance and strength of steam turbines, particularly such a high-performance unit designed for the LMS. His and Guy's development work was crucial to Turbomotive's success.

In advance of their visit, Ljungstrom prepared a briefing pack for Stanier. The front page of one section bore the title 'M.V Lysholm Turbomotive – Operating Instructions'. The title was quickly shortened to Turbomotive, when

Herbert Chambers. (RH)

LMS designers came to describe turbine locomotives in general. In time it would move from plural to singular.

Immediately on their return, Stanier, Guy and Chambers prepared a very detailed case for approval. They were in no doubt

Robert Bailey. (BG)

that their proposals were sound and capable of producing a successful class of locomotives. In early 1933 their paper was submitted. The summary of this seventy-page document reveals the extent of the benefits and recommends a particular course of action:

'The Ljungstrom non-condensing turbine locomotive provides a new prime mover for railways which has the promise of superior economy in fuel and maintenance together with such advantage that may arise from smoother running.

'The precise measure in which these advantages may be realised can be determined only by exhaustive trial and running experience.

'We recommend that such a trial be made by building a 2600 HP Pacific Type locomotive and are of the opinion that to such an extensive user of locomotives as the LMS Rly such an experiment is justified.

'The targets are:
• Reduced coal consumption.
• Reduced consumption of softened water.
• For the same capacity, reduced engine and tender weight.
• Entire absence of hammer blows.
• Completely uniform turning movement and drawbar pull.
• Smooth acceleration from rest.
• Considerably higher sustained drawbar pull.
• Better timings for a particular journey.
• Heavier and faster trains made possible with given limits of axle loading.
• Reduced maintenance and shed hours.'

Stanier and Guy had carefully laid their groundwork and approval was given in February 1933:

'Submitted memorandum (14th February) from the CME and Chief Operating Manager, together with covering memorandum from the Vice-Presidents (Sir Harold Hartley and Mr Lemon) recommending that one of the three four-cylinder 4-6-2 class locomotives, authorised by Mechanical & Electrical Engineering Committee Minute No 142 and Traffic Committee Minute No 3221 of the 27th July 1932, be built as a geared turbine locomotive, in order that comparative trials may be made between this type of driving mechanism and the ordinary reciprocating gear.

'The estimated cost of the new standard engine, without tender, was £8075, and the cost of the same engine fitted with a turbine and gearing, after making allowance for not having to provide cylinders, motion and other standard parts, would be approximately £13500.

'The submission of the proposal had the approval of the Executive Committee, who were of the opinion that it was desirable to investigate this new type of locomotive even if it did not hold out immediate possibilities of financial savings, and whilst the increased costs of interest would be £270 per annum, it is anticipated that there would be a saving of £150 per annum in coal consumption, with additional improvement in performance.'

The tone of this memorandum is cautious, even negative, in the face of Stanier and Guy's optimistic forecast. Hardheaded businessmen and engineers within the LMS would need much more to convince them to invest heavily in a system where success had eluded other designers and their employers. The years ahead would be very challenging.

CHAPTER 3

A LONG BIRTH
(1922–1935)

My father, who was a highly qualified mechanical engineer responsible for many multimillion pound contracts during his career, believed that getting his management board to allow development of a new concept was far easier than delivering a successful product. The promise of significant savings, bigger sales and greater efficiency drew even the most jaundiced opponent of change into his net. The scientific layman could be putty in the hands of a valuable and successful engineer. The trouble is that expectation can run very high and easily turn to severe criticism, especially when the same engineer seeks to journey down a speculative path again. Such is the course of change and innovation.

In their respective companies William Stanier and Henry Guy had, by the weight of their personalities and by exploiting the respect many held for their skills, persuaded sometimes sceptical colleagues to gamble on turbines when success had eluded many other equally accomplished designers for more than two decades. And recent

experimental history, where railway engineers had sought to introduce novel or untried modifications to locomotives, was also against them.

In the late 1920s Nigel Gresley experimented with a high-pressure boiler more usually associated with ships or power stations, and produced a unique 4-6-4 loco, later nicknamed '*Hush Hush*'. The engine had a short and unsatisfactory life

and was rebuilt in a more traditional form in 1935. At roughly the same time Henry Fowler, one of Stanier's predecessors as CME, also experimented with a high-pressure boiler, fitting one to a Royal Scot class engine (named *Fury*). Once again the design proved unsatisfactory, in this case with lethal consequences. While under test the fire suddenly blew back out

Nigel Gresley's experimental 4-6-4, *Hush Hush*, later rebuilt as a conventional albeit streamlined engine.
(Author)

Fury when first built: later converted into a conventional Royal Scot Class engine. (Author)

OPPOSITE:
The Erecting Shop at Crewe, in the mid-1930s, showing the production line techniques adopted by the LMS. (RH/LMS)

of the firebox killing one person and injuring two others on the footplate.

There were other failures, but all areas of science are littered with setbacks and blind alleys. With the benefit of hindsight they will be condemned as wasteful or unproductive by those lacking imagination or ruled solely by the needs of a balance sheet. Yet for every failure there is an advance and no development is devoid of benefit, although this might only be an increase in the pool of collective knowledge that others might use later. Occasionally a designer will stubbornly refuse to drop an idea, even though it is unlikely to show

any benefits. Genius and obsession, as the lives of many creative people can bear witness, are close neighbours in the human spectrum; those blessed with extraordinary skills inevitably have to be handled carefully, if true benefits are to be achieved without damaging the business they are supposed to enhance.

Josiah Stamp and Sir Harold Hartley were in such a position with Stanier. They had carefully selected their man, set him demanding goals and given him the authority and financial freedom to make changes and achieve these objectives. His work was bearing fruit and a new,

improved stable of fine locomotives were appearing, but the development of an experimental engine, in the midst of all this new work, was, to some, an unnecessary distraction. It also seemed incongruous to the long established pattern of life in workshops and offices still living in the past pre-grouping world, where inter-rivalry still existed under the LMS banner.

So the design and building of a turbine locomotive faced many difficulties and a very close watch on this experiment was a natural consequence. For the moment though, Stanier's authority and reputation kept opposition at bay, and a natural curiosity to see what would happen next was part of an engineer's make-up. In this locomotive Stanier embraced a project that brought together many of the problems he faced in giving the LMS new life. It focused attention on the issues that had to be addressed if the company was to meet the challenging goals set by Stamp. What he did with this loco was a microcosm of what he had to do to drag this monolithic company into a new world.

Once the decision to go ahead was given, the design and building teams of both the LMS and Metropolitan Vickers worked together. Stanier and Guy, at the top, were in complete harmony and clear on their targets, but beneath them cohesiveness was less certain. But with the LMS this was a continuing internal problem that years of amalgamation had not settled. In reality much work in bringing these often conflicting groups together had taken place before Stanier's arrival. The main centres of locomotive building and maintenance were the works at Crewe, Derby, Horwich and St Rollox, with Euston as company headquarters. Each had research and development facilities, as befitted their pre-LMS status, and Stamp had brought all these together at Derby. In doing this he strengthened his already well-established credentials as a far-thinking and visionary leader in the world of science. His influence quickly spread and in 1929 he presented a paper entitled *Scientific Research in Transport* to the

Robert Riddles. (RR/LMS)

prototypes, testing new designs using mobile and static equipment, liaising with outside bodies and general engineering issues. It sat alongside the Drawing Office at Derby, but also worked closely with the team at Crewe. So successful was this facility that it lasted longer than the LMS and British Rail, eventually being re-privatised.

Meanwhile at Crewe, where many of the new locomotives would be built, change had been taking place throughout the 1920s; this speeded up with Stamp's appointment. Existing workshops were modified and new buildings appeared, but the biggest changes took place in assembly and repair processes. The car industry in the US led the way in production line assembly techniques and the railways followed suit. The LMS was at the forefront of this work, eventually introducing these principles to their other workshops. Without these advances the LMS would have found it difficult to produce so many new engines in so short a timescale or so cost effectively. As it was, some production work was subcontracted to other companies such as the North British Railway Company and the Vulcan Foundry.

Stanier, as a workshop man, fully appreciated the changes that had taken place, and sought out those responsible for such good work. Of these, the name Robert Riddles came to the fore. Although only in his mid-30s, as Clerk of Works at Crewe he had been placed in charge of this successful reorganisation. He was a

man of exceptional skill and perception and his record of success and innovation recommended itself to Stanier. He was also a product of Crewe, having been apprenticed to the works in 1909, before moving to Derby and then back to Crewe as Assistant Works Superintendent to Frederick Lemon, shortly before Stanier became CME.

Although Stanier was a man of drive and great skill, the size of the task ahead of him meant that he needed effective assistants – men who would embrace change as eagerly as he did and drag along those to whom change was difficult. Undoubtedly Stamp and Hartley would have recommended Riddles to the new CME and on 1 July 1933 he was appointed to Euston as Stanier's Locomotive Assistant. This was an auspicious moment in time because the first of the new Pacifics, 6200 the *Princess Royal*, had just made its appearance and begun tests to prove the value of its design; an event of singular importance to the turbine experiment.

Both men benefited from this relationship. In Riddles, Stanier had a very gifted engineer who he could trust implicitly, and Riddles had a leader of great skill who would teach him much and delegate key areas of work. A lifetime friendship also blossomed. In his biography (by Colonel H.C.B. Rodgers) Riddles described the dynamics of their relationship and touched on Stanier's personality:

'He [Stanier] *trusted everybody and his one fault was a lack of political acumen and he could never imagine any*

influential Institute of Transport. The following year he became the founder of the Advisory Committee on Scientific Research for Railways, in recognition of his great efforts in bringing a unified, more measured approach to railway development.

By the early 1930s this work was bearing fruit and Hartley, under Stamp's guiding hand, set up the LMS Scientific Research Laboratory at Derby, linking it to all research and development functions. By 1933 this impressive facility was operating and its brief was wide. It had responsibility for virtually all technical areas, including metallurgy, aerodynamics, chemical analysis, paint, developing

intrigue against him. But we would talk of such matters and I think that I helped him to a certain extent. I suppose, having experienced first the Lancashire and Yorkshire taking over the London and North Western, and then the Midland taking over the lot, and the intrigue that resulted, I had developed a suspicious mind. I remember him returning from a meeting and saying, "They won't have it, Robert". The matter concerned was fundamental to his position, and I felt that if he gave way he would be surrendering a right inherent to the CME. I talked to the great man, explaining what I meant, whilst he listened staring down at his desk without saying anything. In due course he went home – I not knowing whether he agreed with me or not. In the morning he called me in and said, "It's all right, Robert, they've now agreed".

'He never praised anybody for anything; good results he expected. On the other hand, he could be cutting in his criticism. But he appreciated his staff, and as I got to know him better I realized it was not what he said, but the tone of his voice which gave a clue to his feelings. I came to know him so well that I could tell from his face whether it was wise to say anything or nothing, and no man could have a kinder or more understanding chief.

'I became very close to the Stanier family and frequently visited Newburn, Rickmansworth (their home which was named after Churchward's house at Swindon) …. He was always reading and seldom, if ever, went out to such entertainments as the theatre or cinema. Indeed, his "entertainments" were almost confined to the meetings of the "Mechanicals", to which he was devoted,

and he would delight in discussing technical problems at any time.'

In promoting Riddles to this senior post the vacancy created at Crewe by his departure had to be filled by someone with the same change management skills and the drive to bring new plans to fruition. One candidate, Roland Bond, a product of the Derby engineering apprenticeship scheme, stood out from all others. Although only 28 years old when appointed, his reputation was second to none. A protégé of Henry Fowler, he had specialised in the inspection of locomotives under construction by private companies. He impressed the directors of the Vulcan Foundry so greatly that they recruited him in 1928. But the pull of the LMS was so strong that he returned only three years later becoming Assistant Works Manager at Horwich, where he enhanced his reputation still further, before stepping up to be Assistant Works Manager at Crewe in 1931. With the dynamism of Stanier, Riddles and Bond, under the guidance of a forceful President and Board, the LMS had the key elements it needed to press ahead with modern-isation. But more was needed and other appointments followed.

The role of Chief Locomotive Draughtsman for the LMS was crucial in getting new designs up and running, as well as managing the many modifications necessary to keep a fleet of existing locomotives working effectively. When Stanier arrived from the GWR Herbert Chambers held this position. Like Bond he served his apprenticeship at

Tom Coleman, Stanier's Chief Draughtsman. (RR/LMS)

Derby. He was considered an excellent designer and had successfully managed many projects, but he seemed unable to accept the many changes and innovations being introduced by Stanier and appears to have argued with the CME at length. At a time when Stanier was faced with this huge programme of change, and had few allies, opposition, no matter how well meaning, could not be tolerated for long. At one point Stanier even considered recruiting Sam Ell from the GWR to give more balance, but was thwarted in this by the CME, Charles Collett, at Swindon.

Stanier respected Chambers as a man and an engineer and saw a role for him, but after nearly two years of dispute he needed a slightly more acquiescent, but equally talented replacement. These qualities he found in Tom Coleman, then 50 years old. Having served his apprenticeship at Kerr, Stuart and Co in Stoke on Trent, he joined the North Staffordshire Railway in May 1905, rising to become Chief Draughtsman by the time grouping took place and the LMS came into being. In the years that followed he worked at Derby, Horwich, then back to Derby before transferring to Crewe in 1933 as Chief Draughtsman. His promotion to company Chief Draughtsman in March 1935 was a natural step up in a successful career. In him, Stanier had a natural ally and one who would take new concepts and turn them into working locomotives.

Eager to ensure he did not lose Chambers's undoubted skills, Stanier arranged his transfer to Euston and promotion to Locomotive and Personal Assistant. Chambers was not afraid to ask awkward questions or be a soothsayer, qualities that could prove useful in the battles that lay ahead. There may also have been an element here of keeping Chambers close at hand not only to exploit his undoubted abilities but also curb excessive opposition. Promotion can be a worthy reward, but it can also have the effect of softening the most combative spirit. Sadly, he did not have long to enjoy this new role, dying suddenly in 1937 of a massive heart attack, brought on, some believe, by severe stress.

As the turbine-driven Pacific would be a joint venture between the LMS and Metropolitan-Vickers, the partnership had to be managed carefully, with a successful linkage of staff at all levels. Lines of responsibility had to be drawn and Guy and Stanier spent much time considering how the project should be phased and managed and who should lead, once approval to proceed had been given.

Although Metropolitan-Vickers worked in many spheres of heavy engineering, both electrical and mechanical, a link with another huge company such as the LMS was uncommon. There were usually clear customer–supplier agreements in place for each procurement or a joint venture with smaller companies for experimental work. But here there was a partnership of giants, each providing their own unique and possibly unmatchable technology. Also, the LMS design was itself unproven as a reciprocating engine, let alone turbine driven. One thing is certain – neither saw the project as one likely to reach fruition quickly.

Metropolitan-Vickers was a design and development company with many years of experience in supplying state of the art machinery to companies all over the world. They were used to the risk inherent in experimentation – it was their life blood. This conglomerate had grown from a small company formed by George Westinghouse in the 1890s in Manchester, into one of the biggest and most important heavy engineering facilities in Britain. During the First World War, Westinghouse was absorbed jointly by Metropolitan Carriage, Wagon and Finance Company and Vickers, and Metrovick came into existence, with the aid of huge Government contracts, and continued to grow.

At war's end they, like most engineering companies, were hit by recession and struggled to survive the loss of work, and increasing levels of industrial unrest slowed performance. But, with substantial redundancies, they struggled on until their fortunes changed in the mid-1920s with the formation of the Central Electricity Board, which placed a great deal of business with Metrovick. As always in the business world, change is constant and mergers are a way of life. In 1928 they joined with British Thomson-Houston (BTH) and then this combined company was purchased by the Associated Electrical Industries (AEI) as a holding group. But Metrovick and BTH had been rivals in the same market and their merger caused constant headaches for AEI, which seemed unable or unwilling to control the animosity or competition. Sometimes antipathy can generate a creative edge that benefits the holding company, if the market is strong. The Great Depression that began in 1929 made this impossible and both struggled to survive, their workers again being the primary sufferers.

A young trade unionist, Hugh Scanlon (later president of the Amalgamated Engineering Union and a Lord), cut his teeth with Metrovick, having joined as an apprentice instrument maker in 1927. He was an active union member who, in the early 1930s, was elected a Shop Steward and fought many tough battles with Metrovick's

Board in the years that followed, before promotion to Works Convener. He was an ardent fighter for workers' rights and in Metrovick he had great scope for this work. Undoubtedly the collision between capital and labour caused delays in production and added to the problems faced in exploiting new developments and new markets. But the scope for improved working conditions was huge and a new, fairer way of doing business was essential if the company and its workforce were to prosper and survive. The Victorian principle of worker exploitation had to be abandoned due to the growing aspirations and conditions the war generation knew they had earned by their sacrifice.

In many ways Metrovick's predicament mirrored the position in which the LMS found itself in the decade after its creation. Both were struggling to make their way in a hostile and yet expectant world. The turbine Pacific programme began as this expectation and the problems of industry were at their height.

The linkage between Metropolitan-Vickers and Ljungstrom was more straightforward, based, as it was, on an established business and scientific relationship. With this link already in place, and in advance of approval to go ahead, Guy and Stanier, with Robert Bailey acting as their focal point, had given Ljungstrom their specification for a turbine unit and received a broad estimate of costs and outline drawings in return. Also, Ljungstrom had completed some preliminary work on grafting the

turbine onto the new Pacific locomotive. In the submission to the LMS Board this work was described as follows:

'In order to examine the possibilities of a Ljungstrom Turbine Locomotive the Ljungstrom engineers were asked to prepare a proposal for a 2600HP Pacific type locomotive suitable for the Euston-Scottish express service.

'The steam conditions recommended were 250lbs/sq in g, and a total temperature of 850 F and with a supply of steam to the prime mover of 30000lbs per hour.

'Their proposals are attached.

'At starting the turbine locomotive is expected to develop a tractive effort of just over 40000lbs, while at 70mph the tractive effort expected is just over 12000lbs. The expected increase in the tractive effort of the turbine over the reciprocating locomotive to exceed by 30% for all speeds above 35mph.

'The turbine will be designed for maximum efficiency at 60mph at which speed the turbine will rotate at 760rpm. At 90mph the maximum speed of the turbine will be 10220rpm.

'The turbine drives through a double reduction gear, a gear wheel coupled by a quill to the driving axle. A separate reversing turbine is provided which drives the main turbine high speed pinion through a wheel clutch and an additional reducing gear.

'We have received a quotation for the turbines and gears of Swedish manufacture of £4330 at the current rate of exchange (offset by a saving of £1950 on reciprocating parts).'

Shaping a joint team of designers and workers from such diverse organisations required strong

6202 nearing completion at Crewe in April 1935. (RR)

leadership and political acumen. Many saw Metrovick as natural leaders. Although Stanier and his Board were the primary recipients of this work, Guy, Bailey and their company were leading the way. In later years Bond summed up how this relationship worked:

'I was fortunate to be concerned with its building, which involved many visits to the Trafford Park Works of Metropolitan-Vickers, who, with Ljungstrom, designed and made the

turbines and gear transmission. Henry Guy was in general charge of the project. I was much impressed by the high standard of workmanship and later by the meticulous care which Guy took during discussions in my office, in probing and analysing the cause of early troubles in service with some of the turbine and transmission components with which we were unfamiliar.'

Normally a company such as the LMS would issue a detailed specification and ensure the sub-contractor produced an item within specific targets in a fully costed, technical framework. With the turbine Pacific they departed from this norm and placed greater freedom in the hands of their supplier. The level of trust between Stanier and Guy was such that the LMS did not seem to baulk at this arrangement, although it may have caused raised eyebrows amongst some employees. But it was a time when the designers and managers, at Euston, Derby and Crewe, had their hands full with such a massive modernisation programme, so perhaps the freedom Metrovick were allowed was a practical solution in the circumstances.

The LMS's locomotive building programme, now including a turbine Pacific, was daunting by any standards. From a modest 17 new engines in 1933, it rose to 164 in 1934 and a peak of 358 in 1935, before dropping back to 319, 201, 131 and 34 in successive years. This made a grand total of 1,224 locomotives of 8 distinct designs. The initial batch of three Pacifics, produced under Lot 100 of Order 371 (1932), could easily

have been lost in this plan if they had not been such a high-profile project. In reality the turbine locomotive replaced a standard Pacific in this first batch, which should have been completed in 1933, and its success was dependent on the first two proving a successful design capable of adaptation. The early signs were promising, although there were some inevitable teething problems when trials began, the most significant being the steaming quality of the new tapered boiler and firebox. As a result, crews found themselves nursing these two new engines along to get the best from them and also learn a different firing technique.

The problem seemed to stem from Stanier's insistence on continuing the GWR practice of achieving a low degree of superheating in boiler design and this depended on near-perfect steaming for best performance, something that on LMS lines was difficult to achieve. Many thought that a good engine could be made better if the sixteen element superheaters were modified, a fact not lost on journalists at the time who had witnessed the early trial runs:

'It may be said that an express locomotive working for a large percentage of its time with steam at a high rate of expansion requires more superheat than goods engines where the steam is not used at such a high expansion rate. It is questionable whether full consideration has been given to this point.

The Railway Engineer.'

In fact, the use of low superheat had proved successful on the GWR

for thirty years or more and its use on the LMS was justified. But the two railway systems were different and the long distance, nonstop requirement of the London to Scotland route necessitated a different approach. The solution proved to be a simple one to achieve: a new boiler containing thirty-two superheater elements, not sixteen, and a longer firebox. The second batch of ten Pacifics, authorised in 1935, received these new boilers as did the original two locomotives in 1934 and the turbine engine when built. As one driver commented at the time, 'the modifications made a good engine exceptional'.

So with the new 4-6-2 design proving itself in service, a turbine unit under development, plus a working relationship between the LMS and Metrovick taking shape, the main elements of the project to produce the turbine engine were in place. Now it only remained to marry designs together and fit the building programme into the tightest of schedules.

In 1945 Roland Bond was asked to prepare a paper for the Institution of Locomotive Engineers, eventually given the title *Ten Years Experience with the LMS 4-6-2 Non-Condensing Turbine Locomotive No 6202*. On 30 January the following year he presented his findings to an audience in London. Although Stanier and Guy had led in producing this engine, they both felt that the privilege of presenting such an important paper should go to a man who had served the project and the LMS so well. In a well balanced

and carefully thought out lecture, Bond gave a most detailed account of the project from inception to operation. In an early draft, to Stanier, then no longer with the LMS, he touched on the main technical issues that had to be resolved during design and building. In the draft he wrote:

'Very early in development consideration was given to the best engine design to be used for the turbine experiment. The 4-6-0 was rejected as being too limited in capacity as was the 2-8-0, even though the Swedish turbine example was proving successful in operation. The newly developed 4-6-2 seemed to offer the best solution. It was larger and so offered more space within its frames to fit the turbine, its gears and ancillary equipment. It was also an experiment in which modification and refinements were expected.

'The main features of this new locomotive that we had to consider and our solutions were:

'Turbines, Transmission and Control Gear.

'It was decided that there should be two turbines, one for forward running and one for reverse, arranged on the left and right-hand sides of the main frames roughly in the positions occupied by the outside cylinders of a normal locomotive. The ahead turbine was of 2600hp nominal maximum capacity at 62mph. There are 16 stages and the internal arrangement of the blading ensures maintenance of high efficiency over a wide speed range. Steam passes from a normal design of superheater header through a strainer mounted on the outside of the firebox to a steam chest immediately above the turbine. Thence the steam is passed by way of one or more of six valves controlled by hand from the cab, to the nozzle group in the turbine casing. The valves are opened in succession, the number passing steam at any time determining the power output from the engine.

'The turbine is permanently connected through a double helical triple reduction gearing to the leading coupled axle, giving a ratio of 34.4 to 1 and a turbine speed of 13500rpm at 90mph. The final drive gearwheel surrounds the axle and is connected to two arms, forged solid with the axle, by means of

6202 in the Paint Shop at Crewe. (RR)

four pivoted links and a yoke, which also surrounds the axle, in such a way that relative motion between the gear wheel and axle due to the rise and fall of the axle-boxes in the guides is freely permitted. The gear wheel itself, which runs in white-metalled bearings, rigidly attached to the gear case enclosing the whole train, consists essentially of three main parts, a gear rim and two wheel centres. Power is transmitted from the gear rim through a series of laminated springs arranged circumferentially round the wheel, which relieves the teeth from shocks which would otherwise be directly transmitted to them from the wheels.

'The reverse turbine, on the right-hand side of the engine, drives through an additional single reduction gear, giving an overall ratio of 77 to 1, and is normally out of mesh with the main gear mesh with the main gear train. It is smaller and less powerful than the ahead turbine, as it is only required for light running and occasional low speed shunting movements. It is engaged by means of a sliding splined shaft and dog clutch, operated by the controller in the cab through a hand operated gear. When originally built this clutch was engaged by a small steam motor, but this proved troublesome and was quickly replaced by the manual gear.

'The main control box is situated in the cab in the position normally occupied by the reversing screw. One handle operates the steam admission valve to both turbines, rotating in a clockwise direction opening valves to the ahead turbine, and in a contrary direction to the reverse turbine. An inter-locking mechanism prevents the reverse turbine clutch being engaged until the handle is in the neutral position

with all valves closed. It cannot be opened until the reversing clutch is properly engaged and the ahead turbine valve cannot be opened whilst the reverse turbine is connected to the gear train.'

During the many design meetings held between the LMS and Metrovick teams, Guy and Bailey expressed the view that a single turbine, capable of managing both forward and reverse movement, was feasible and would be easier for the loco crew to manage, but would require more, possibly lengthy, development time. Despite this the two turbine solution was deemed the best and most practical solution by the railway company. It was a debate that Metrovick would resurrect later. Bond's paper then touched on the remaining elements of the locomotive's design:

'Lubricating Systems.

'Research and development work by Metropolitan-Vickers on ship and industrial turbines had highlighted the essential requirement for efficient lubrication of the turbine bearings and gears. Within a locomotive subject to greater movement and negative forces this requirement was even more critical.

'The solution was effected by a closed force-feed oiling system in which three pumps draw oil from a sump integral with the gear case and pass it under pressure to all the bearings and through sprayers on to the teeth. One pump, situated behind the gear case, is a reversible one, driven by the main slow-speed wheel through an increasing gear. Consequently, this pump only works when the engine is running, and the pressures and quantity of oil which it

delivers varies with the speed of the locomotive. The two other pumps are steam driven Worthington-Simpson reciprocating pumps which supplement the gear pump supply at all times, particularly when starting and running slowly. They are kept working after the engine has come to rest, to provide oil for carrying away heat conducted along the turbine shaft to the journals. The feeds from the gear pump and one of the steam pumps, combine and pass through an air radiator type of cooler situated under an elevating fall plate at the front of the smoke box. Thence the combined steam is distributed to the ahead turbine bearings, the gear train bearings and sprayers, whether the engine is running forward or in reverse. In forward gear a small feed passes to the reverse turbine through a plunger valve, which, in reverse gear, is a automatically opened to allow a full pressure supply to the reverse turbine unit. The feed from the second pump passes direct to the reverse turbine unit only.

'An Auto clean strainer with magnetic inserts is fitted in the sump and requires cleaning daily. A certain amount of contamination by condensed steam, which is not entirely removed by the turbine gland ejectors, takes place, and approximately one gallon of water is drained daily. The oil is changed completely after approximately 6000 miles running.'

In describing the turbines, gears and lubrication system Bond covered the primary work undertaken by Metrovick in Manchester. In reality these elements took longer to complete than the modifications to the locomotive being developed to hold the turbine

Turbomotive pulled out into the yard for an early publicity photo session. (RB)

Painted and waiting numbering and lining. (AE)

mechanism. Consequently, work at Derby and Crewe was often put on hold awaiting the completion of development tasks at their partner's factory. If anything, the task facing the LMS was simply one of creating a space large enough to take the turbines, gears and ancillary equipment, then modifying the rest of the locomotive to take account of the lessons learnt from the first two Pacific engines already in service. In his paper Bond listed the changes made to the original design:

'Engine 6202 differs in five important respects from the two original "Princess Royal" locomotives:

'The boiler has a larger superheater.
'Attainment of maximum economy from non-condensing turbines demands the use of a really high degree of superheat.

The boiler for the turbine engine was, therefore, provided with a 32 element superheater.

'The firebox has a greater volume, obtained by increasing the length of the combustion chamber.
'No great significance attaches to the provision of a firebox of greater volume in the boiler fitted to the turbine engine. A further series of 10 four cylinder 4-6-2 locomotives were being built concurrently with 6202, and in the course of development, improvements were made in the firebox design. So far as the external dimensions are concerned, the boilers are interchangeable, and the fireboxes have the same grate area and volume.

'A double blast pipe and chimney were fitted.
'The provision of exhaust passages of large area is a simple matter with the turbine locomotive, and the double blast pipe and chimney enables full advantage to be taken of the reduced back pressure thus made possible, at the same time ensuring an adequate smoke box vacuum. The LMS had no previous experience with double blast pipes, nor was there any data available from comparable engines which could be used as a guide to fixing the design of the blast pipe arrangements for the turbine with its continuous, non-pulsating exhaust.

'A feed water heater, in series with the exhaust steam injector and supplied by steam bled from the ahead turbine, was provided.
'On the advice of Metrovick advantage was taken of the economy offered by the principle, well established in turbine

practice, of bled steam feed heating. A tubular feed water heater was arranged transversely across the engine immediately behind the oil cooler, and was supplied with partially expanded steam bled from the forward turbine. It was connected in series with a No 12 Class Davies and Metcalfe exhaust ejector, fitted under the footplate on the fireman's side.

'Timken roller bearings were fitted to all axles, both on the locomotive and tender.
'The development by Timkens of roller bearings offered us the opportunity to improve performance of the locomotive and maintenance. In 6202 all axle bearings, of the locomotive and tender, were so fitted. During the early stages of design, it was doubtful whether weight restrictions would permit a complete installation, and it was intended to confine their use to the leading coupled axle and the trailing pony trucks. In the end, however, it was possible to fit them throughout. These roller bearing axle-boxes have given thoroughly good service and, in general, have shown no appreciable wear so far.'

Within the LMS and Metrovick Drawing Offices progress on the turbine locomotive was slow. Competition with other tasks was the key problem but so was the continuing debate over the final shape of the engine. Eric Langridge, who was then a Leading Draughtsman at Derby, and directly involved in the design of both the new 4-6-2 locomotives and Turbomotive, later recalled the process of development in his

FEED WATER HEATING
by the Exhaust Steam Injector

Photograph by courtesy of The London, Midland & Scottish Railway.

is adopted on the New
L. M. S. Turbine Locomotive

HIGHEST IN EFFICIENCY
LOWEST IN FIRST COST AND MAINTENANCE
LOWEST IN WEIGHT • 20,000 LOCOMOTIVES FITTED

DAVIES & METCALFE LTD.
ROMILEY NEAR MANCHESTER

SAY YOU SAW IT IN "THE RAILWAY GAZETTE"

autobiography *Under 10 CMEs* and during several recorded conversations. Having been aware that the contract for the first three 4-6-2s had only resulted in 6200 and 6201 being completed, 'mysterious rumours' surrounded the third of the class. Parts for 6202 had been manufactured, but were stored at Crewe Works. Surprisingly, word did not leak out. Finally, the third 'came out of the mists' and the plan was revealed by Herbert Chambers who had accompanied Stanier and Guy to Sweden and helped produce the paper and outline drawings for the Board to consider:

'It came as a bit of a surprise. Experimental jobs weren't too popular when our hands were so full of other work, but the Drawing Office staff were interested nevertheless and the idea of working on something new was appealing.

'In between other jobs I was told to get out a tube plate for the third boiler, as engineers at Metrovick said they must have hot, dry steam otherwise the turbines would be inefficient and their blades damaged by drops of water. Drawings were completed and the boiler constructed but Metrovick were not ready with their equipment, so this boiler became a spare for the first two engines and was soon fitted to one to try out the effect of higher superheat. The boiler for the next batch of 4-6-2s (6203 to 6212) was the same design as the turbine. One of this batch was modified by drilling 40 flues and this was exchanged for the one originally built for the turbine.

'During its development Guy and his assistant Struthers often visited Derby to discuss the work we were doing and we went through the many drawings their Drawing Office prepared showing the two turbine units, gears and other equipment. It surprised me how well it fitted into the frames of the 4-6-2, but the locomotive was a very flexible design.

'I was given the design of the boiler and Willie Armin got on with the frames, wide hornblocks for the roller bearings and drillings for the two turbines. My next job, as work

Photos of 6202 were distributed to main parts suppliers by the LMS's PR Department for use in their publicity campaigns. These images would appear many times. (Author)

progressed and Metrovick provided more information about the turbines, was to do the pipe and rod arrangements.

'I always found Guy very pleasant to deal with. He had the ability to talk to people at all levels and understand the problems they faced in developing their ideas. He seemed to lead on many issues concerning the turbine locomotive and Chambers, Coleman and Bond seemed happy to let him do so. Stanier kept in touch, but having delegated responsibility and given us clear targets he let us get on with the work.'

The weight of 6202 and the other new 4-6-2s was a concern. The hammer blow of reciprocating engines had to be minimised to reduce wear and tear on the permanent way. Consequently, the civil engineers restricted the maximum permitted static axle loading to 22 ½ tons. 6202 was a heavier engine than her reciprocating sisters – 6 tons more when loaded – and so exerted greater downward pressure on the track, but as the turbines removed the hammer blow a higher axle loading was possible and the greater weight of the turbines and gears could be absorbed. The theory was agreed and 6202 was allowed a static axle loading of 24 tons. Even at that level wear would be considerably less on the track. Without experience in service it was a leap of faith, but the risks seemed acceptable with only one locomotive of this type ever likely to be built, or so many believed. Meanwhile at Derby, Langridge continued with the boiler design:

'The specification I received said – nickel steel rolled plates, mild steel flanged plates, three rows of large tubes and a 'combustion' chamber. It was well known that the GWR designers had always advocated vertical tube plates: on this new boiler for 6202 and in all subsequent 4-6-2 boilers this prejudice was overcome and this so called 'combustion' chamber introduced.'

When Stanier's appointment to the LMS was announced in early 1932, Drawing Office staff had quickly tried to familiarise themselves with GWR locomotive designs, predicting that their new CME would introduce many of these ideas. There was some resistance, but on the whole draughtsmen and engineers accepted these changes with polite scepticism, ready to point out flaws in these proposals as far as LMS engines were concerned. Langridge recorded one such incident:

'There was an idea that this [the vertical tube plates concept] should follow the lines of the many jointed affair of the proposed "Fowler" ill-fated compound 4-6-2, but after drawing out one or two schemes, Chambers got HQ agreement to a deep flanged plate idea which would avoid any extra joints and all 'scarfing'. It all depended on what the plate presses at Crewe could handle, so I was told to go to Crewe and measure the gap available. It was found possible, after allowing for the depth of the shaping blocks themselves, to press a plate to approximately 3ft in depth, allowing a 1ft 6in chamber, shortening the original 4-6-2 tube length by that amount. It thus became possible not only to reduce the tube lengths to a more manageable figure of 19ft 3in, but, what was of greater value, to increase the firebox volume and its surface subject to radiant heat from the firegrate.

'I got out a sketch showing how the plates would overlap for Chambers to submit to Stanier. He came back and told me to get a scale model in wood made by Hunt, the Derby Pattern Shop foreman, and a sheet of lead to represent the plate being flanged…. I was next told to take it to Euston; there I met Cox and Fell the Crewe Boiler Shop foreman, who, after explanation, went into the inner sanctum for half an hour with Stanier, while I waited outside…. I had got my idea accepted and was told to proceed.'

Stanier was a pragmatist by nature and did not believe in confrontation, as a rule. He realised that some of his 'GWR' ideas might run contrary to established practice within the LMS, but although standing firm on principles he knew worked, he could be flexible when necessary. He encouraged his team to think for themselves and come forward with new ideas, provided that they were submitted in a positive spirit. Many of these ideas could be impractical or poorly thought out and he relied upon his managers to act as filters to make sure good concepts were developed and unacceptable ones buried or refocused. He was quick to accept workable solutions and ever ready to reward endeavour. Very quickly most saw the benefit of his working style and rallied round, although, undoubtedly, there were others who wished to see him fail. Such is human nature.

1934 was largely a year for development of the turbine locomotive and it was not until late

The Turbomotive

Labels on illustration:

Double chimney

Regulator valve

Steam from superheater going to turbine

Water supply to boiler from tender

Steam-entering steam pipe to superheater

Four safety valves

Coal supply

Firebox

Regulator handle

Water supply

L M S

6202

Exhaust pipes

6202

Steam valves

Rod from drivers cab for operating steam valves

Fire-tube not boilesse

Rod from drivers cab to steam valves of reverse turbine

Reverse turbine for driving locomotive backward

Steam chest Forward turbine

Cold air entering to cool lubricating oil pump

Blades of turbine

Crank

ing es

Exhaust opening for used steam from turbine

ving els

Connecting rod coupling driving wheels

Shock absorber to insure smooth running

Oil sump in which gears run

Gear wheels turning front driving wheels

HOW THE ENGINE WORKS

THE general layout of the turbine locomotive is as follows. The main motive power unit comprises a multi-stage turbine and treble reduction gear, the turbine being mounted on the L.H. side of the main engine frame. For reverse running a separate turbine is provided, having an additional single reduction gear, making in all, inclusive of reversing, a quadruple reduction gear between the turbine spindle and the driving axle.

In the main turbine, the number and type of the stages have been chosen so that a high turbine efficiency is maintained over a wide range of engine speed. The steam from the boiler is led to a steam chest formed as a steel casting containing six control valves, which are hand operated from the cab. From the steam chest the steam passes through flexible pipes to groups of nozzles in the high pressure end of the turbine cylinders, each nozzle group being controlled by one of the six valves. The speed of the turbine which governs that of the locomotive and train, is controlled by hand from the cab by opening these control valves progressively, the steam from the turbine exhausting to the atmosphere through the smokebox and chimney in the usual manner.

The turbine spindle is directly coupled to the high-speed gear pinion, and a thoroughly flexible drive is ensured by an intermediate hollow quill shaft fitted with a pair of flexible diaphragm couplings. The treble reduction gear is of the double helical type completely enclosed in a fabricated gear case.

The first and second reduction pinions have been made slightly flexible to equalise the pressure along the teeth.

To take up any relative movement between the engine frame and the driving axle, the final drive from the slow speed gear wheel to the crank arms formed on the main driving axle is a very flexible one. The slow gear wheel encircles this driving axle and is coupled to it by a series of floating links. Leaf springs between the rim and the boss of this slow speed wheel prevent transmission of shocks to the high speed gearing.

One important point with regard to the operation of the turbine locomotive is that the engine cannot be reversed until the locomotive comes to a stand. This is achieved by means of a dog clutch situated between the reverse turbine and the final drive on hen the

engine is in the reverse drive the forward turbine, which is permanently connected to the transmission gear, rotates in the reverse direction, but steam being shut off, no power is developed in the forward turbine.

Another point of interest is that until the reversing gear is located in its position by the locking gear provided in the control gear box in the cab, either forward or ahead, steam cannot be admitted to either the forward or reverse turbine, as the case may be.

It will be appreciated that an express locomotive with 6 ft. 6 in. coupled wheels requires very careful consideration in the choice of the transmission gear between the turbine and the coupled wheels. Thorough investigation of this problem, however, resulted in a speed ratio of 34.3 to 1, or, expressed another way, for a locomotive speed of 60 miles per hour, the turbine shaft speed is approximately 8,900 revs. per min.

The whole of the transmission gear is carried in a gear case which is of a three-point suspension type. This was decided on as it was necessary to ensure that, whatever flexing took place in the locomotive frames when running at high speeds, there would be no distortion of the gear case that could interfere with the sweet running of the turbine or transmission gear.

This turbomotive will also be recorded as the first attempt in this country of providing roller bearings for all the axle journals of the engine and tender.

---

in the year that assembly of parts from the Works at Crewe and Trafford Park began in earnest. Word soon reached the railway press that something unusual was taking shape and the Editor of the *Railway Gazette* was invited to witness firsthand the gradual evolution of 6202 and was given an open brief: he could ask

any questions he wished and observe the experiment for himself. Today 'good PR' is deemed essential to any group, public or private, and it is difficult to understand that in the early part of the twentieth century these principles of business were still in their infancy. But the medium for selling ideas or products

was spreading quickly and growing more refined, stimulated, at first, by the need to encourage a war-weary nation to keep fighting, as catastrophic casualties mounted. By the 1930s more newspapers and magazines existed than at any time in history and advertising sponsored most, the cinema was rising to a

The LMS made sure that detailed descriptions of Turbomotive appeared in the press and 'in-house' magazines. (LMS/RH)

George Loftus-Allen LMS publicist par excellence. (LMS/RH)

peak, radios were now commonplace and TV was just round the corner. Business had to manipulate and exploit the media to make sure their voices were heard and positive messages were conveyed to the marketplace.

The LMS had been slow in developing their public relations arm, unlike the LNER, GWR and Southern Railway. But in 1927 Thomas Jeffrey, the Advertising and Publicity Officer, retired and was replaced by George Loftus-Allen, his deputy. He was a veteran of the First World War and a man well versed in publicity and capable of developing a very active and attractive image for the LMS. As a 34-year-old, he was a man of the modern age, aware of changing needs and fashions. He had also been well schooled in new methods of public relations – not only identifying the needs of

customers, tailoring messages to suit identified audiences, lobbying and managing the flow of positive information but also how to handle negative news. When attached to the War Office in 1915 he had seen how the military badly mishandled public relations, seeking, by censorship, to hide bad news, making matters worse when the truth was eventually revealed. He was determined not to make the same mistake but tackle issues head on. As an assistant to a man nearly thirty years his senior he must have struggled against the conservatism of the older, mid-Victorian generation. Certainly when promoted the LMS found a new, dynamic voice in public relations and change was rapid and spectacular.

Loftus-Allen (born G.H.L. Allen, but later hyphenated) was also a supporter of the arts and saw the aesthetics and grandeur in many elements of the railway world. In this he reflected the way art was changing to mirror an industrial reality common to most working people of that age. Through his many connections he promoted all these elements and, with an effective team around him, successfully portrayed the company and lifted its profile to new heights.

As a result of his efforts the artist and art advisor, Norman Wilkinson, was recruited and through him the artists Charles Pears and Murray Secretan were employed. Between them they produced artwork that displayed what the company did and what it offered. These images remain eye-catching to this day and

worked spectacularly well when first appearing on high-street billboards, in the press and on station hoardings. Publications were also produced that highlighted the railway's attractions and many focused on the technical advances being made. The quality and comfort of railway carriages, locomotive modernisation and performance, and, in partnership with holiday resorts, glowing brochures covered with scenes that many in recession-hit Britain would have found alluring. Loftus-Allen and his team exploited fully every aspect of life on the LMS and the regions it served.

With his encouragement the press became fully involved in the development of new locomotives, and 'parties' for particular events became commonplace. In this the LMS was catching up with the other regions, particularly their main rival, the LNER. The launch of the first 4-6-2 locomotive, in 1933, and early speed trials, were covered fully in newspapers, magazines and, through British Pathé newsreels, on the silver screen. Railway magazines were, of course, at the forefront of this news gathering and, despite some reservations among the operational managers, their journalists were embraced and allowed a level of access unknown today, where image is more carefully manipulated and constructive criticism not invited.

Glamour was the key to good PR and the turbine locomotive held this promise and so she quickly became public property as construction reached its end. Loftus-Allen and Stanier, possibly for different reasons

Traditionally, each new locomotive was photographed at the 'works' with the background removed, during photo developing, to show the locomotive to best effect. (RR)

– one selling the company and the other selling a new experimental locomotive – were very keen to make sure that the engine received as much good publicity as possible.

As 6202 moved down the assembly line at Crewe, sandwiched between other new locomotives, the editor of the *Railway Gazette* prepared then ran the first of his articles that would announce the birth of this new engine. The style is rather pompous, but it captures the age and conveys the way journalists then wrote:

'The LMS Turbine Locomotive June 28, 1935

'It has become the fashion when referring to any development of an outstanding character in locomotive practice to label it a "bold experiment". We do not, however, propose to follow this example in dealing with Mr

Stanier's new turbine express recently completed at the Crewe works of the LMS Railway; not because of inability to realise that the adoption of the principle of utilising steam for locomotive purposes still remains largely an experiment, and that courage is required in taking such a step, at the present juncture. Rather it is for the reason that, having had ample facilities for studying the design and seeing the engine grow up in the works from the time the frames plates were laid down to that at which the complete locomotive stood ready for painting and testing, we have been able to convince ourselves that in this design every effort has been made to simplify the general layout and follow as closely as circumstances permit what may be termed orthodox locomotive lines. The main and, indeed, the only real difference from a structural point of view is the substitution of turbines and geared transmission mechanism for the

more usual reciprocating machinery consisting of cylinders, steam distribution valves and other motion details....

'The first question one is inclined to ask oneself in a matter of this sort is why a departure of this kind here involved has been undertaken at all. Turbine locomotives have already been tried out in this country and abroad, more particularly in Sweden, and a great deal of patience and ingenuity expended in the effort to make them show up advantageously in comparison with the reciprocating form of locomotive. Have the results been such as to warrant further trials and experimentation or not? Such a question is natural enough, but the main point for the Chief Mechanical Engineer and other officers of a railway company to decide is whether the theoretical advantages of the turbine can be turned to profitable account on their particular line for dealing with the trains they have to haul under the conditions that actually apply. Once they have satisfied themselves that this can be done the next step is plotting a design which, in the judgement of those principally concerned, is the best to meet the circumstances of the individual case....

'There will, as a matter of course, be criticism of the design of the locomotive apart from the principle on which it operates, and among such criticisms we expect to find one based on the fact that it is of the non-condensing type. It is, we know, urged by some that the absence of condensing apparatus robs the system of half its value....

'We congratulate Mr Stanier on his latest achievement , and it is with a feeling of confidence, that we predict a measure of success which will justify the enterprising step he has taken in introducing this type of locomotive which incidentally marks a new stage in the locomotive history of this country by the construction of a turbine locomotive in railway company's works.'

To mark the occasion, this editorial acted as an introduction to a ten-page article in that month's magazine, which described in great detail 6202's development, and included numerous drawings and photographs taken during the locomotive's building. A little later the article was produced as a booklet and sold through WH Smith and other outlets, priced 1 shilling, one of a number sponsored by the LMS at that time. The project's 'sub-contractors', Metrovick and Timkens, also produced versions of the article and circulated copies to their employees. The level of interest

Another official photograph taken at Crewe, but now 6202 looks a little more weather beaten. (RB)

in 6202 grew rapidly and the engine became something of a celebrity even before she ran and expectations ran high.

On the assembly line construction did not run smoothly. Hold-ups as design changes were made, plus significant downtime waiting for Metrovick engineers to complete their tasks and run tests on the turbine system, held up progress. This situation was made worse by constantly changing production priorities, despite the best efforts of the Works's managers. But with more than 350 locomotives under construction and many more requiring maintenance at Crewe, the Works were running at near maximum capacity throughout 1935. The suspicion forming that 6202 would be an unnecessary distraction was coming true. But, in fits and starts, work proceeded and gradually the new locomotive took shape.

Her next ten sister engines were being built at the same time at Crewe, although passing through the Works in considerably less time than 6202, and this allowed various interested groups to compare the two designs. Both types were deemed very attractive, with a poise to their shape that caught Loftus-Allen's artistic eye particularly. If anything, most thought 6202 much sleeker with its pleasantly curved casing around the turbines smoothing the lines. But it did have a slightly lopsided look because the forward turbine casing ran the length of the running plate, and the reverser side was

shorter, the unit being much smaller. Loftus-Allen noticed this and asked whether both sides could be the same. In the rush to get the work finished his suggestion was not taken seriously.

In April 1935 the locomotive was complete. She was married to her new tender and entered the paint shop for priming. Steam had been raised and the engine had moved under her own steam for the first time. Before her crimson top coat was added she was photographed from many angles, with a written brief and pictures being widely circulated to the press and advertisers.

Design and building had been a long process and Hartley, in particular, had questioned whether

the project was ever likely to be completed. Also, he could read a balance sheet and was aware of the risings costs of the locomotive and worried that its benefits would never outweigh expenditure. The accountants now estimated 6202 would cost £9,000 more than each of the second batch of 4-6-2s and more than £7,000 more than the original estimate. For the moment his and Stanier's correspondence was polite, but revealed these underlying concerns. All hoped that when running 6202 would quickly confirm the value of this experiment, but for that she had to get out on the road and prove herself in full view of a very interested audience.

Engine Cold at Crewe and awaiting a return to duty. (RB)

June 1935 and 6202 makes her first appearance at Euston. This and many other photos were taken or collected by Alfred Ewer from many sources. He was the LMS's District Locomotive Superintendent, based at Camden, from 1934 to 1947 and was responsible for Turbomotive for most of her life. He carefully recorded and documented life in his district.
(AE/LMS)

CHAPTER 4

TRIALS AND TRIBULATIONS
(1935–1936)

The first few weeks of 6202's life followed the course of so many engines that had gone before. So much new metal needs to bed in gently, with a posse of engineers fussing around, scratching their heads and making adjustments to make sure she was safe to use and safe to run on the mainline. With an experimental locomotive this process is prolonged, especially when two technologies are being married. Teams from the LMS and Metrovick had worked hard to get the engine this far and had resolved many problems during building, but a working, breathing engine presented a much bigger challenge.

Henry Guy and William Stanier had visited Crewe Works many times during building and saw the slow evolution of their 'baby' and, although hardened engineers, had displayed a paternal interest in all elements of its birth. Later Guy recorded his impressions of this time:

'To see this new engine gradually come together and to assess its potential was an enthralling business. In looks alone it was an impressive engine and certainly nothing else I had seen approached its handsome good looks, especially when compared to other turbine driven engines. After several weeks of tests with the turbine drive uncoupled, the various elements of boiler, gears and drive were finally joined together (but not the coupling rods) and steam raised to test these parts of the engine. Two days of adjustments followed in which we solved a number of problems, one fitter describing it as "giving it a good tune up". Finally, the coupling rods were fitted and the locomotive moved for the first time under her own steam. Initial grinding sounds of new metal bedding in soon passed with a liberal supply of oil. The turbine and gears had already run for many hours at Metrovick on a rigid test bed, so worked smoothly when the engine moved for the first time. There was no cheering or handshakes, but Stanier and I were quietly pleased that the engine was finally moving, but much work lay ahead to prove the experiment worthwhile.'

The two months to June 1935 saw 6202 go from an unpainted, unpolished but assembled engine to

A common scene at Euston in 1935. (RH)

a fully completed, highly lacquered crimson locomotive looking the thoroughbred the designers hoped she would be. Once certified for use beyond the confines of Crewe Works she ran a number of 'running in' turns, to Shrewsbury and then south along parts of the mainline to London. Each journey was carefully monitored, with loads gradually increased. The footplate crew varied considerably during these trials and, for that matter, her entire working life, but it became established practice for one of two fitters to accompany each run, to be on hand to make sure the turbine system ran properly and correct any simple defects. This remained so until she was withdrawn from service as a turbine engine.

Much later, Stanier stated that the locomotive might have performed better in service if the footplate crew had been limited to a small number of drivers and firemen, who could have gained greater experience of her own particular needs. But as CME he did not manage the LMS's Running Department so could only suggest, not direct this policy. Whether this was a deliberate snub or a result of the problems related to running a complex, very busy system is hard to determine, but for Stanier to raise this issue many years later suggests it might have been the former. It stands to reason that any machine can be operated better if the user has specialist skills and experience.

Once in service passenger locomotives were invariably named and 6202s twelve sisters were each given the names of princesses – *Elizabeth* and *Margaret Rose* amongst them. But for some reason the turbine engine was not formally named. The question why has never been answered. Perhaps most predicted a short life for her or felt that it was unnecessary to name an experiment. But as time passed and the engine proved herself in service this policy, if that is what it was, did not change. In such a vacuum nicknames were adopted. One of her fitters called her the 'clockwork engine', the forward turbine cover looking as though it had a fixture for a very large key, whereas Stanier and Guy (as John Chacksfield relates in his excellent biography of the CME) liked the nickname 'Gracie Fields – because it sang as it went'. But the name that stuck was 'Turbomotive', lifted from the cover of the driving instructions prepared by Ljungstrom in 1933.

Turbomotive evoked a modern high-tech world – a world that found a voice in the many comics of the period that hinted at superheroes and space flight to distant galaxies. It also had an appeal to the publicity department and the headline makers, so to many on the railway and the general public the name stuck. Some derided the title and frowned at its use, but in the absence of a real name and buoyed by a desire for something futuristic and

Turbomotive eases back onto her train in June 1935. (LMS/RH)

glamorous it remained a potent title that has lasted to this day.

In many ways the name Turbomotive harked back to an earlier development. In the late nineteenth century the pioneering engineer Charles Parsons produced the first turbine-powered boat. This huge leap forward would revolutionise ships and naval warfare, but in the 1890s it was an experiment that confounded traditionalists and drew much criticism. In its earliest trials it reached 34.4 knots and sustained that speed for some considerable time. To make sure this invention was accepted Parsons realised that publicity was a key ingredient for success. He named his boat *Turbinia* realising that this title suggested modernism, a shedding of old, unimaginative shackles. It would also grab headlines, which it proceeded to do following an electrifying performance at Queen Victoria's Diamond Jubilee Fleet Review in June 1897. Many of the men who worked on Turbomotive grew up knowing about *Turbinia* and may have consciously or unconsciously made a connection between these two ventures.

By June, Turbomotive was deemed ready to begin the next stage of her development and was allocated to Camden Shed in London to run from Euston. Although the railway press had described the engine in some detail during building, its first turn at the London terminus was a major occasion, fully exploited by George Loftus-Allen and his team, with journalists and

photographers, as well as VIPs and directors from the LMS and Metrovick in attendance.

Two weeks later British Pathé was invited to film Turbomotive in operation. During a fully loaded test run, a second engine ran ahead of her on the adjoining up line with several carriages, the last of these containing a film crew. Turbomotive from some distance back

accelerated alongside, slowed briefly and then pulled ahead. This manoeuvre was completed several times, managed with hand signals and shouted instructions, until the film makers were happy. Throughout the shoot the fireman and driver looked quizzically back at the camera, their expressions giving little away. The short sequence when shown in cinemas

Stanier explains some technical aspect of Turbomotive to Josiah Stamp, his Chairman, and the locomotive's driver (June 1935). (RH/LMS)

6202 awaits departure and receives close inspection (June 1935).
(LMS/AE)

6202 would always carry a fitter on her footplate. Here, a final check is undertaken before departure (June 1935).
(AE/LMS)

across Britain in early July, under the banner 'News in a Nutshell', was overlaid with a commentary typical of the time – clipped speech around a succession of dramatic words and phrases:

'A great new LMS locomotive is undergoing speed trials. It's nearly 75 feet long and weighs over 163 tons. That's not the only reason why it's outstanding. Actually it introduces a startling new principle of engine design. Instead of being driven by the old type of steam engine with a piston working up and down in a cylinder, it's driven by a turbine – like a ships engine. The steam is forced under tremendous pressure against a series of fan blades causing them to revolve at high speed. Now watch this new form of speed then come aboard and feel the absence of vibration and noise. This engine can develop over 2000 horse power which assures a very high speed.'

Appeasement was in the air, particularly in Britain where the population still bore the scars of the Western Front and hoped for prosperity not conflict. The development of new technology such as Turbomotive fed the fantasy that all was well or would be better, so was well received.

During her first few weeks at Camden, loco crews familiarised themselves with this new locomotive. A detailed set of instructions were produced for them and she ran a number of excursions that were no more than a continuation of the trials begun at Crewe. The driving technique was different, but seemed to be easily adopted by drivers and firemen. Conversion to full operational use

was eagerly anticipated, but in mid-August a routine inspection revealed that water had seeped into one of the roller bearings and an oil leak from the casing around the turbine bearings was discovered. By early September these defects had been repaired by Camden's fitters and on 11 September she was rostered to take the express from Euston to Liverpool Lime Street. This became her regular turn until 24 September

when she failed at Liverpool. Her record card reveals that the 'reverse turbine dog clutch failed to engage' rendering her unusable.

She was towed to Crewe where she remained until 21 December 1935, the opportunity being taken, when out of service, to complete a light overhaul, jointly conducted by LMS and Metrovick engineers. Apart from the failed dog clutch the rest of the locomotive had bedded in well.

Her return to traffic was brief though. On 15 January the clutch failed again, this time at Euston, and to Crewe Works she returned until 4 February, before being allocated for two months to Edge Hill Shed on Merseyside, presumably because it was closer to Crewe, so any more problems would mean a shorter tow to the Works. In April she was reallocated to Camden, the operating base for the rest of her life.

During an early test run, 6202 was photographed passing another train. Although the quality of these pictures is poor, they do catch the power of this elegant locomotive. (RR)

During these early days, Turbo-motive's progress was followed avidly by enthusiasts, particularly the Railway Correspondence and Travel Society (RCTS), which monitored her movements. In January 1936 they recorded:

'6202 has several times recently worked the down Merseyside Express and it has been particularly interesting to witness a start from Mossley Hill with a load of 16 or 17 bogies. In the first place a continuous roar is heard, becoming louder as the train accelerates (which it does rapidly) and then a high pitched whistling as speed increases. Owing to the more uniform power transmission this engine has never slipped once in starting, though Royal Scots and Pacifics rarely get away without some trouble.'

After these initial problems Turbomotive settled down to regular, unbroken service for three months during which her performance came under close scrutiny, the company wishing to see if their investment would prove wise. At the same time her twelve sister engines were proving their worth, but the testing regime for engines was not all that the CMEs of the LMS and LNER wished it to be and the need for more effective testing had been advocated by Nigel Gresley and Stanier for many years.

In his Presidential address to the Institution of Locomotive Engineers in September, Gresley had described in some detail these concerns.

When developing his P2 class of locomotive he had found it necessary to ship the first engine over to France where a new testing station had been built at Vitry, there being nothing as large or effective in Britain:

'What have we here in England? A small locomotive testing plant of 500hp capacity, installed at the Swindon works of the GWR thirty years ago by Mr Churchward, whose tragic death last year we all deplore. He was without doubt one of the most eminent engineers of recent times, and we see evidence of his influence in the designs of the most up to date engines of each of the great railways of this country. The Swindon plant is, however, much too small for modern locomotives.

'There are four dynamometer cars in existence on British Railways, all of which I regard as almost obsolete when compared to modern cars (used overseas).

'The building of locomotives has been a national industry for over 100 years, and during the last few years has been more depressed than almost any other industry in the Country. Owing to the lack of facilities for carrying out research work our locomotive designers and builders are working under disabilities when in competition with builders of foreign nations.… The need for a locomotive experimental and testing station is of national importance.'

His comments found support across the railway industry and were echoed by Richard Maunsell, CME of the Southern Railway, when

Euston 1935 – 6202 at rest after a test run. The driver appears to be Laurie Earl, a Camden-based driver of great repute. (WS)

proposing a vote of thanks to Gresley at the end of his address:

'I have always held there is too wide a gulf between the scientific side of engineering and the practical side, and I feel convinced that if this experimental station were erected it would be the means of bringing these two sides of engineering more closely together than they are at the present time, and I feel certain that if science and practice will advance hand in hand it will be for the betterment of engineering in this country.'

Stanier had been asked to second the vote of thanks, but had been warned by the Institution's Secretary to do so with discretion. One assumes he felt strongly on this subject and had been less than cautious in his criticism of those who had the power to authorise improvements in testing facilities:

'I do not know why I should be so warned, but the Secretary evidently thought I should be.

'It gives me particular pleasure to second the vote to Mr Gresley, firstly, because of his very kind reference to my old chief and secondly, because of my admiration for anyone who can get up such an Presidential Address as he has just given us. The work Mr Gresley is doing is an inspiration to all of us who are trying to follow in his footsteps, and it is particularly pleasing to me that he has the same admiration for my old chief that I have myself.'

Engineers in Britain had long been aware that the testing regime was limited and could retard the development of new, complex designs that might need longer to bring to a successful completion. All recognised that 'on the road' tests had their place and could reveal much about performance and design, but did not exploit the full range of scientific techniques available in a fully equipped testing station, complete with a rolling road. Gresley had been arguing since the mid-1920s for such a facility and in a previous period as President of the Institution had canvassed widely for support. But with such a deep economic recession affecting investment, no railway company felt able to inject the capital needed to build such a facility and so the idea remained unexploited.

With the huge leaps forward in design being made by Stanier and Gresley, and with ever greater emphasis on locomotive capacity, performance and economy of effort were even more important. The CMEs felt that these goals would have been better achieved by a more scientific approach to design and building. French engineers had seen the way forward and built the advanced testing facility at Vitry. Envious eyes were cast at this state of the art centre from across the Channel. None more so than from Stanier's office.

There seems little doubt that despite the investment by the LMS in research at Derby and the influence of such a great scientist as Harold Hartley, as its manager and advocate, Stanier felt that there was still a significant gap in the development process and sought, with Gresley, to create a facility to meet this need. After much canvassing and consideration, approval was finally given in 1937

and work was well advanced, on the facility at Rugby, as war loomed and priorities changed. Work was suspended during 1940 and only resumed in the last months of the war and finally opened in 1948, long after Gresley and Stanier had departed the scene and the decline of steam had begun.

With such high-performance locomotives being developed on the LMS and LNER, testing was limited to dynamometer trials only, so

Camden Shed's Locomotive Arrangement Board for 1 September 1936. 6202 is marked down for a 10.40 run to Liverpool. (AE)

limiting scientific analysis, or so designers believed. Turbomotive's development could have benefited significantly from more thorough testing on a rolling road. There is no evidence to suggest that the LMS considered using Vitry, as the LNER had done when developing the P2, but the thought may have crossed Stanier's mind, especially as a turbine locomotive was on the drawing board in France at the time, clearly influenced by 6202's development.

Three separate trials were planned for 6202. The first two would see her compared to sister engines over the same routes with similar-sized loads. The third would study the coal and water consumption rates when working the Royal Scot train between Euston and Glasgow. Each test served to examine the basic principles behind the great experiment – would a turbine engine run as well as her sisters and produce the savings both Guy and Stanier predicted in their 1933 concept paper. Other elements of performance – maintenance, availability, the practicalities of daily use and so on – would be monitored by fitters working on the footplate, shed and workshop staff, so could have lacked a degree of scientific impartiality, or so many thought at the time.

The first tests took place between April and July 1936 on the Euston to Carlisle route and involved 6212, as the comparison engine, both pulling loads of between 449 and 548 tons. Two weeks after the first runs on April 20– 29, 6202 was withdrawn for a light overhaul at Crewe and did not return to traffic until 24 June. Her performance had raised concerns that something might have been wrong, but nothing untoward was found. The second set of trials took place between July 16 and 19, while the engine was, according to her record card, out of service for a heavy overhaul at Crewe, being fitted with a new boiler and having an oil leak repaired. This time only 6202 was involved, running between Crewe and Carlisle, pulling loads of between 337 and 457 tons. The report from the April tests stated that:

'The general steaming of engine No 6202 was not completely satisfactory, as it was found necessary to coast with the regulator shut on several occasions in order to effect an improvement in the boiler pressure and also to create a working level of water in the boiler. The steaming of engine 6212 was more satisfactory, but as in the case of engine 6202, when working heavily and with correspondingly greater demand on the boiler, a satisfactory boiler pressure was only effected by maintaining a minimum level of water in the boiler.'

When the final report (number 61 in the LMS series) was published in August it concluded that both engines were affected by the severity of the load, but combustion in 6202's was at times worse than her sister engine. It went on to state that 'taking the whole combined service the turbine engine used 6% less coal

6202 awaits departure. The fitter is chatting to a member of the station staff or the guard while the driver, Laurie Earl, looks on. (AE)

Poor driving conditions were commonplace in a Britain powered by coal, here captured in all its smoke laden heaviness (AE/RH)

6202 picks up speed, her fireman looking back along the carriages while the fitter prepares for a quiet journey. (Author)

June 1936. Turbomotive returns to Crewe for some attention. (AE/LMS)

and 7% less water than the standard reciprocating engine'.

On 27 July Hartley, having heard some critical comments about 6202's development and performance, wrote an internal memo to Stanier seeking assurances that all was well. He had been pressing the CME for regular updates for some months and, with the first trials completed, expected a more detailed briefing note on the engine's condition and any problems it had faced. Two days later Stanier replied:

'With reference to your letter of the 27th, the turbine engine is at present at Crewe works. It failed at Euston on the 14th May, owing to the overheating of a bearing in connection with the reverse turbine. The engine was sent to Crewe and the turbine taken down and sent to Messrs. Metropolitan Vickers, where examination revealed that the failure of the bearing had caused the blades of the rotors to be stripped, and it was necessary to reblade this part of the reverse turbine.

'The turbine was sent back to Crewe, refitted and the engine was turned out of the works on 24th June. It ran satisfactorily so far as the engine was concerned, but a considerable amount of oil was being used, and an examination was made from which it was found that oil was leaking between the joints of the gear case. It was necessary to return the engine to the works on the 14th of this month, where further examination revealed that the copper jointing was defective, and it was decided to replace it with new stainless steel rings. As this necessitated the stripping down of the whole of the gear, the opportunity was taken of changing the boiler and fitting one that, having five rows of superheater

Liverpool Lime Street Station in the 1930s, Turbomotive's regular destination for her entire working life. (AE)

tubes instead of four, an increased degree of superheat will be obtained, and should give a much better performance than those obtained on previous tests.'

Stanier attached a complete statement of all failures and their causes since June 1935, but did not offer a view on future availability or performance, one assumes to avoid becoming a 'hostage to fortune'.

Before the second set of tests took place, 6202 returned to her usual duties, spending most time running to and from Liverpool Lime Street very reliably, no workshop time being recorded in her record cards. During this period, Edward Livesay, an engineering journalist, began a close association with the locomotive that would last for four years and resulted in articles for *The Engineer* magazine. He was allowed unfettered access to 6202 and the men that maintained her and worked on the footplate. He began with a review of turbine development, moving on to building and ended with a vivid description of the engine in action. Over many months he analysed all that he saw with an experienced and dispassionate eye and his draft notes capture the excitement of this new engine and the joy of steam locomotion:

'I will now take you with me on the footplate, where I soon discovered that there are more things in Heaven and Earth – or rather in the cab of No 6202 – than I had previously dreamed of in my locomotive philosophy.

'A trip on a strange type of engine is always interesting to a locomotive enthusiast. One looks for differences, in design and performance, and contrasts

strike one with double force. Comparisons with other types are made; judgement is passed on this and that. Directly I entered the cab of 6202 at Camden Shed my critical faculties were aroused, and I looked for novelties. I soon found them – she gave me full scope at once.

'The engine left the shed tender first, and this at once brought an interesting feature into prominence. The reverse turbine is not permanently in gear, but has to be brought into association with the drive by means of a dog clutch. Motor car drivers sometimes discover that dog clutches can refuse engagement and must be persuaded to take up their duties by a partial revolution of half the

dog. This little objection cropped up when 6202 prepared to leave the shed, but was quickly smoothed over by the use of a device Fitter Whiston, who accompanied the engine, called the "inching gear". It is a simple fitting, quite effective and quick in action…. After this, 6202, got underway, running down to Euston to pick up the 10.40 am train for Liverpool and for the first time I experienced the smooth, seemingly effortless thrust of turbine power applied to a locomotive. It was altogether novel; I felt confident of having an unusually interesting run, and that I would gather further valuable information about the engine from Driver Worman, Fireman

6202 receives attention at Lime Street. (ET)

Turbomotive at high speed. (AE/RH)

Ruffell and Fitter Whiston, who made up the crew.

'Whilst waiting to pull out of Euston, my attention was attracted to the unusual fittings and controls in the cab that must be fully understood if the handling of the engine is to be followed intelligently.

'Many of the fittings are similar to those found on the usual types of engines, but turbine propulsion has naturally called for the introduction of others that are novel - at any rate, they were to me. The chief difference centre around the control box, which is on the left of the cab, in front of the driver's seat. The driving handle opens the valves successfully in the steam chest of the turbines; its manipulation controls the power and speed. This takes the place of the regulator and reverse gear of the orthodox locomotive – one control rather than two and a very simple one at that. It is turned clockwise to open the ahead valves and counter clockwise for the astern valves. The main regulator is used simply as a stop valve, and is kept fully open when running. There is a valve indicator showing how many are open; six ahead notches forward of the neutral position, and three astern notches behind it corresponding to the number of valves. There is a safety handle, which must be raised to the locking position before the reverse turbine can be engaged, this cannot be done unless the engine is stationary.

'To the left of the control box is the liquid meter, which indicates the amount of oil in the gear-box sump. The oil pressure explains itself, but on the right of the fireman's seat are two oil temperature gauges, one showing the temperature of the oil after it has circulated through turbines and gears, but before it enters the cooler in front of the engine, the others gauge oil temperature after it has cooled. The steam pressure gauge is now on the driver's side of the cab, over his head. Another unusual feature is a gauge that indicates the back-pressure of the exhaust in the ahead turbine.

'6202 got away punctually from Euston at 10.40 am, the start naturally being watched closely. The train weighed about 400 tons gross, so I expected sand to be used, but it proved unnecessary. Acceleration was absolutely smooth, and fairly rapid, though not exceptionally so. Two valves were opened for the get-away, and as the engine began to pick up speed I was struck by the novelty of my auditory impressions. The familiar staccato exhaust-beats were missing; I could hear nothing from the front end, the continuous flow of spent steam being so soft as to be practically noiseless. But another sound was at once perceptible – a musical singing note from the turbine-pinion, which sounded directly the engine began to move, rising to a pitch as the speed increased, until at about 15 mph it disappeared; I suppose because of the inability of my aural mechanism to follow it further up the scale. This musical accompaniment gave point to the nick-name bestowed on 6202 – "Gracie Fields".

Another valve was opened on the 1 in 70 Camden Bank, bringing three groups of nozzles into action; there was no slipping, and the evenness of acceleration was striking. It felt very strange – the complete absence of any of the vibration, thus or thump so often noticeable with the normal type of engine. A speed of 30 mph was attained in about half a mile, rising to 35 mph, at which the rest of the bank was mounted. The top, roughly 1 ¾ miles from the start was passed in 3 ½ minutes. Whiston, whose enthusiasm for 6202 was very obvious and creditable, drew my attention to the fine acceleration, so I diplomatically agreed with him – one learns tactfulness on the footplate! – but candour now compels me to admit that on this particular occasion, though good, it was nothing to write home about. I have done equally well on Camden Bank with other Pacific engines. But the steadiness of it, the feeling of power – that, I agree I have never before experienced to such perfection.

'Willesden, 5 ½ miles, was passed in 9 ½ minutes at 60 mph. No, Whiston, there really was nothing extraordinary about that! Again, it was good, but not astonishing. I'm not suggesting that 6202 could not have done better – I merely record that she did not, and that three nozzle groups were in action. But it must be conceded that Euston is an awkward station to pull out of – on a curve, with a very heavy gradient immediately following. The 3 ½ to North Wembley took about the same number of minutes; the speed was 60-65 mph, and here I first caught another unfamiliar sound, when I had cancelled out the other assorted footplate noises – a deep, very musical hum, the combined chorus sung by the gear train. It was not at all obtrusive; in fact, one could easily miss it, "Gracie Fields" was living up to her reputation.

'Up most of the long 31 mile rise to Tring, two valves were open, and the speed held steady at 60 mph; Kings Langley, 21.5 miles was passed at 11.06 am, 26 minutes from the start; Tring Station, just beyond the top of the bank, the speed had fallen to 55 mph…. Drifting steam caused no difficulty…. The draught was under, rather than over-fierce: I was told that the smoke box vacuum roughly corresponds to 1in per valve. Once over the top at Tring, the cut-off was shortened – sorry, I mean Worman cut out one group of nozzles – I'm not used to the turbine phraseology yet! The speed increased on a gently falling gradient and Cheddington was passed on one valve at 75 mph; 36.5 miles in 41.5 minutes. The Linslade Tunnel as usual called for shut dampers and firebox and the covering of ones face. This is a twin bore tunnel, and the area is very circumscribed so heat and smoke swirl into the cab directly it is entered. Bletchley was passed at 11.31 ½ am, 47 miles in 50 ½ minutes; here the engine was again running on two nozzle groups, the speed being 72 mph.

'Steaming was very good, the pressure remaining close to blowing-off point with a consistency I have never seen equalled. The draught being continuous and the blast soft, there were no signs of the fire being pulled about. I presume it is possible to adjust the cones in the blast pipe if it should prove

With Euston's magnificently sweeping roof as a backdrop, 6202 comes to rest. (RB)

6202 running light through the troughs at Bushey. (HH)

necessary, but they are no longer raised or lowered automatically according to the number of steam- chest valves that are in use, as was originally the case; it cannot be done while running. The best position has been chosen for normal working and there it stays.

'Wolverton was left behind at 11.35 am and the succeeding 7.5 miles to Roade, mostly on an up gradient of 1 in 326-410, were covered in 7.5 minutes. Weedon, 10 miles on, was reached in 9 minutes; 60-65 mph seemed a favourable rate of travel on this run; there were no intermittent "peak" speeds. Steam was shut off coming out of Kilsby Tunnel; the engine drifted down to Rugby, passing at the usual restricted

35 mph by the through line at 12.04 ½ pm. The average speed over the 82.5 miles from London had been 58.5 mph and we were 1.5 minutes ahead of time. We had been slightly ahead ever since passing Willesden, as a matter of fact and the average speed was higher than I realised, but the running of 6202 is very deceptive. It seems so effortless and casual, and speed variations so slight, that I failed to do her justice. She makes so little fuss about her job.

'After Rugby, seeing there was time in hand, the speed was moderated yet further and the fireman's movements became even more unruffled. The needle of the pressure gauge seemed glued to the 245 lbs line; it is evidently easier to

keep the steam at the required figure on a turbine engine than with a normal type. I find this was noted in my pad; it was apropos of a statement to Ruffell. From Rugby to Nuneaton passed at 12.20 pm, 1 minute early; 14.5 miles in 15.5 minutes, only one group of nozzles in action. 6202 seemed to spin along like a sleeping top. One group remained the allowance until we struck the slight rise to Lichfield, after water had been picked up at the Hademore troughs, when two valves were open. Tamworth had been passed at 12.32 pm, a minute ahead – Lichfield 6.5 miles in 6.5 minutes; even time once more. Stafford showed that 6202 apparently had got the bit between the teeth again – we were two minutes ahead here, passing with steam shut off at 12.57 pm. A couple of miles after Stafford 14 miles of an easy rise to Whitmore troughs begins and, as things were placid indeed in the cab, I allowed the engine to pursue the musical tenor of its way unwatched, while I lunched.

'I enjoyed the lunch in spite of its Spartan simplicity. But there – any sort of fare is grateful and comforting when one is in good company, and happy! As the Psalmist had it, "Better a dinner of herbs where love is, than stalled on an ox, and hatred withal!" I had brought neither stalled ox nor herbs into the cab with me – I dined on sandwiches, garnished with coal-dust and flavoured with engine oil. There was certainly no hatred in that cab – only such an atmosphere of good fellowship that it seemed almost a pity that 6202 had not been given a name in keeping with it. "Agapemone" for instance!

'I have said nothing about riding yet…. It was one of the chief features I had anticipated finding of exceptional

interest. The entire absence of reciprocating weights – the never changing torque of the turbine in place of the uneven thrust of pistons, from maximum to zero – was very good indeed, but I am quite unable to decide whether it was any better than that of a "Princess Royal", so evidently there can be actually little difference. As obviously there are no disturbances on a turbine engine due to internal forces, it follows that the balance of the "Princess Royal" class must be extraordinarily good. Against 6202's riding I have, therefore, no complaints to lodge, and so I will leave it at that and return to the run.

'Being 2 minutes ahead of schedule at Stafford, things were taken afterwards

Turbomotive in pristine condition awaits her turn of duty. (RH)

6202 photographed at Hatch End. The dynamometer car attached just behind the engine suggests that this was one of her test runs. (AE)

Euston, now in regular service. (AE/RH)

more legitimately and at Whitemore, passed at 1.20 pm, my sandwiches being finished, I began observations again, to find we were dead on time. From the troughs it is sharply downhill into Crewe and 6202 drifted to a stand at the station at 1.30 pm, two minutes to the good. The 24 ½ miles from Stafford had been covered in 33 minutes. No wonder 6202 had done most of the distance on one nozzle group! The 158 miles from Euston had taken 170 minutes, an average speed of 55.8 mph, over which the engine had handled the train with effortless ease, never having approached anything like hard work. At Crewe Whiston's place was taken by Fitter Parker. I had found the former's help invaluable and his thorough knowledge

of the engine, and his keen enthusiasm for it, very infectious. Worman and Ruffell carried on northward.

'Getting away from Crewe with the 400 ton load was easier than it had been at Euston, as the track is level; there was no slipping and again sand was not used. It was done with two valves open, but on the chiefly falling gradient to Weaver Junction – at which point the Liverpool line branches off from the main route to the north – one valve sufficed. I could not help noticing how simple the handling of 6202 was – I really believe a fairly creditable performance at the controls would have been in my own powers at a pinch!

'Weaver Junction was passed slow at 1.48 pm, a minute ahead of time, the

1 in 100 climb to South Weaver calling for three open valves. 1.57 pm found us passing Ditton Junction 2 minutes early, so we slowed down making an easy way along this somewhat hilly, curving section into Lime Street Liverpool, which was reached at 2.15 ½ pm under the booked time. The average speed over the 193.5 miles from Euston, with the stop at Crewe included, was 53.9 mph.

'I went with it to the shed, as I had been told this was a place very difficult to access, so there seemed promise of a good chance to watch the engines power of manoeuvre – that 'inching gear' interested me. And so it proved: I have never seen a shed so awkward to get into and out off. Forward and backward movement must alternate frequently, *but 6202 gave no trouble. Once or twice the "inching gear" had to be used, but it seemed quite simple to operate.'*

Livesay made the return trip to London later that day (this time with Driver Eborall, Fireman Jones and Fitter Parker, again) and over the months that followed gradually produced a critique of 6202 that he passed to Stanier for comment. No alterations were made and in due course *The Engineer* ran his article spread over a number of editions in 1940; long delayed and only published when the magazine ran short of material as the needs of war placed an embargo on technical information released to the press. Stanier and Guy no doubt would have found Livesay's summary encouraging:

'I make no secret of the fact that 6202 appealed to me considerably as a very fascinating machine, for which I could easily form an attachment. Fitters Whiston and Parker had evidently fallen under its spell; their loyalty was quite touching! The enginemen had no vital complaints on any score – or if they had they kept them dark. Fireman Ruffell had such an easy time of it heading north that he could not possibly have been anything but satisfied; but I gathered that Jones would have been a trifle happier had there been some means of intensifying the blast when causes beyond his control found him struggling with a pressure of 90 lbs below the proper figure.

'There is little doubt that 6202 represents a bold and most deserving excursion into a little explored field; in fact, in some degree, an unexplored one, as the design differs in important respects from previous turbine
locomotives. It follows that answers to many questions and problems associated with the engine can only be given after lengthy operation in ordinary service; and another point worth remembering is that little risk of failure as possible has been incurred, and the cost of construction reduced, by grafting a turbine drive on to an already existing design, the Princess Royal Class. It is not as though the engine were an entirely new conception throughout; if it were so, this would have resulted in increased possibility of trouble and greater cost.*

'One of the chief reasons that led to the construction of this engine was the expectation that, in spite of the absence of a condenser, economy in fuel consumption would result. I am not in a position to say whether this has been achieved or not. Merely watching the fireman, and listening to their remarks did not constitute a sufficiently accurate means of gauging consumption. During my runs I had no means of accurately measuring the coal used, but Mr Stanier has kindly filled the omission, and the figures dealing with 6202's runs with the "Royal Scot" show very clearly that her consumption, to say the least, is anything but excessive. To handle trains weighing nearly 500 tons between London and Glasgow at an average speed of over 55 mph with a coal

At Camden. (AE/RH)

6202 in her prime. Footplate crew seemed to have found her a worthy and generally reliable locomotive despite the time she spent at Crewe for maintenance and repairs to her turbines. (AE/RH)

expenditure of only 42.4 lbs and 40.2 lbs per mile on the respective trips seems to me exceedingly good. I cannot say whether the anticipated 15% saving theoretically looked for has been attained in practice.

'I was told that the smoothness of running of the turbine engine shown up in the fact that piping, utilised for various purposes lasts longer than usual; that things do not shake loose to the same extent as the normal type and that the roller bearings found on all axles have given no trouble whatever…. This alone speaks well of the design.

'My criticisms are very brief – I have none. The riding was good, acceleration quite up to normal, attained without a trace of slipping, which was no doubt the outcome of the constant, unvarying torque. The running was deceptively smooth and quiet, and it was very easy to under-estimate the speed. It is evidently equally deceptive to an onlooker; platelayers have been known to sing out "Here comes the Ghost Train!" [a play, later made into a film, of the same name was doing good business at this time] when 6202 looms up in the distance. It is a graceful machine in action.

'So ends the account of my turbo motive experience. I have travelled on many interesting engines lately and all have a place in my regard – with one diabolical exception! – but none was *quite so intriguing as this unusual machine, 6202, I wish her well and shall watch her subsequent career with interest.'*

In October 6202 and 6210 began four trial runs each running the full length of the West Coast mainline from Euston to Glasgow and back in one day. On 19 October and 26 October *Lady Patricia* and *Turbomotive*, respectively, ran the 10.00 up and 22.45 return. Then between 20/21 October and 27/28 October each ran the 14.00 to Glasgow and the 14.00 back the following day. A number of shorter trials took place on both engines earlier in the month to make sure they were in good shape for the long distance exercises during which 'trouble developed with the left crosshead [on 6210]' and with 6202 'steaming was not satisfactory'.

A week after the last run Stanier prepared a short summary of the results for Hartley, dispatched before the Vice President could hasten the CME again. His notes were becoming regular features of Stanier's working day:

'Each engine worked two trips Euston to Glasgow and return with the usual train loadings and a statement is attached showing the average results obtained from which it will be noted that the turbo motive shows a saving of 4.02% in coal.

'The maximum superheat recorded with the turbo motive (5 row element boiler) was 720F, as compared with 600F with the standard boiler on engine 6210.

'It should be noted, however, that the above results in the case of the turbo motive exclude one run between

Glasgow to Euston on the 26th October when unusually severe weather conditions obtained together with a gale of wind particularly on the northern section of the road.'

In fact the statement shows that on average 6202 burnt slightly more coal per mile than 6210, but used marginally less water. However, the final report (number 64), when issued early in 1937, made it clear that the stormy weather had affected 6202's trials on 26 October and 27 October, and this distorted the results considerably, raising her coal consumption from an average 43 to 50lbs per mile. 6210's trials had been conducted in much better weather so consumption had a smaller variation.

As 1936 drew to a close the results of the experiment were inconclusive. There were some positive signs: she

ran well, seemed capable of excellent performances, economy in fuel and water seemed possible and the crews found her a good working engine. But on the downside her reliability was questionable and the costs were very high, with little firm evidence that she would produce the savings predicted.

Ever wary of burgeoning costs, Hartley, as early as February, asked Stanier to report expenses incurred in building the first three Pacifics and set these figures against the outlay predicted in 1933. He duly reported that 6200 was £5,453 more than estimated, 6201 £4,155 and 6202 £7,813. Overall the programme was £17,421 over budget. Hartley and the Board recognised that development and experimentation cost money and eventual outlay

An everyday drama unnoticed at Hatch End. (AE/RH)

At speed and time to look out from the cab and observe a lineside photographer. (AE/RH)

could vary considerably as work progressed and unforeseen problems cropped up, but 43 per cent more seemed excessive.

Despite any misgivings there may have been among Board members, the desire to build new engines was undiminished and Stamp made sure that any opposition or criticism was kept in check. Progress and competition were in the air and work on the Princess Royal Class and Turbomotive would soon be eclipsed by an even bigger development – the Coronation Class. But this new programme began as an extension to the Princess Class – an extra five ordered in July 1936 on the back of the success of the first twelve reciprocating engines. The change, when it happened, seemed almost unexpected – spurred by competition with the LNER, where huge advances were being made in train design and service. This new development would soon eclipse the Princesses and threatened to push the turbine development into the background, unless its performance could be seen to be exceptional. So far the results were inconclusive and the months ahead would, some thought, be make or break time for the locomotive.

6202 pauses at Shrewsbury. (AE)

CHAPTER 5

COUNTDOWN TO WAR
(1936–1939)

1936 was a pivotal year in European history. The rise of fascism in Germany, Italy and Spain had begun to cause great concern worldwide and even Britain had its extreme right-wing element, though here it was a more muted affair. In Germany and Italy re-armament and expansion were well established and gaining ground, and here appeasement, even sympathy towards Germany, held sway. Many saw the danger, but hope seemed to triumph over reality and after years of recession people looked for an improvement in their lives, not the awful grind of poverty or a slide towards another cataclysmic war. But newsreels, newspapers and the 'wireless', now in many homes, gave voice to a growing feeling that this period of peace was ending.

Wilson Harris, editor of the Spectator, expressed these thoughts most clearly as 1936 closed:

'Life goes on; trade slowly but consistently expands; stock exchange values mount, unemployment diminishes; slums are cleared and houses built. But through it all penetrates ceaselessly the recurrent thought that all our building is for destruction, all our wealth is being amassed only to be destroyed in the work of destroying, all the wise expenditure of the nation on the education and health of its children and the support of its unemployed, its sick and aged will be checked or disastrously contracted by the need for laying on ourselves and future generations insupportable burdens in preparation for a new war.'

As the recession receded so commercial life expanded. Investment increased and when Britain, finally taking heed of re-armament in Europe, began to replace aging military equipment,

In the late evening light 6202 rushes past. (AE)

this too gave a massive boost to industry and employment. While it lasted the railway companies felt able to continue with their investment programmes, particularly on glamorous express services. In reality, the building of better goods engines was a far wiser outlay, as it boosted company profits considerably and also gave more practical support to a country facing war, where industrial might had to be exploited to the full. But it was passenger trains that made headlines and appeased shareholders growing tired of low dividends. And they still remained remarkably effective marketing tools, even though few Britons would have the resources to make use of them.

The rivalry between the LMS and the LNER for the trade from London to the north was reaching an intense pitch. Nigel Gresley had fully exploited the Pacific design and in 1935, as Turbomotive and the final ten Princess Royals appeared, introduced the next step in this evolution – a streamlined Pacific, the A4. When set alongside its stablemates the locomotive looked like something from a new age – sleek and sophisticated – though in reality it was only an updated version of other LNER A Class Pacifics already in service. But Gresley had gone further in another way. He, and his designers, produced a completely new deluxe train, locomotive and carriages, as a single streamlined, aerodynamic unit. The first engine, *Silver Link*, entered traffic on 7 September 1935, shortly followed by three class mates, *Quicksilver*, *Silver King* and *Silver Fox*. On 27 September the LNER ran a special press trip launching its new high-speed service, the *Silver Jubilee*, running from King's Cross to Grantham (when in service the train would run to Newcastle and back). Its impact was immediate and stunning, reaching speeds in excess of 110mph. In due course two more streamlined services appeared in 1937 and 1938: the *Coronation*, between London and Edinburgh, and the *West Riding Limited*, between London and Bradford.

The publicity this new class of locomotives and the *Silver Jubilee* service received was immense. The loco even appeared in the popular film *Oh, Mr Porter!* getting 'star billing' with the comedian Will Hay in 1937. The boardroom at Euston could hardly fail to note this sudden leap forward, at a time when they could offer little competition – on speed or quality of service. They had the Princesses and Turbomotive giving some glamour and good headlines, but thirteen new, high-performance engines could only offer limited competition to a fleet of more than eighty tried and tested Pacifics on East Coast routes. But the major cities along the West Coast line were bigger and had greater potential for trade. The challenge set by their rivals had to be taken up and exploited fully.

6202 was still, occasionally, making the headlines because of her

A return to Crewe Works for some attention. (LMS/AE)

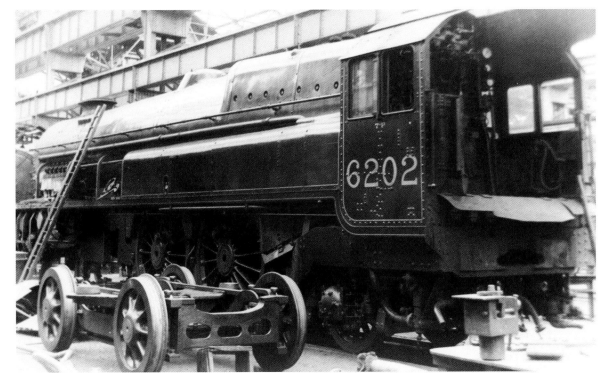

novelty, but was not doing anything spectacular; and the Princess Royals were performing well, but more was needed. So in 1936 the LMS undertook a well-publicised high-speed run between Euston and Glasgow. Its aim was to travel non-stop at the highest average speed in the quickest time. To achieve this, in November a special train of only six carriages and a dynamometer car, all weighing 225 tons, were coupled to 6201, *Princess Elizabeth*, increased to 255 tons for the return journey. The two runs took place on 16 and 17 November in mixed operating conditions and shaved 6 and 15.9 minutes off the schedule set specifically for this trial, averaging speeds of 68.2mph and 70.15mph. An impressive performance, as witnessed by Robert Riddles, who oversaw the trial:

'The locomotive had been fitted with a speedometer for the occasion and was gone over with the proverbial fine tooth comb. 6200, the Princess Royal, was similarly prepared as the standby engine. Driver Clarke, Fireman Fleet and reserve Fireman Shaw were on the footplate for both runs.

'Before leaving Willesden I had impressed on the Mechanical Inspector that he must make sure that all steam pipe joints were tight in the smoke box. Judge my consternation when at 5.15 pm he telephoned to say that the left-hand main steam pipe had failed. No replacement was available locally and one had to be rushed down from Crewe overnight not arriving until 2.30 am, leaving precious little time for fitting and testing. But we managed it and at 9.50 am we were given the "right-away"

from Euston and covered the 401.4 miles between Euston and Glasgow in 353 minutes 38 seconds. The maximum speed reached was 95.7 mph and 83 mph was sustained for 12 miles on practically level track.

'We had tea at the Central Hotel in Glasgow, with passengers, LMS Officials and the press, all were most enthusiastic over the day's experience. Later Ernest Lemon, briefly CME and now a Vice President got hold of me and "suggested" that we ought to try and run even faster on the return to London next day. I was opposed to trying higher speeds, but suggested adding an extra coach (making the train a weight comparable to the LNER's Silver Jubilee service). Lemon agreed to this.

'Whilst at dinner that evening an examination of 6201 was taking place and the fitter found all the metal out of the left hand block. With no suitable replacement available we had to repair the engine overnight and by 5.30 am work was complete and we were coupled up again ready to leave at 1.15 pm. Warned

that film people and more pressmen would be waiting for us at Euston I wondered if we would ever reach Beattock with a newly metalled slide block. We did, but my heart was in my mouth for much of the journey. In the two days we had run an aggregate distance of 800 miles, some in very bad weather, at a mean speed of 69 mph, which was a World record for steam traction.

'At Euston the train was met by Sir Josiah Stamp, Chairman of the LMS Railway, Sir Harold Hartley, Vice-President, Mr C R Byrom, Chief Operating Manager and Mr Aston Davies, Chief Commercial Manager, who congratulated the train crew on their remarkable dual performance.'

Such was the pressure for success that most Board members turned out to greet the train, eager to increase the impact of this record-breaking run. Riddles also, much to his surprise having moved mountains to make the trials a success, recalled that Sir Ernest Lemon, not in humour or light ribbing, queried the

6202 going at speed, but very quietly in comparison to her more conventional sisters. (AE)

6202 is prepared for duty. (AE/RH)

loss of a minute in the run-up to Beattock! William Stanier did not attend having been seconded to an inquiry being held in India to consider the parlous state of the railways there. UK members of this team arrived in Bombay during November and did not get home until March the following year. But he kept in touch with Riddles and sent a telegram of congratulations when the good news reached him.

Although proving the concept of long, non-stop journeys feasible, and gathering much-needed publicity in the process, these tests revealed that much of the main line was unsuited to high-speed running – a legacy of poor investment and the parochial attitudes of the pre-grouping railways. Before the new service could begin the Civil Engineering Department had to rebuild some junctions, realign track, remove loading restrictions, re-profile station platforms and correct subsidence in many places. In only six months the

transformation was complete and numerous speed and safety restrictions had been removed allowing a standard high-speed service to begin in June 1937 – twenty-one months after the LNER Silver Jubilee service commenced regular running and one month before their next special train, the Coronation, began. All the plaudits seemed to be going one way and belatedly the LMS tried to catch up.

During 1936, planning work had begun on five extra Princess Class locomotives. Orders for materials were prepared and the numbers 6213 to 6217 allocated. While waiting approval to proceed Derby Drawing Office examined the design and performance of the first twelve engines to see if improvements were feasible. A new shorter firebox and coupled wheel base were considered, as was a reduction in the total locomotive and tender wheelbase. But these developments remained a paper exercise only until

the high-speed trials took place and lessons learnt could be absorbed.

It soon became apparent that there was a need for a more powerful locomotive to supplement the Princesses and one that could equal the glamour created by the streamlined A4 hauled service on the LNER. So the specification was reviewed and Tom Coleman's team began redesign work. What emerged was a streamlined design capable of speeds in excess of 100mph, with larger, 6ft 9in coupled wheels, a bigger boiler and cylinders, a shortened wheelbase and two rather than four sets of Walschaerts valve gear operating four piston valves.

Throughout the 1930s streamlining was in vogue, although it was a concept that had long been studied. But in the decade before the Second World War it became very fashionable, science and art combining in a way that seemed to mirror the desire for a modernistic, high-tech world.

In reality streamlining evolved from the developing sciences of hydrodynamics and aerodynamics. As long ago as the early eighteenth century an understanding of these concepts materialised, but it was not until the means of measuring and collecting empirical data were understood and developed that the true worth of these sciences emerged. By slow degrees and experimentation the flow effect of air or liquid over a moving object, and the resistance they created, were identified and shape was seen to have an effect on reducing resistance. A blunt, angular shape created turbulence that impeded forward movement by creating a vacuum behind the moving form. One experiment in the mid-nineteenth century described this effect as 'sucking a forward moving object backwards into an eddy of disturbed air'. Streamlining the shape of an object, to reduce or eliminate drag, was identified as the solution to this problem.

As science deepened understanding of these concepts, the need to visualise and measure the effects of resistance emerged and a solution gradually suggested itself. In 1871 Francis Wenham, a Marine Engineer, who was fascinated by the theory of manned flight, had, with his colleague John Browning, noted during experiments that a strong breeze affected flight. Taking this further, they realised that different body and wing shapes reduced drag and increased lift and improved forward movement. They then considered how to measure this phenomenon in a controlled, scientific way and came up with the concept of a wind tunnel; in 1871 they built the first tunnel at Greenwich.

Over the course of many decades the concept of streamlining and the means of measuring performance had emerged and in time these ideas would be refined and used to great effect in designing ships, aircraft, road vehicles and trains.

The 1930s saw a crescendo in this development: art and science, form and function combined with a changing fashion to produce a look and style that became infectious.

Some felt that the science of these dynamics was sacrificed for a modern look. This was nowhere more apparent than on the railways, where directors were always seeking to make their trains more efficient and more eye catching.

Even from the earliest days of locomotive design some engineers had seen the value of a sleeker shape. In the 1840s Medhurst proposed a railcar tapered at both ends and in 1867 the Reverend Samuel Calthrop, of Massachusetts, applied for a patent that incorporated a steam engine, tender and carriage in a single streamlined tapered body. Neither project went beyond the drawing board, but they encouraged others to develop the concept, as the twentieth century dawned, and US designers led the way. By the late 1920s many streamlining projects had been proposed and some built, but the impact of these was minimal. Then in 1932 Roy Shelden and Egmont Arens, industrial designers, stated that the railway system needed to modernise. Through their book *Consumer Engineering* they

Frederick Johansen, scientist and aerodynamics specialist, employed by the LNER and later the LMS to oversee streamlining experiments. (FJ)

asserted that passenger services would become obsolete if the 'public be damned' attitude among railway companies continued – improvements to speed, economy, comfort and beauty were essential for survival and growth. The practical and beautiful had to be wedded. They saw the streamlining of shape and

How 6202 might have looked if streamlining had been applied to the Princess Royal Class. One of Johansen's Models. (FJ/LMS)

service as one. This work found a ready audience in their own country, with designers Henry Dreyfuss, Otto Kuhler, Raymond Loewy and Norman Bel Geddes leading the way. In a few short years they were producing many iconic streamlined locomotives and carriage sets. These advances were noted in Europe.

From late 1927 to 1932, a scientist in his early thirties, Frederick Johansen, employed by the National Physical Laboratory at Teddington, had conducted experiments into aspects of fluid motion and the dynamics of resistance. His work greatly benefited from a wind tunnel the NPL had had built. Although not a locomotive engineer, he used rail vehicles as a basis for much of his work, modelling and testing various shapes and designs to arrive at ideal solutions for reducing resistance. Some of this work was sponsored by Gresley, and Johansen did a great deal of research work for him on the possible shape and aerodynamics of the LNER's experimental locomotive 'Hush Hush'. With the company's designers he came up with a novel body shape for this locomotive and played an active part in its development. His work was soon taken up by the other railway companies, but it was on the LMS, after the LNER, that his efforts had most impact. Harold Hartley, ever aware of the need to improve the skills pool of his scientific department, recruited Johansen in 1932, basing him at Euston so he could continue using the facilities at Teddington.

Although his research on fluids, air resistance and streamlining

resulted in a considerable amount of new, valuable material, it was not made public until 1936 when he presented his findings in a paper to the Institution of Mechanical Engineers, years after his research had found favour with the LNER, but less so with his employer, the LMS. Some would later say that streamlining was too radical a departure for conservative traditionalists at Derby and Crewe. In their defence, others argued that air smooth casing would produce only minimal benefits in performance and economy; not enough to make the expense of streamlining worthwhile.

However, Gresley continued to embrace the concept, had various shapes tested in the wind tunnel at the NPL, under Johansen's guidance, and produced his classic A4 design, plus modifications to the P2 class and two B17 4-6-0s. By 1937 the A4s were performing good work on high-speed runs and gathering much credit and publicity for the company and its service. With the Coronation Class taking shape, it seems that Stanier and Riddles felt under pressure from Board members to follow the example of the A4 and produce a sleek, modern design. So a series of experiments were carried out at Derby, with Coleman and Johansen taking the lead, to determine the ideal shape for the new Pacific.

Although Johansen had, in his first years with the LMS, carried on using the wind tunnel at NPL, he argued that a similar structure should be built at Derby, so that

locomotive, carriage and truck design could be tested more thoroughly and conveniently. In 1936 building was complete, in time to test various streamlining options for the Coronation Class. But with air smoothing in fashion, Stanier was encouraged by Hartley and Stamp to consider converting the Princesses and Turbomotive as well. Coleman's team prepared two drawings to show how the class of twelve could be modified and assumed that 6202 would follow suit, some adjustments being made for the casing that covered the turbines and ancillary equipment.

In an internal memorandum, on 21 July 1936, T.M. Herbert, Head of Research, briefed Johansen on the proposal for 6202:

'Mr Stanier writes that it is intended to change the boiler in the above engine and says further that he considers it an ideal engine for trying out the effects of streamlining. He is anxious for this to be done as soon as possible and has written to Mr Coleman telling him to get out a scheme in conjunction with the Research Department. I shall be obliged if you will do your best to meet Mr Stanier's wishes in this matter.'

Some would later claim that Stanier was opposed to streamlining and felt that it was a distraction. If so, he might have felt that offering the experimental Turbomotive up as a test vehicle might deflect attention away from his primary purpose – to evolve and develop the Princess design. This may say something about a changing attitude towards 6202 – a growing realisation that, despite her achievements, turbine

Cowans, Sheldon and Co of Carlisle, which manufactured turntables, requested photographs of 6202 and other new, high-profile locomotives for publicity purposes. These two shots, of a group of five, were taken on a very murky, wet London day for the company and featured in their adverts. (AE/LMS)

Leaving Euston on another trip to Liverpool, something, now long forgotten, proving of great interest to the fireman and fitter. (AE)

drive would go no further with the LMS and her days were numbered. So nothing would be lost if she were streamlined and lip service would have been paid to the latest panacea in locomotive design.

Through August, Herbert and Johansen corresponded on modifications to 6202:

'5 August 1936

'Referring to our conversation, Mr Stanier is agreeable to postpone the streamlining for a month, and I should be glad if you would see Mr Bellamy as early as possible regarding the production of the necessary model in the Patten Shop. I am very anxious that everything possible be done to complete the work within the month.'

In the early 1960s, not long before his death, Johansen recalled, in a letter, his memories of these debates and the work he did:

'My work for the LNER certainly caught Hartley's attention and he encouraged me to consider how the LMS might usefully adopt streamlining. With Gresley it was very clear from day one that he wanted express locomotives modified in this way and would not stand any opposition. But his position with the LNER was different to that of Stanier at the LMS. He had greater authority and could do as much as he pleased.

'I was in the very strange position of working for the LMS but producing and testing designs for the LNER at the NPL. Hartley seemed unconcerned by this and even encouraged it, I assume because this work could have a wider significance and be adopted by the LMS.

'By 1936, with the A4s making such a huge impact, Hartley felt that I should only involve myself with LMS design tasks and be based, part time at least, at Derby. I convinced him of the need for better testing facilities there. He agreed with my proposal for a wind tunnel and authorised expenditure.

'Many of my colleagues at Derby had reservations about the benefits of streamlining, but the A4s clearly impressed some of them. Overall, though, there was a muted response, which I hoped my paper to the Institution in 1936 would improve. It certainly encouraged much debate, and with Hartley's solid backing work began on bringing some of these principles to bear on the LMS Pacifics – those already built and the next group, then under consideration by Stanier and Coleman.

'It was difficult to see how a programme to modify the Princess Class might be fitted into their running and maintenance schedules; the need for them to remain in service on the long route to Scotland took precedence. But the turbine locomotive appeared a more realistic option; being experimental and with considerable time in works, as teething problems mounted up. So our test and design work focussed on this engine only. Drawings of a streamlined Princess had already been prepared and soon after a wooden model, with changeable sections, had been constructed. From these we were able to extrapolate the likely effects on the turbine loco, as well as the rest of the class and decide on the most effective streamlined shape. Soon after this work was completed (in August), at a meeting with Herbert and Coleman, it was made clear that our efforts would now be redirected towards the new class of

Pacifics then under consideration. No one said that streamlining the turbine engine or the rest of the class had been dropped permanently, just that the priorities had changed.'

One can only imagine the conversations that took place over the costs and benefits of all these projected developments, particularly if, as some believe, Stanier was not an enthusiastic supporter. If so, his departure for India in November, and a five-month absence, took him away from these debates until design work on the first batch of Coronations was virtually complete.

Most tasks on the railway were hard, mundane and repetitive, a far cry from the high-profile record runs

that craved headlines. Life, even for 'glamorous' engines such as Turbomotive, was one of workshop time and hard running. Less of the former, more of the latter was the recipe for a successful railway and, as 1937 dawned, she fell foul of this commercial necessity. At the end of January she again failed, this time at Willesden when the forward turbine motor jammed.

She remained out of traffic until mid-April and, as soon as he had returned from India, Stanier received a slightly testy note from Hartley seeking news and explanations about 6202's latest breakdown. Sandham Symes, ex-Principal Assistant to Henry Fowler and now the Chief

Stores Superintendent, acting as Chief Mechanical Engineer in Stanier's absence, had kept Hartley briefed and tried to smooth, what seemed to him, 'troubled waters':

'21 January 1937
'Engine No 6202 failed at Willesden on January 3rd, it being found impossible to move the engine either forward or backwards, and it was necessary to jack up the driving wheels before it could be hauled to the shed. The forward turbine was released from the driving gear, and it was then found that the driving transmission was free, but the turbine itself was fast.

'The turbine was taken down and sent to the works of Metropolitan Vickers, Trafford Park Manchester, and

A photographer's dream – a locomotive running at high speed, working hard with a sheen of steam and smoke stream flowing back along the train. (AE)

here it was opened up yesterday and a preliminary examination showed that several of the rotors in the centre portion of the turbine were found to have the blades stripped, and these were jammed between the rotor and the casing.

'I have not received a report from Metropolitan Vickers as to the reason for the stripping of the blades, but when this is to hand I will send you further information.'

Nearly two months later, having heard nothing more, Hartley hastened Stanier. He replied:

'11 March 1937

'Mr Guy reported on the 5th ultimo that as a result of their investigation into the cause of the damage to the blades and diaphragms, it was found that the rim of

diaphragm No 9 had come in radially over 1/8" on the bottom half, this being the maximum at the vertical central line. This was the final result of a progressive movement resulting from working between the diaphragm and the cylinder groove during the times when the temperature of the diaphragm was higher than the cylinder. This progressive movement would in future be prevented by forming a lock between the diaphragm and the cylinder groove when the new blades are fitted.

'I am informed that the Turbine repairs are well in hand, and it is expected that it will be despatched from their Works to Crewe on the 15th instant.'

Whether appeased or not by this response, Hartley very tersely

scribbled at the bottom of Stanier's memo, 'Who does the tests ? Who bears the costs? W Taylor will see that reply is sent.' Stanier's response was brief and to the point:

'With reference to your endorsement on my letter of the 11th instant, the cost of all repairs to the turbine have been borne by Messrs. Metropolitan Vickers where they themselves have done the work in Manchester and no charge has been made by them. We, on our part, have not charged them with any work done in connection with the dismantling of various engine parts for them to have such parts in their Works for repair. In other words, each side at the moment has borne its own costs. This, I think, is an equitable arrangement and until such time as the engine is definitely of a satisfactory design, is one I think, should be continued.'

It seems likely that Hartley felt that the joint project was going too slowly and diverting attention and funds away from other more pressing matters. He had already, influenced by concerns expressed by company accountants, questioned the costs and looked for some substantial benefit to accrue from the experiment. As a leading scientist himself he knew only too well that in every experiment a time would come when ends ceased to justify means. With Turbomotive he was reaching the point where evidence of success was minimal, costs seemed excessive and notable future benefits unlikely. Another major breakdown would hardly reassure him.

For his part, Stanier still believed in the project and would later say that the LMS should have built fifty

6202 at Shrewsbury. Trips to Shropshire from Crewe were used as running in turns for new engines or those just out of long-term maintenance periods. (AE/RH)

or more turbine locomotives. With these numbers operating there would have been an economy of scale and a spares regime in place to cope more adequately, and cheaply, with breakdowns. He also believed that 6202 should have had specific crews assigned to her, on the footplate and in the workshops, suggesting that she would have run more effectively if specialist teams with detailed knowledge of the type had been in place. With only one engine this would not have happened and all 6202 had as 'expert' support

were the two fitters who were assigned to her footplate crew.

It was a debate that would roll on for some time. While it did, Turbomotive returned to traffic and did what she was designed to do, with many interested and critical eyes looking over Stanier's shoulder to see what happened next. But his reputation was so high and his mastery of design deemed so complete that his advocacy of this cause was likely to keep the experiment going far longer than lesser men might have allowed. For

their part Metropolitan Vickers still strongly believed in the concept and absorbed their costs in repairing the turbine without complaint – new orders remained a possibility.

Support for 6202 also came from the footplate crew who worked the experimental locomotive, as Alfred Ewer, the District Locomotive Superintendent covering Camden, later recalled:

'My arrival at Camden in 1935 coincided with 6202's entry into service. I can honestly say that she was greeted with enthusiasm by drivers and firemen

A heavy load handled with ease. (AE)

Running backwards with a heavy load was not one of 6202's strong points. The reverse turbine was unsuited for such heavy duty. (AE/RH)

and there was competition amongst them to work on her footplate, moreso than the other Pacifics coming into service during those years. This attitude didn't change in all the years I worked there. I took the opportunity to ride on her footplate on a number of occasions and went as far as Liverpool, taking the controls over from Driver Earl through the Trent Valley.

'Even though Camden and Willesden received many new engines at that time 6202 always attracted most attention, particularly from higher management. Mr Stanier visited a number of times and closely questioned all those who worked with the engine – drivers, firemen, fitters and managers. He sat in my office on each visit and talked about the turbine, very keen to understand how she performed and how she might be improved. Mr Coleman, from Derby, also took a close interest and on one

occasion was accompanied by Mr Lemon and two representatives from Metropolitan Vickers, whose names escape me. There was a long debate about the best ways or running and maintaining 6202. I can't say there was agreement and Mr Lemon strongly supported the view that due to the engine's unreliability that a fitter should continue to ride on the footplate at all times. Mr Coleman felt this was unnecessary because there was little the fitter could do in the event of a breakdown and routine maintenance – checking the engine over and oiling – could easily be carried out by the driver and fireman. But Mr Lemon, who remembered the problems with "Fury" gained the support of Sir Harold Hartley and the fitter remained. I disagreed with this.

'Tom Coleman became a close friend and during his visits closely examined 6202 and did some sketches of her in

modified form. Though a reserved man by nature he talked openly about the engine and his wish to modify the design. He wanted to improve the reverse drive, change the cab controls, modify the frames and fit 6'9" driving wheels. He left me two drawings of the engine in streamlined form.

'Although the engine had a reputation for being unreliable, I think this was unjustified. On many occasions fitters at Camden could have fixed the problems, but Mr Lemon directed that she should be returned to Crewe for repairs. This was time consuming and unnecessary on many occasions. It would also have reduced her time out of service if spare parts had been more readily available.

'From my point of view the engine was well liked by the drivers and firemen. It ran well and if my fitters had been allowed to do more, would have *given me no more problems than the other Pacifics, possibly even less.'*

Interest in Turbomotive still existed and Hartley received many requests for information from railway companies and designers in the US, Germany, France, and Japan. Raymond Loewy, who was designing a series of modernistic locomotives and carriage sets in the US, visited Britain, saw 6202 in operation and commented in his classic 1937 book *Locomotive* that she is:

'In the writer's opinion, a truly splendid engine, and an outstanding example of the "British School." The cut in the rear top section of the tender might have been omitted , creating a longer horizontal outline. However, it is as a whole one of the most beautiful pieces of machinery ever designed by man. It has poise, the rhythm and balance reminiscent of some magnificent ship. This engine probably represents the apex of the pre-streamlined era.'

Loewy wasted little time in considering 6202's performance, seeing her only with his artist's eye, so form easily triumphed over function in his review. But the aesthetic quality was not lost on many conservative engineers. The old saying among designers that 'if it looks right, it probably is', would strike a common cord and many engineers had a good eye for such things. And she was such a sleek, very good-looking locomotive, that streamlining was unlikely to improve her.

Loewy's contemporaries among the American Railway Association took a more straightforward view and sought a detailed technical assessment. Hartley and Stanier carefully deflected this request, being unsure of the benefits of turbine drive and wishing to keep their discoveries secret from competitors for as long as possible. Instead they sent a copy of the 1935 *Railway Gazette* article, which was then published in the American press. Other enquiries met with a similar response.

Once back in traffic, after her breakdown in January, 6202 performed well for many months. During June, her third and last trial was run on the Euston to Glasgow route, but this time without another Princess as direct comparison. By this stage all twelve were in full operation, over many routes, and their performance was understood and well documented. On 27 October Stanier sent a copy of the latest report (Number 71) to Hartley, plus copies of the previous reports from 1936, 'as requested'.

It seems likely that Stanier preferred to keep the trial results to himself until he could present a complete assessment of the engine's performance and potential, suggesting that he did not necessarily see Hartley as an ally in this cause. In November the Vice President wrote to Stanier, forwarding another request for information from overseas, and his note suggests a slight degree of discord.

Hartley made it very clear how the reply should be worded:

'25 November 1937

'…. I should then explain (to the correspondent) that the turbo locomotive is a joint experiment with Metro-Vickers and that until the locomotive is in regular service after the experimental period we

Two of 6202's crew lean out to watch the photographer. (AE/RH)

do not propose to give the detailed information required, as this might give quite a wrong impression with regard to the locomotive's performance.

'The locomotive is the first of its kind to be built in England and a good many changes have been made, which have kept it out of service for a considerable time, but we do not think the statistics asked for would serve any useful purpose at the moment, though you are ready to give any technical details that he wishes for [Hartley heavily underlined the last part of this sentence in ink].

'I think this is the only fair attitude we can adopt, in view of our relations with Metro-Vickers.'

This is a strange letter in many ways, because its terseness suggests disharmony. In one way Hartley is simply setting out a policy for communications with other companies, but in another way there seems to be implied criticism of Stanier and the turbine programme. One can only wonder at the politics and confrontations taking place in the LMS at the time, but clearly relationships between both men were strained if Hartley felt it necessary to write in this way. Stanier's response, if there was one, has not survived.

An interesting development was taking place in France at this time and it is curious to wonder if Stanier and Henry Guy had some involvement. Links between French and British locomotive designers were close, with Gresley and Stanier greatly impressed by the work of Andre Chapelon, in particular. During 1937/38, the Compagnie des chemins de fer du Nord (often shortened to the Nord Railway Company) began developing a streamlined Pacific turbine locomotive that was clearly influenced by Turbomotive.

It seems an odd coincidence that this company should produce an engine using many design features from the British experiment without some contact with the LMS or Metrovick. Its air smooth shape also bore a strong resemblance to streamlining designs being developed at Derby for the Princess and Coronation Classes. So perhaps Hartley's restriction on releasing information to foreign competitors was influenced by a sense that the links between engineers was too close. If so, he need not have worried about the Nord Company's turbine work. In the late 1930s French railways were nationalised and the project was soon abandoned. Another attempt was made to resurrect the concept in 1939, but the invasion of France brought this to an end too, though the engine built remained in existence for some years.

The report for Turbomotive's final set of trials, which had taken place between 22 and 25 June, showed promise. Much had been in her favour. Weather conditions were ideal on all four days, the engine was well run in, with a total mileage of 102,915, two months free of problems had seemed to settle earlier running issues and its crew were experienced 'turbine men'. As usual a fitter rode on the footplate, this time accompanied by a representative from Metrovick.

Only two problems materialised during the trials:

'Trouble was experienced in the working of the Exhaust Steam Injector, which failed to pick up water cleanly when working with three steam nozzles in operation, and during the first two trips the live steam injector was used for considerable periods. The injector was dismantled, cleaned and cones examined, and finally a new delivery cone end was fitted, but, although, there was some improvement, the working of the injector could not be considered satisfactory.

'Throughout the tests sectional timekeeping was affected by an abnormal number of speed restrictions, which for the first two days of tests resulted in a late arrival at Glasgow and Euston respectively.'

The June results proved promising with average coal consumption reaching 41.6 lbs per mile, but water consumption, at 37.1 gallons per mile, could 'not be regarded as representative of this engine, because of the trouble experienced with the Exhaust Steam Injector which made the water figures too high'. The locomotive was usually capable of using 2 to 3 gallons a mile less and did so on the last two runs. When all test material was analysed average consumption for engines 6210 and 6212 during the 1936 trials was compared to 6202's performance over all three trials:

Coal – 6210 – 42.9 lbs per mile.
6212 – 45.0 lbs per mile.
6202 – 43.46 lbs per mile.
Water – 6210 – 36.0 gallons per mile.
6212 – 37.0 gallons per mile.
6202 – 35.53 gallons per mile.

6202's results were disappointing, but average readings can be misleading because they can distort the picture or ignore the vagaries of each run: weather, operational restrictions, mechanical issues and the skill of footplate crew. Rightly or wrongly, Stanier viewed all four test runs in June as being the most accurate for coal consumption, but only the last two for water. The earlier tests, although interesting, were disregarded as 6202 was under development then, so some way from full operational efficiency.

Delaying publication of the second and third set of tests until October 1937 seemed tardy and suggests that Stanier wanted to prepare the ground properly before revealing these mixed results. He obviously expected some opposition to his proposals and common sense dictated a measured approach if the turbine experiment were to lead to more locomotives, as the CME wanted. But to Hartley and Stamp the balance seemed wrong and the potential benefits in cost were far from proven, especially when the chequered maintenance record of the engine were included in the equation. The question any good manager would ask could only focus one issue – does this engine improve on anything we have or can get from more traditional means? On performance alone the only answer to this would be no, especially when streamlining was being developed and advocated by Hartley's own department as a

Awaiting right of way.
(AE)

cheaper, more efficient way of improving high-speed performance.

By the time 6202's reports had been published and distributed the first five streamlined Coronation Class locomotives were operating from Camden Shed. Very quickly these impressive engines drew the public gaze, all the stops being pulled out by the PR team to sell the new locomotives and the trains they would pull. Under this barrage of publicity the thirteen Princesses quickly slipped from view. The addition of fifteen more Coronations, including five non streamlined engines, before war was declared in September 1939, completed the domination they had over all other express classes on the LMS.

Despite its limited success, Turbomotive continued in service but any

chance of more turbine locomotives being built seemed to fade.

Sadly, many records were destroyed and only conjecture, fuelled by memoirs and a few surviving documents, remains to illuminate these decisions. It is likely that Stanier remained a strong advocate of 6202, but became increasingly isolated. Hartley may have thought that the CME had lost sight of company goals in his advocacy and hoped to move him forward and away from a gallant, but ultimately flawed concept. Stamp and his other directors would have been driven by financial necessity and satisfied by the public relations glow emanating from the new streamliners. They would also have seen their huge re-equipping programme reaching fruition and trade picking up as a result. Against these advances Turbomotive had become a costly irrelevance and her future must have been discussed. Conversion to a standard design or withdrawal and scrapping may have been considered, but nothing happened. One can only assume that Stanier put forward a strong case in her defence and no one was prepared to overrule him. So 6202 remained in service, warts and all.

By 1938 Stanier's position in the company was an interesting one. Recruited specifically to modernise its fleet of locomotives, he had, after five difficult years, brought this ambitious plan to fruition, but completion of this design work changed the dynamics of his role as CME. Even though he was 62 years old he was at the peak of his powers

and authority, but what lay ahead? Eager to keep such a talented man in the company, when the CME role was changing from development to one of process, would be a challenge. Two secondments to India to conduct major reviews, Presidency of the Institution of Locomotive Engineers, then Presidency of the Institution of Mechanical Engineers offered valuable outlets for his energy, but being the CME remained of prime importance to him and this meant designing and experimenting. So, for the time being, 6202 remained under Stanier's protecting hand and slipped into regular service on the Euston to Liverpool route.

Following Stanier's death, in 1965, Hartley was invited to write a biographical memoir for the Royal

Society, to which the CME was elected in 1944. Although their relationship remained cordial, Hartley did not let the moment pass without a passing, but oblique reference to the professional differences that had existed:

'Although Stanier was not altogether happy in his relations with the Research Department, they did help him in various ways, particularly in the metallurgical problems associated with metal fatigue of tyres, axles and laminated springs and corrosion fatigue of boilers. Their studies of combustion led to improved firing, little and often as it was called, that gave savings of from 5 to 10% of coal. Cinematograph records showed the relation of steady riding to the coning of the tyres and also the tendency of coupled wheels to lift slightly from the rails at high rotational speeds. Measurement in a wind tunnel showed the saving in wind resistance given streamlining at high speeds.'

Later in the same piece he touched, very briefly, on Stanier's turbine experiment. Even after thirty years Hartley felt it necessary to have the last word, albeit in a very measured way:

'It ran successfully until the war and, with certain modifications showed itself capable of performing the heaviest tasks…. Being different to the standard types it needed special supervision and under war conditions it ran into trouble. Subsequently it was decided that the advantages it offered did not compensate for the exceptional treatment it needed and it was rebuilt in a standard pattern.'

H.A.V. Bulleid, in his book *Master Builders of Steam*, touched, very briefly, on the professional

Another arrival and 6202 still draws attention. (AE)

The Liverpool run again, this time
captured by Eric Treacy. (ET)

differences that seemed to exist between both men:

'Sir Harold Hartley naturally took a strong interest in the whole project, and told Stanier to be sure to have wind tunnel tests made at Derby to ensure the best streamlined shape…. Then doubt was expressed at Board level as to whether the streamlining was really necessary. "Why argue," thought Stanier, "rather please a fool than tease".'

Although Stanier contributed to this book, provenance of the story is unclear, but, if true, it is a contemporary account of the differences that may have existed and adds to the few strands revealed by surviving documents and memoirs. Wherever the truth lies it seems to me that disagreement and debate will foster a creative edge, especially if both 'protagonists' wish to achieve the same thing, but from different routes. In this case two men of great substance and skill wished to achieve what was best for the LMS, ever aware that this was not a public body, able to draw research funds from Government, but a private company where profit and loss were paramount. To have speculated, at great cost, on the turbine experiment demonstrated openness of thought and scientific curiosity. For this Stamp and Hartley deserve praise. But they felt that the idea had been taken as far as it could and had to find a way of ending the experiment without offending their CME.

During 1937, after her failed forward turbine had been repaired, 6202 ran well, spending only twenty-one days in the workshop for routine repairs, plus some modifications and additions.

Between these two maintenance periods she ran a creditable 43,315 miles and seemed to be bedding in well. But her reverse turbine failed again on 2 November and fifteen more days were lost while the turbine was completely overhauled. Again she ran without any recorded problems until June 1938 when she entered Crewe Works for a planned period of routine repair and maintenance lasting 123 working days. She emerged from the workshop in October and worked effectively throughout the winter, but after four months a failed forward turbine afflicted her for the second time. In 1946 Roland Bond recalled this incident:

'The failure occurred when the engine was travelling at over 60 mph near Leighton Buzzard on the up journey from Liverpool. Conditions on the footplate had been completely normal immediately prior to the casualty, which was due to the breakage of the end of the main turbine spindle at a screwed portion under the nut retaining the thrust collar. The breakage allowed the turbine rotor to move laterally until fouling occurred. Internal damage was naturally severe…

'These two failures (of the forward turbine) naturally caused some misgivings as to the suitability of turbines for locomotive work, particularly bearing in mind the long periods out of traffic which entailed thereby. It is fair comment to say that had a spare turbine been available, the engine would not have been in the Shops any longer than is required after a reciprocating engine has had a serious inside big end failure, to which these casualties may well be compared. Inside big end failures are not unknown and often cause damage to cylinders, motion and crank axle more extensive than was the case with 6202, in which damage was confined solely to the turbine itself.'

Guy visited the Works shortly afterwards and agreed to transport turbines and gears to Trafford Park for detailed assessment and repair. Stripped of her drive for an indefinite period, staff at Crewe took the opportunity to undertake other work on the loco. This included fixing new top frame bars to the leading bogie, fitting a new control box and attaching smoke deflectors; drifting exhaust had long been a problem by obscuring the crew's forward view.

The locomotive was finally reassembled and back in traffic at the end of July as events in Europe reached fever pitch. After months of shadow boxing, as Hitler slowly spread his insidious empire across Germany's neighbours, he met a country prepared to fight, though ill-equipped to do so. Poland stood in his way eastwards and on 1 September his forces invaded, despite Britain and France pledging support to their ally. They both declared war later the same day.

Few, if any, could predict what would happen over the next few years, but institutions across the country activated contingency plans or just muddled through, hoping that the conflict would not last long or reach these shores. Government decanted offices away from London;

Back to Crewe again and stripped of motion, wheels and turbines. (RR/RH)

museums placed many precious items in safe stores; hospitals, where they could, were evacuated, as were families or at least children; industry geared up for war production; non-essential products disappeared from shops; and the building of Anderson Shelters became a basic part of life for those with gardens. A country at war was soon stripped of its peacetime facade and the generation that had lived and fought through the First World War slipped into a pattern of life they had hoped never to experience again.

The railways were central to Britain's war plans and the investments that had seen so many improvements during the 1930s would soon pay many unexpected dividends. But the glamorous express services that had seemed so important a few years earlier now appeared to be an unnecessary extravagance for a country soon to be plunged into wartime austerity.

Good, strong, reliable engines were essential, but anything falling short of this standard would be stripped away. Very quickly it was decided that Turbomotive, with her poor maintenance record and lack of readily available spares, could not be kept in service and within days of war being declared was mothballed; it was condemned to the Paint Shop at Crewe, while awaiting a decision about her future. Few expected to see her re-enter service.

CHAPTER 6

RESURRECTION
(1940–1945)

There was little time to stand and watch when war came. The time for appeasement had given way to a solemn, sobering reality. Memories of the First World War were still fresh and the martial instincts of many old soldiers were stirred by these events. But with this feeling came a horror of what lay ahead for their children. Survivors from the First World War had been given a brief taste of what any future conflict might hold when Britain was bombed by airships, then large twin-engine aircraft. Although damage and casualties were light, when compared to the carnage on the Western Front, civilians glimpsed the terror that might befall them if these weapons were developed in greater numbers. Newspapers and films during the 1930s graphically predicted an Armageddon for our cities and the civil war in Spain, where Hitler's Luftwaffe had run riot, gave these horrors a vivid voice. No one could predict the future and the worst was imagined. But even the most lurid imagination would have been hard pressed to even glimpse the extreme violence that lay ahead for civilised nations.

Railways and shipping were key to Britain's survival. Without them service personnel, civilians, food and war material could not be transported and our army, navy and air force would soon be depleted. The Big Four railway companies slipped into a war footing on day one, each activating their own mobilisation plans while moving under a measure of State control. The LMS, being the largest of these companies, had a great deal to offer. By 1939 it was carrying 434 million passengers and 125 million tons of freight per year. It owned and managed extensive workshops, 25 harbour facilities and 66 steamships, 4,000 motors and 3,000 trailers, a fleet of aeroplanes and 535 miles of canal. To serve these needs they had 19,000 miles of track, 250,000 staff, 7,500 locomotives and 303,000 individual items of rolling stock. Due to Josiah Stamp, the LMS Board, William Stanier and others, much of the company had been modernised and was in good condition to meet the trials ahead.

It is strange that among all the stresses and strains these preparations for war created, one locomotive, 6202, should be singled out for mothballing, especially when she had just passed through a heavy overhaul, was fully operational and judged to be an effective engine capable of good work, even under war conditions. Years later, when talking about her withdrawal, Stanier expressed his dismay at this 'knee jerk' reaction. The excuse that in war she would be difficult to run and maintain, in his view, 'held little water'. No documents seem to have survived to explain this decision so we are left with conjecture. One hopes it was a decision made for the right reasons, but Stanier did not manage day to day running of the railway and there was a coolness between those who did, in the Operations Department, and his own organisation. While Ernest Lemon ran the operational side as Vice President there were differences, but these were handled diplomatically. But in 1938 he was seconded to the Air Ministry as Director General of Aircraft Production. His replacement, Ashton Davies, failed to grip the work effectively, or so it seemed to H.G. Smith, Lemon's Personal Secretary, who remained with the LMS. He wryly observed the deterioration:

'Ashton Davies is solely hanging on for "Sir Ashton" to come along, as he is certain will do out of the war. He will hang on until his teeth drop out. He is entirely selfish and No 1 comes first every time. He is a skater on the surface, and does not get down to the root problems, and since you went there has been no real criticism of the Operating Department. And some criticism is needed. Royle swallows everything Fisher tells him, and moreover, Royle is getting a swelled head, which is not good. AD will not stand up to anything Royle tells him… I do hate to think that all the initiative and drive you put into the two Departments (Operations and Commercial) a few years ago should be allowed to run to seed.'

Thomas Royle, an ex-Lancashire and Yorkshire man, was appointed Chief Operating Manager in 1938 and S.H. Fisher was Operating Superintendent at Euston. Both had been selected by Lemon but fell short in the way they managed the operational side of the LMS when their Vice President joined the Air Ministry in 1938 and Ashton was unable to control them. It seems that they both fell prey to making arbitrary decisions based on a prejudiced or preconceived view, unsupported, it seems, by evidence.

Occasionally the relationship between the CMEs and the Operating Department became hostile, sponsored, it appears, by Royle and Fisher's poor performance. Lemon was intrigued by the new locomotives that the CME was producing and took an

FEBRUARY 1938

Already 3 years old and Turbomotive is still being used for publicity purposes, even though it is only the LMS's own magazine. By this time the streamlined Princess Coronations were attracting all the attention. (Author/LMS)

Euston – another arrival at Platform 1. (AE)

active interest in Turbomotive. While he remained in office any criticism of this experimental engine by his staff was quashed. But throughout the four years of her life, 6202's trials and tribulations had become a sore point with Royle and Fisher particularly. Stanier believed that more could have been accomplished if they had followed his advice and supported the project more wholeheartedly and professionally. He must have wondered whether the decision to mothball 6202 at the outbreak of war was an expression of this prejudice dressed up as a sound operational reason. If so, the problem was deferred, not resolved.

In April 1939 the Minister for Transport published an order containing the instruction that in an emergency he would be responsible for the provision, allocation and co-ordination of internal transport services. In reality this gave him direct control of all railways. He created the Railway Executive Committee to act as his agent and advisor in this work. They would consider and plan the movement of war materials and men and the distribution of supplies, then allow the four railway companies to manage these requirements as they would in peacetime. But the needs of war would place even greater demands on their resources. Well-

equipped workshops would be used to build armaments (the LMS had been doing so since 1938), tens of thousands of children had to be evacuated and many members of their workforce would serve in the armed forces, reducing the pool of experienced men available. An effort was made to restrict enlistment by introducing reserved occupations status, but this did not stop 44,375 determined young men and women joining up (and more than 1,500 would die).

As the Phoney War and evacuations gave way to the invasion of Western Europe, then the Battle of Britain, the railways continued moving to a war footing. It took time to adjust and absorb so much extra work. All locomotives, whether passenger or freight, were worked to their limits and even time in works, let alone cleaning, became a luxury. Once-elegant high-speed express engines became no better or worse than the oldest shunting stock. All that was asked was that they do all that was requested of them and do it without fuss. But such an approach is one of diminishing returns, as engines, carriages, trucks, the permanent way and all the people who made the system work, gradually wear out under the stress of long hours, an impossibly heavy workload and the threat of bombing.

As the war raged around her 6202 continued to languish in store, not so the people who had driven her creation.

Having visited the US in 1939 to help promote the successful tour of one of his engines, 6220 *Coronation*,

Two final views before smoke deflectors are added. (AE)

Stanier returned to a Britain gearing up for war and found himself equipping workshops to support wartime production. With locomotive building curtailed any spare capacity was quickly absorbed, but, as he noted later, this additional task meant that other essential locomotive maintenance tasks could not be completed and standards would quickly drop. It was his task to make sure performance kept pace with all demands. In 1942 he was seconded to the Ministry of Munitions as one of three scientific advisors. At the same time he became Chairman of the Mechanical and Electrical Sub-Committee of the Railway Executive Committee and also undertook work for the Ministry of Labour. Professionally he was given the ultimate accolade of being elected President of the Institution of Mechanical Engineers in 1941. Well beyond normal retirement age and exhausted by so many commitments, he resigned from the LMS in 1944, his post being filled by his deputy, Charles Fairburn. He was knighted in 1943.

In 1938 Josiah Stamp became a Baron and three years later a casualty of war. During a bombing raid on 16 April 1941, his house in Bromley, Kent took a direct hit and he, his wife and oldest son, Wilfred, died instantly, in their air-raid shelter. His vision and effort in transforming the LMS from many diverse companies into the organisation it became was a fitting memorial to a man of huge skill and determination. Without his

farsightedness in recruiting Harold Hartley, William Stanier and many other talented managers, the rebuilding of the railway and its locomotive fleet might not have happened or would have been a very muted affair by comparison. There would have been no new Pacifics, no sturdy freight engines to support the war effort, no second tier express locomotives to do unglamorous but essential day to day running, and noTurbomotive.

Hartley remained with the LMS throughout the war, but acted as advisor to many government bodies, his extensive scientific knowledge being brought to bear on various diverse subjects, including chemical and biological warfare. This was a subject in which he had become an expert during the First World War, rising to the rank of Brigadier General in charge of the Chemical Warfare Department. In 1946 he retired and was replaced by Robert Riddles. He was knighted in1928 and became a Companion of Honour in 1967.

Henry Guy remained with Metrovick until 1941 before resigning to seek new challenges, but still pursued his dream of turbine power. The company had manufactured many units across different industries and profited from his work, but, as an ex-railwayman, Turbomotive was a project close to his heart and he returned to it many times, convinced, as was Stanier, of its eventual success.

During the war, he chaired or sat on many scientific committees for

the Ministry of Supply and was knighted in 1949.

He and Stanier had become great friends and when elected President of the Institution of Mechanical Engineers he became its Secretary with Stanier's support, and remained in this challenging role until the end of his life. Much later Stanier wrote:

'His wise counsel and considered judgement did much to raise the standard of mechanical engineering in this country and it is largely through his guidance that the status of the Institution became accepted by industry, the Government and national undertakings, as a standard of high qualifications of professional engineers.'

Roland Bond was appointed in 1937 to manage the design and building of the National Testing Station that Nigel Gresley and Stanier had advocated for many years. With construction well advanced on a site near Rugby, the war intervened and the facility was not completed until 1948, when its main supporters were gone. If, as hoped, the testing station had been completed in 1940, it seems likely that Turbomotive might have been one of the first engines to be tested, so keen was Stanier to develop the concept. With suspension of this project Bond was posted to Scotland as Acting Mechanical and Electrical Engineer, replacing Robert Riddles. In 1941 he returned to Crewe as Works Superintendent where he remained until the end of the war.

Ernest Lemon returned to the LMS on 1 August 1940, with Ashton Davies moving sideways to take responsibility for 'special war time functions' and to provide cover for any other senior staff absences. In short order Lemon brought the Operations Department back under tighter management, but much of his and the company's work was being driven by forces beyond their control and this presented many problems. One was the supply of engines and rolling stock for military use, at the same time as demand increased on the domestic front. This greatly concerned all railway companies and they sought the Railway Executive Committee's permission to build additional locomotives to meet these pressing demands. While awaiting a response the erosion of numbers continued and the position reached a critical level. H.G. Smith summed up the effect this lack of action had:

'The tentacles of the REC octopus were now beginning to twine around every activity of the railway transport service, and, slowly but surely, the Civil Service machine was strangling initiative and resource of staff whose lifelong task it had been. The amateur was superseding the professional.'

While awaiting official approval the LMS looked for ways of boosting engine numbers. In February 1941 fifty-four locomotives written off as scrap were repaired and reinstated. Alongside this work many other options were considered and here Turbomotive's future lay. She had been stored in full operational condition and it required little effort to get her running again. It was a risk, as her reliability was in question and the chances of a major

breakdown high. In which case Metrovick, being fully employed on war work, would be unable to repair the turbine system or build spare parts. And Crewe did not want the added responsibility of a temperamental locomotive. But the need for powerful engines was so great that Lemon, Stanier and Hartley believed the risk worthwhile and on 9 August 1941 she re-entered traffic, allocated once again to Camden Shed. Seeking to extend her life as long as possible, 6202 was reassigned to duties that best suited her performance, so back to the Euston to Liverpool line she went. There was a suggestion that the turbines be stripped out and

reciprocating gear installed, but the cost and time in workshop to rebuild the engine was deemed excessive. With hindsight it might have proved a more sensible option, but with the war going badly, invasion still possible and the future uncertain, such a commitment would have seemed foolhardy.

Sadly, she only ran for little more than a month until her reverse turbine failed again. She remained out of service until the following July, a long time at Crewe for a comparatively minor problem. A full record of this failure has not survived so one can only assume that spare parts caused this extended stay. Undoubtedly the

Work complete, 6202 reappears in traffic. Smoke deflectors and extended casing are the most obvious changes. (AE)

echo of 'I told you so' may have reached the CME.

But back into traffic she went in August 1942 and ran without problem until November when oil leaked from both turbines. On 9 January 1943 she was operational again and for six months ran trouble free when, as Roland Bond reported:

'*A serious failure occurred in July 1943, after arrival of the engine at Camden Shed on completion of her normal working from Liverpool. The coupled wheels locked without warning during shunting operations in the Shed yard. A preliminary examination showed that a number of teeth on the high speed pinion had broken, but it was not clear whether this was the initial cause of failure or was damage consequent upon some other fault in the transmission.*

'*The engine was hauled dead to Crewe Works with the leading coupled wheels packed up clear of the rails and the coupling rods removed. By this time it had completed 249,261 miles, of which 71,848 had been run since the engine returned to traffic after the period in store.*

'*The examination carried out at Crewe showed conclusively that the trouble leading to this failure had originated in the flexible drive between the slow speed gear wheel and the driving axle. As a result of wear which had taken place, in the normal course, at the driving pins and bushes connecting the gear wheel to the floating link and driving axle, clearance between the nuts securing the driving pins and the access hole in the gear wheel centre discs had become reduced sufficiently to cause contact…. The knock set up caused the locking device to be damaged and the nuts both became unscrewed. Excessive slackness in the drive caused by the loss of these nuts resulted in the transmission of heavy shocks, particularly when changing direction from forward to reverse. These shocks were sufficient ultimately to fracture one end of pin No 2 and the teeth of the high speed pinion, ten of which were found to be broken. Other damage to the flexible drive was rather extensive…. Of the total of 256 spring plates, 68 were found to be broken.*

'The failure, serious and expensive though it was, did not denote any unsoundness in the principles of design, but should properly be regarded as part of the price to be paid for new experience. From the lessons learned it has been decided to make an inspection of the flexible drive after 100,000 miles running in future.

'In view of the mileage run and the fact that the forward turbine had not been opened up for inspection since 1939, it was decided to give the engine a heavy general repair and to make a full examination of the turbines on this occasion.'

It was lucky that Bond was Works Superintendent. He was a disciple of Stanier and saw himself as the custodian of this unique locomotive. It is likely that anyone else in that position would have condemned her to another long stay in the Paint Shop at Crewe or worse.

So Bond persevered with the experiment, still seeing huge potential in the design. Undoubtedly he and Stanier thought with one mind on this subject. But this latest breakdown, followed by heavy general repair, kept her out of service for nearly fourteen months.

Between this latest return to traffic and the end of the war, 6202 would experience two more periods of repair. The first was in December 1944 following a failure at Rugby when the oil passage became blocked restricting flow to her reverse turbine bearing. It was found, on examination, that the blockage had been caused by work undertaken during her last maintenance period at Crewe. On 18 January she returned to traffic, but was withdrawn in April when oil was again found to be leaking from the turbine bearings. A pre-planned period of light casual repair

followed in July and then 6202 ran without problem until March 1946 when another period of scheduled heavy general repair began. This would last until April 1947.

It was during the last months of 1944 that a young naval aviator en route to Canada arrived at Euston and was overjoyed to find

To some the smoke deflectors, though improving visibility ahead, broke up 6202's smooth lines. But the unusual angular shape of the deflectors was unavoidable due to the bulge of the turbine casing. (AE)

Turbomotive ready to pull his train to Liverpool. In pre-war Britain he, like many young boys, had followed the development of locomotives on the LMS and LNER, keeping a scrapbook of press cuttings and photographs. As a 13-year-old he had seen 6202 twice and was entranced by her and her sisters. He kept notes of all these encounters and painted several images for his scrapbook; now he was about to travel behind her:

'We were taken by a camouflaged Army lorry from our Wardroom at Yeovilton shortly after midnight. It was cold and uncomfortable in the back of the truck and certainly no creature comforts were provided; a wooden bench along either side and our kit bags piled between them, where we rested our feet. Cigarettes were soon lit and a dense fug of smoke soon descended. So early in the morning no one was eager to talk and we were all slightly overawed by leaving Britain, most for the first time.

'Entering London, close to my home in Worcester Park, we passed two heavily damaged areas where Doodlebugs or V2 rockets had recently crashed. The clear up was underway. We didn't linger long. Having lived in London through the Blitz these scenes had become commonplace. I was just glad my family were safe, but we had lived with such dreadful uncertainty for so long that losses were always expected.

'Euston was a gloomy sight when we decanted outside its Great Hall. Even before the war it had been a grimy, dirt laden place, but the smoke that congested the air in great, impenetrable waves had engulfed London for so many decades that all buildings fell prey to its cancerous effects. But it didn't reduce the excitement I always felt when entering one of London's great stations. It was the buzz generated by the thought of travel, but also the look, sound and smell of locomotives.

'We arrived too early for our train to Liverpool, fully expecting to spend much of the day waiting for a gap in the traffic. But we were directed to the train, minus engine, and found seats in the front part of the train. With time to kill and wishing to enjoy my recently acquired Sub Lieutenant status by parading up and down, I wandered to the end of the platform to watch the engines passing to and fro. Within minutes a Princess Class engine appeared in the distance and slowly backed down towards our train. To my surprise it was a very dirty Turbomotive with an "ancient" driver at the controls. The only difference to her pre-war state seemed to be the addition of unusually shaped smoke deflector plates.

'The crew seemed happy to chat to one lone spectator and I was invited on to the footplate and asked all sort of questions. Becoming a pilot was my great passion, but engineering came a close second. Before volunteering for the Fleet Air Arm I had begun my technical education and so I found all I saw on Turbomotive fascinating, as the driver and fireman talked to me about all her special features. I was struck by the obvious pride they had in being footplate crew with the LMS and in charge of such a prestigious engine.

'Loth to return to my carriage, hoping that my uniform might allow me to remain on the footplate, I dropped the window in the front door and hung my head out to experience all the sensations of power and delight these powerful

engines evoked. I wasn't disappointed. Used to great volumes of hissing steam and smoke, then violent slipping as the wheels of a Pacific tried to grip the track, I was surprised when Turbomotive took up the strain of her 17 carriage train without fuss. We seemed to move forward so smoothly, with little snatch, accelerating up Camden Bank effortlessly then continued to Harrow where we were brought to a halt for a few minutes. But again she moved forward without protest when the signals released her.

'It was a stop and start journey northwards, as you would expect in wartime where priority was given to freight traffic. At Lichfield Trent Valley we stopped for 30 minutes or so and a tea trolley appeared on the platform to be quickly swamped by hungry and thirsty servicemen. I went to see my friends on the footplate for another chat and watch three long freight trains amble passed. The crew were regulars on the Liverpool

run and were used to these delays, but explained that these big Pacifics were so strong that they could make up time if given a clear road ahead. They proved this when moving again and seemed happy to push the engine to her limits, despite any wartime restrictions.

'I said goodbye to them at Lime Street hoping that I would survive the war to relive this wonderful experience. Before I left the driver gave me a battered copy of "Carry On" the LMS War Time Newsletter, with his name, Harry Baraclough, scribbled on the top and his photo on the front page.

'Bernard Graves, Sub Lt (RNVR)'

And so peace gave way to war and the country and its railways faced a huge and daunting rebuilding task. Even before the conflict ended the LMS had begun surveying the state of its railway, estimating costs and planning the work needed to restore it to something close to its

6202 in her new guise still proved popular with crew and lineside train spotters. (AE)

The LMS insignia is soon to disappear, to be replaced by the nationalising emblem of British Rail. (AE)

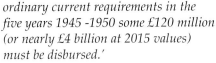

former glory. What the Board found was a railway infrastructure in a far more dilapidated state than they expected and in need of a massive injection of capital to bring it back to pre-war levels. In their summary they concluded that:

'It has been computed that to pay for the effects of war, to overtake the lag in new construction and to meet the ordinary current requirements in the five years 1945 -1950 some £120 million (or nearly £4 billion at 2015 values) must be disbursed.'

It was an ambitious programme, but one doomed to failure in a country that faced bankruptcy after six years of war. The railways, although central to commercial life, would see some investment to make good war damage, but insufficient to restore them to pre-war levels. But the political map of Britain was changing and, even before hostilities ended in the Far East, a Labour Government had won a landslide victory on the promise of a radical programme of change and nationalisation. The railways, struggling under a weight of expectation and a backlog of rebuilding, would be one of the first organisations to feel the effect of this cultural shift.

Against all odds Turbomotive still existed in her experimental state and few, if any, questioned her right to exist, especially if she continued to work effectively. But with so many pressing demands on the railways the fate of one locomotive was of little consequence except to those who still saw turbine development as a worthy concept. Although now retired, Stanier and Guy remained potent advocates of turbine power and through ex-colleagues within the LMS and Metrovick continued to encourage development. Like Turbomotive the concept refused to die, but many challenges lay ahead and other voices, pushing alternative methods of locomotion, began being heard.

CHAPTER 7

TIME FOR CHANGE
(1945–1950)

Peace when it came took many by surprise. The war in the Far East was expected to last into 1947, at least, and Britain's commitment was expected to increase as Europe embraced peace, releasing forces for service in the Pacific. So certain of this were the British and American governments that Lend-Lease, the backbone of our war effort, was extended by another eighteen months. With this backing Clement Atlee, the new Labour Prime Minister, hoped that this would enable industry to move smoothly from war to peace – from manufacturing weapons to producing domestic goods. But Japan's rapid collapse, once the atomic bombs had been dropped on Hiroshima and Nagasaki, took the Allied Nations by surprise.

The unexpected end of hostilities, in August 1945, terminated the Lend-Lease agreement and so the support this scheme offered to Britain's depleted coffers ended equally abruptly. Rebuilding was dealt a severe blow that could only be corrected by a huge loan from America. Lord Keynes, who led the loan negotiations, had analysed the extent to which Britain's economy had suffered during the war and valued the damage to industry and private property at £2billion. This, of course, did not take into account the many other costs of war: financial, social and emotional. To pay its way in a recovering world he estimated that Britain would have to export 1 ¾ times as much as before the war. With the state of the country and its economy so distressed this level of business could not be achieved before 1949 and so the British Government sought a loan of £1.25 billion, a capital sum to be boosted by the sale of foreign investments. The loan, when granted, fell short of this amount and the economy struggled even more severely for the next decade. Society entered a period of extreme austerity and industry struggled to make good its resources and find markets. The railways were affected as deeply as the rest of the community and the ambitious targets they set for recovery would lay dormant.

But the new Government was set on a course of nationalisation, greater social care and better education, and this would absorb precious resources at a critical rate.

In pre-war Britain 11.3 per cent of government expenditure went on social spending: housing, health, education and welfare. By 1950 this had risen to 18 per cent and the demand did not slacken. And although the cost of its armed forces had reduced significantly with the war's end, it remained a major drain on resources as the Cold War spread its tentacles and the Empire needed to be policed.

Nationalisation or privatisation was, as it is now, a matter of political doctrine and economic interpretation. The Labour Party believed that so many of industry's ills were caused by too much wealth being placed in the hands of too few, and those who laboured for this wealth shared few of its benefits. Central control of essential industries seemed to be the way of correcting this imbalance and, at the same time, make them work more effectively for society as a whole. There is still no consensus on these issues and we continue to play out these extremes of policy – swinging one way and then another in a macabre economic dance.

With Labour in the ascendancy the Bank of England, gas and

electricity suppliers were nationalised, then coal and transport followed, in January 1947 and January 1948 respectively. But both industries were in a very poor condition when taken over. The mine owners had not invested in mechanisation so the pits could barely maintain a basic level of production, let alone expand to meet growing markets. The railways were little better and faced prohibitive costs in bringing the system back to pre-war levels. Economists at the time saw the shortsighted nature of nationalisation and urged that social spending be curbed and industry boosted. But this was not to be. To adapt a quote made famous in the 1930s, 'Britain chose butter, other countries chose industry'. And so the railways, whether privately or publicly owned, faced an uphill task in restoring and developing their services.

In the 1945 film *Brief Encounter*, we see a Britain apparently untouched by war – hope, aspiration and a comfortable reality conjured to appeal to cinemagoers tired of conflict and 'making do'. Much of the filming took place on the LMS station at Carnforth. People go about their business, express trains thunder past and relationships are formed and broken. But if you look closely beyond the film's homely veneer you will see signs of wear and dilapidation on the railway. The locomotives going past look and sound well worn, with a particularly dirty streamlined Coronation Pacific steaming by on the way to Crewe. Filming at night hid many realities. Beyond the arc lights the illusion of peace and prosperity quickly dissipated and the grimy Pacific was thundering into a world of cold and sober reality.

Arthur Roberts, a fitter at Crewe, recalled:

'Throughout the war manufacture of weapons took priority in the workshops, the locomotives certainly came second. It broke your heart to see all those engines we'd looked after so well before the war gradually fall into disrepair. But we built them solidly and they stood up well to the battering they received. We did cut corners many times, though, and sent locos out when we knew they should be worked on longer. It's a wonder to me that there weren't more accidents.

'The Coronation and Princesses suffered most. They were race horses by comparison to the other classes and they required more work because of it. They were in many ways precision made for high speed work and so the wear was more excessive. By 1945 most were in a sad condition, particularly the turbine loco. The maintenance was poor and accounted for the long periods she spent in the works. Things didn't improve for a long time after the war. Make do and mend was how we approached our work. We were told there just wasn't the money to do more.

'The workshop equipment was in an equally bad condition. They also suffered from lack of maintenance and by 1945 many were in a positively dangerous condition. But we just had to get on and use them.'

After her long period of heavy general repair, Turbomotive reappeared on the main line in 1947, being spotted by a Railway Correspondence and Travel Society (RCTS) observer in July:

'London Area. On Friday 11.4.1947 Turbomotive 6202 was seen on the

In BR black livery shortly after receiving her BR crest. (RH)

8.30 am up express from Euston to Liverpool painted in its new livery (black). It returned on the 5.25 pm express from Liverpool and has since been working this duty regularly.'

But on 20 July she failed on the 08.30 and was not back in traffic until 9 September. In one way this was lucky because the engine rostered to take her place the next day, 6244 *King George VI*, was involved in a serious accident near Grendon. Due to a track defect and inadequate maintenance the streamlined locomotive was derailed when travelling at 65–70mph and fourteen of the seventeen carriages followed suit. Five people were killed and sixty-four injured. Luckily an anxious signalman had the presence of mind to stop an up

express before it reached the scene of the crash.

6202 ran until 23 September and then was back in works for four weeks, re-emerging on 15 October. Her record card does not specify why she was being repaired, but simply records the reason as 'not classified'. Come December another five weeks of maintenance took place and on 7 January 1948 she was spotted by an RCTS member in London back 'at its usual job'.

One criticism levelled at 6202 was that she spent too much time in the workshop, and from April to December she lost sixty-five weekdays at Crewe under repair. By comparison the other Princess Pacifics spent an average of 65 days under repair during the same

period, though individually this varied from 30 days to 100 days. So, even from this simple analysis, it seems that Turbomotive's record of reliability could be as good as the remainder of the class. But the turbine, without careful, regular maintenance and without easily accessible spares, could always present a problem. Neither of these conditions were likely to be forthcoming on a railway trying to rebuild, short of funds and with nationalisation just round the corner. She was on borrowed time and the next breakdown was likely to be her last.

But the concept of turbine power would not go away. Although William Stanier and Henry Guy had left the railway scene, they followed

An unusual square on view of 46202, now in British Rail guise. Her three-man crew look relaxed. (RP)

14 up and working hard. Alfred Ewer wrote alongside the original print of this photo, 'the *Merseyside Flier*'. (AE)

developments worldwide and lobbied those in authority, through the professional institutions to which they belonged; before, that is, nationalisation struck home and the railways lost their independence to pursue new ideas.

By some means the argument that Turbomotive was an experimental engine held sway for more years than could justifiably be claimed for any machine in development. Valid arguments, based on her lack of reliability and cost and the valuable workshop time she consumed, seemed to have no effect and each time a halt could be called to the project it gained a new lease of life. Luck was on her side. She had strong supporters and fate took a hand through the increasing demands of

war, but this should not have been enough to keep the experiment going. The truth seems to be that the men who crewed and maintained her, senior management and the general public regarded her highly. She had become, rightly or wrongly, an icon and enjoyed the status and blindness to reality this can cause. But she also acted as a potent guide to encourage more research.

In 1945, as the LMS looked to the future and considered new developments, Ernest S. Cox, who had risen through the ranks of the pre-war LMS and was now working as Technical Development Manager, visited the US, to observe advances made on its railways. It was the only country in the world where war had boosted industrial strength, not

destroyed it, so it acted as a beacon to locomotive designers. He was one of a party of six, from the LMS and LNER, who spent seven weeks studying locomotive design in all its forms, but in terms of competition to steam not viable alternatives, such as diesel or electric. Such a debate seems flimsy now, when we look back and wonder how steam traction lasted for so long in this country. But with such huge reserves of coal and little money to invest in change, Britain's fixation with steam is understandable.

His report to the LMS Board in early 1946 concluded that:

'There were large sections of the job where not only was there nothing to learn from the Americans but our own practice is far in advance…. America is

The result of a PR collaboration between the LMS and a magazine popular in the late 1930s. (RH)

Express drawn by Stanier's Experimental "Turbo-Motive", since converted to steam

John and his sister, Janet, are keen "train-spotters". They live quite near a railway. They are looking at a London—Liverpool express.

"The locomotive is a steam-turbine, sometimes called a 'turbo-motive'," John explains to Janet, with pride.

The smooth, sleek blue monster thrills Janet, and she decides that if ever she travels from London to Liverpool she'll go by it.

Childhood memories of Turbomotive. (Author)

"WHO RUNS MAY READ"

LIVERPOOL
TO
LONDON (EUSTON)

Illustrated description
of the Journey

Along the Viking Border

L M S Route Book No. 2

PRICE ONE SHILLING

The LMS Publicity Department produced travel guides for each major route. Alfred Ewer kept a set and here is his copy of the Liverpool to Euston booklet. (AE)

A momento of a last trip drawn by Turbomotive. (BG)

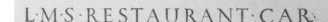

L·M·S·RESTAURANT·CAR

Lower Darwen Mutual Improvement Class

L U N C H E O N

3/4

Thick Mock Turtle

Roast Beef   Horseradish Sauce
Baked & Mashed Potatoes
Spring Greens

Windsor Pudding

Cheese,   Biscuits,   Salad

Coffee, per Cup, 4d.

PLEASE DO N PAY ANY MONEY UNLESS A BILL IS WRITTEN AND TORN OUT OF THE BILL BOOK IN YOUR PRESENCE

Gratuities in respect of this meal are included in the price

In the general interest Passengers are requested to refrain from smoking immediately prior to and during the service of meals.

Part of the Metropolitan-Vickers site at Trafford Park, Manchester, in the early 1930s. (Author)

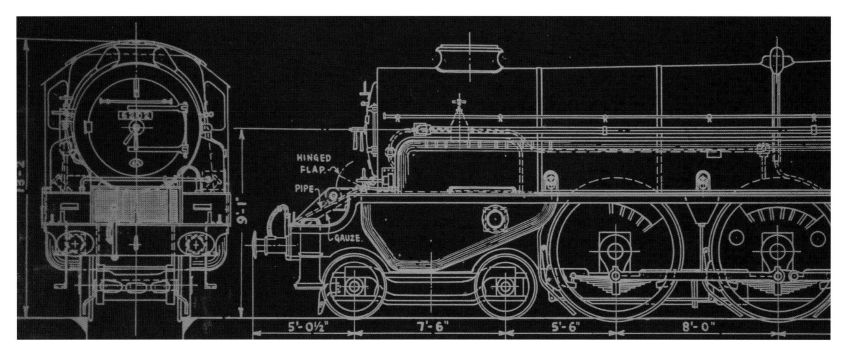

HINGED FLAP.

PIPE

GAUZE.

5'-0½"   7'-6"   5'-6"   8'-0"

6202 comes together on the drawing board.

WILL'S CIGARETTES

TURBINE-DRIVEN LOCOMOTIVE, L.M.S.R.

More publicity reflecting the 1930's attitude to smoking. (BG)

The United States ultimate steam turbine locomotive is justifiably publicised by its manufacturer.

One of 46202's history cards recording her last few weeks of service and her eventual fate. (RH)

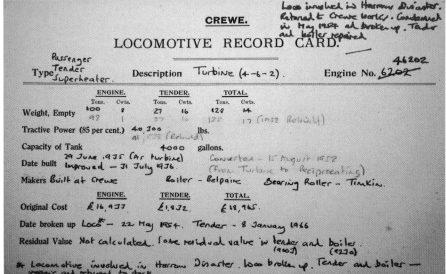

Vol. 1. Nº 3.

PRICE 6ᴰ

The BEYER-PEACOCK QUARTERLY REVIEW

JULY 1927

"LJUNGSTRÖM" TURBINE CONDENSER LOCOMOTIVE
ON MANCHESTER-LONDON EXPRESS, NEAR MILL HILL, L.M.S. RAILWAY.

Beyer Peacock
herald their turbine
development.
(Author)

Now post war and publicity booklets appear again for the major passenger routes. (BG)

a land of contrasts. The best is very good and we can learn from it. The worst is of far lower standard than anything we have here.'

Before leaving for the US, Cox was asked by Roland Bond to look at the way US designers were developing turbines. Three pages of his thirty-two-page report focused on the issue, assessing steam, gas and electric-powered developments. For steam he found that:

'Only one turbine locomotive is at work at present, the Pennsylvania-Westinghouse 6-8-6 locomotive. This was completed in September 1944 and follows closely the principles and design of the LMS turbo motive. It is in daily operation over a round trip of 580 miles from Crestline to Chicago and back with start to stop average speeds of up to 64 mph and train loads varying from 900 to 1200 English tons. I was

fortunate in securing a footplate trip on which 100 mph was held or exceeded for 12 consecutive minutes with 930 tons trailing load.

'Compared with the LMS turbine engine the following points stand out:
- *The method of control gives finer graduation of power output and more indication to the driver what the engine is doing.*
- *The engine is operated at 85% of full power output for the greater part of each journey.*
- *The engine has been built for power not economy, so no appreciable economy over reciprocating types is obtainable.*
- *Turbines and gears have been free from trouble so far (about 50000 miles). The performance of this engine is being watched with great interest by other American Railways.'*

He then listed other companies investigating the steam turbine concept, but added that they were tending towards electric or gas-based systems as alternatives. In his final paragraph he added a brief note: 'While great interest is being taken in the possibilities of these new designs, none of them is ready yet to meet the competition of the diesel…. The road performance of the diesels is most impressive and mechanically it is able to do the job…. Whether it does it more cheaply than modern steam traction is not yet clearly established…. Until this becomes clear most railways make best use of both worlds (steam and diesel) for their shareholders'. The US was pointing the way ahead for railways around the world and Britain would eventually follow in these footsteps, but until sound

Turbomotive at Brinklow running fast. The new smoke deflectors seemed to help the forward view for the crew. (RO)

46202 waiting attention outside Crewe Works in late 1948. She would not return to traffic until March 1949. (RH)

alternatives were available steam would still dominate.

Cox had, with Stanier and Bond, been a strong advocate of steam turbines, and had written in 1942 of Turbomotive's success, suggesting that 'a most valuable trial would be to equip a standard 2-8-0 with turbine drive' as a means of developing this idea still further. But by the end of his visit to the US his thoughts had moved on and his advocacy of steam turbines quietly subsided. Not so Roland Bond, who at Stanier's urging prepared and delivered his paper on Turbomotive to the Institution of Railway Engineers in January 1946. It received wide attention in the railway press and the response was, on the whole, positive. But it is hard to say, at this distance in time, whether the paper's intention was to inspire more research in this field or simply justify the effort expended on the project. In his summary, which echoed Stanier's views, Bond made plain the core issues in the debate that had run for more than ten years:

'It is only natural that an unusual engine, the only one of its kind and not too reliable in its early days, should be regarded as a nuisance by those responsible for its care and maintenance. No doubt in other countries, as in Great Britain, the first Diesel locomotives were similarly regarded. And while the locomotive must fit into the pattern and organisation of the transport machine of which it is a part, the machine itself must not be so inelastic that no adjustment can be made to enable full advantage to be taken of new developments. A turbine locomotive inevitably requires some re-education of footplate and maintenance staff if its possibilities are to be fully exploited – its method of control can never be exactly the same as the familiar reciprocating engine – this fact must be recognised and accepted.

'On present indications, the next five years should show up the turbine in an increasingly favourable light. It has, in the author's opinion already proved itself well worth persevering with, and it is not beyond the bounds of possibility that *a limited number of non-condensing turbine locomotives in a more highly developed form based on the experience with 6202 will be regularly employed on the heaviest and fastest express trains, with profit to the owners.'*

Stanier added a brief footnote to Bond's presentation in which he touched on the need for footplate crew with specialist knowledge of the locomotive:

'At one time, when the engine was stationed at Liverpool, it was worked by 20 sets of crew, and there was little hope of an experimental engine being successful in those conditions.'

He acknowledged that he had been wrong in assuming Great Western practice in boiler design was always right and admitted that a two-row superheater was insufficient for LMS high-speed, long-distance needs. But he had seen the light and agreed that a larger superheater was needed and had proved itself in the Princess and Coronation Classes. He also felt that modifications to the turbine controls would have removed the need and expense for having a fitter permanently attached to the loco all the time. Guy had proposed just such an improvement in 1939, but the onset of war, the engine's mothballing and then the lack of workshop capacity had ended this development. In conclusion, he added that 'I have always felt that the engine had been very successful', but did not express his opinion on future development, allowing Bond's assessment to speak for him.

During his career, Stanier had been loath to set his thoughts down in writing and gain direct credit for his work. He had great trust in those he chose and promoted their careers whenever he could. For a man of such drive and ambition this was remarkable. Bond was just one of a number of people to benefit from this generosity, but at the same time it did allow Stanier to present a façade of arbitration when, in fact, he was leading. This was a sound political move that suggests he had learnt much from Robert Riddles while Chief Mechanical Engineer. Even so, he must have realised that the world was changing rapidly and in the aftermath of war, with a government committed to nationalisation, the steam turbine programme, although successful, stood little chance of further development. And Cox's US report must have made this clear to his Board. The future lay with diesels and, as reinforced by the Southern Region's rapidly spreading modern-isation programme, electrification. But for the moment steam ruled in most parts of the country and the attention it received from the public in the late 1930s was revitalised, but with a more direct focus.

Post-war years saw an interesting trend emerge among boys and young men. It became fashionable to be a trainspotter, encouraged by Ian Allan who in 1942 began producing a series of booklets that listed locomotives, their numbers and names. Soon stations, even in wartime, attracted spotters who would gather at the ends of platforms, or other vantage points along the line, collecting the details of trains as they passed. Soon each region had its ABC Ian Allan Booklet and sales reached 250,000 copies. This was supported by a Locospotters Club, which Allan and his wife began in 1943, which by 1946 had a membership of 150,000 and a new magazine, *Trains Illustrated*. All this coincided with a revival of model railway collecting, Hornby having restarted production, and a boost in sales of established periodicals: the *Meccano Magazine*, the *Railway Gazette* and the *Railway Magazine* among others.

There was a void in many young lives created by many long years of war and hardship. Simple things could lighten the austere gloom and the drama of life on the railways, with the magic of steam locomotives at its centre, was alluring. With so many people becoming interested, and with Ian Allan providing a focal point, news about railways became an essential part of life for a new generation of young people. Much of this was centred on the glamorous locomotives that had plied their trade before the war, but Turbomotive again attracted much attention too, even though LMS and then British Railway managers saw her as a back number, to be discarded as soon as possible. In truth she had become famous not for the technology she championed but for being unique and, as Raymond Loewy had opined in 1937, for being 'one of the most beautiful pieces of machinery ever designed by man'. It is a view that I for one would not dispute.

In the few years left to her she would appear in the children's

46202 in weathered working condition, the photographer again attracting attention from the footplate. (RH)

reading book *Janet and John*, with a glorious, but inaccurate, painting of her in experimental blue livery, without smoke deflectors. *Meccano Magazine* ran an article spread over three issues from November 1946 to October 1947. At the same time the *Railway Gazette* produced a long article sponsored by Bond's presentation to the Institution of Locomotive Engineers, which led to wider discussion of Turbomotive's achievements.

And many more items appeared in the railway press, none critical. To the growing band of trainspotters she became an icon and was much

photographed and remained a firm favourite of the footplate crews who manned her. The LMS seemed aware of this interest and encouraged the attention, allowing journalists wide access to the engine and her footplate, as a journalist for *Meccano Magazine*, calling himself 'North Western', discovered. His article tells us so much about the engine, her performance and the crew who worked her, but it also captures very vividly a world then so familiar but now long disappeared:

'"*Come early*," *said the District Locomotive Superintendent, "then you can see something of the preparation of*

the engine for the up run. "Nothing loth, I did as suggested; for I had been charged by the editor of MM with the pleasant task of making, by courtesy of the LMS authorities, the return journey between Liverpool and London on the footplate of the LMS "Turbomotive" number 6202, the only engine of its kind in the world until the appearance last year of the Pennsylvania Railroad 6-8-6 turbine locomotive referred to in the January 1946 MM.

'*So, one Autumn afternoon, armed with the necessary footplate pass, I presented myself at the office of Edge Hill Motive Power Depot. "My" engine had not yet come round on to the shed,* so while waiting I was given some details of the working arrangements of 6202 and her various crews. The "Turbo" as she is often called, belongs to Camden and her normal working had for some time been to work down on the 8.30 am from Euston to Liverpool, a heavy train with several stops; then, after servicing at Edge Hill, she takes back the 5.25 pm from Lime Street stopping at Crewe only, the train often referred to in pre-war days as the "Liverpool Flier", though it did not carry this title (officially).

'When 6202 had come round I was taken along to her, and it seemed unusual nowadays for such a big engine to have no outside cylinders and motion, the coupling rods being the only visible moving parts. She was standing undergoing the various ministrations necessary between one journey and another. Driver J Worman and his mate Fireman E Robinson, both Camden men, were already busy; the one oiling round and the other superintending operations connected with his part of the job. The fire had been cleaned, a hot and dirty task, and made up so that it should have plenty of fire and a good head of steam by starting time; and the footplate was hosed down and fittings generally tidied up. A Fitter attached to the Chief Mechanical Engineer's Department always travels with the engine, and Fitter F Broach of Crewe, who has been on the job for some time, immediately appointed himself my guide, philosopher and friend for the journey; so I felt as if I "belonged" to the crew right away.

'Preparations being complete, we moved away from the pits, and over the tricky layout of the locomotive depot and I had the opportunity of seeing how

readily manoeuvred is 6202, in spite of her unorthodox design. Driver Worman, whose service dates back from 1897, was one of the first enginemen to handle 6202 and his complete mastery of the engine made the job look simple.

'So we made our way to the coaling plant – one of the earliest fuel plants in this country, and one that has been in use for over 30 years – and the coal supply was quickly made up. Back again now to the head of the yard where a "Black Stanier", in other words a Class 5 4-6-0, was waiting to accompany us down to Lime Street.

'We are due off the shed at 4.50 pm so with the Class 5 leading and thus virtually in charge of us, we drifted out on to the main line to that sort of "hole in the wall" as it looks from passing trains, by which engines leave the shed premises. We coasted backward through Edge Hill Station and down the cavernous slope by which the line goes

down to Lime Street, through a cutting with sheer and grimy sides of red sandstone, remarkably deep and intersected by bridges and short tunnels carrying the streets and property above.

'The Turbo ran easily and quietly, for she has roller bearing axle boxes throughout, the only noise I would discern being the rumble of the wheels on rails, punctuated by the impact of the rail joints and occasionally a hiss from the driver's brake valve. We came down to Lime Street and after a little manoeuvring backed on to our train standing at No 7 Platform. Starting from Lime Street is not an easy job, as from No 7 to the up main several crossovers have to be negotiated. At most terminals with engines standing or constantly passing in and out, the tracks are inclined to be greasy, and Lime Street is no exception. Driver Worman was taking no chances; before we left he filled the spare shovel with sand and

Cleaned and ready for duty, driver and fireman posing for the cameraman. (AE)

walked ahead literally "hand sanding" the rails over which we were to pass.

'Looking back from track level to where our train was standing it was striking to notice how even the giant 6202 was completely dwarfed by the lofty road bridge and high side walls at the cutting leading out of the station. From the front end 6202 looked very businesslike and was plainly eager to be off. Smoke was showing at the chimney, and the fire, brought into good shape by Robinson and urged by the blower, was causing the safety valves to hiss furiously. This "music" was quickly checked by putting the injector to work, and at this point the "landing party" returned to the cab. I was installed on the fireman's seat on the right hand side. A few last moment touches, setting of

dampers, adjustment of injector feed, breaking of coal and the inevitable hosing down, and Robinson leaned out behind me to catch the "right away", the station platform here being on the fireman's side.

'Five-twenty-five and a shrilling of whistles on the platform; "Right Jack", and almost imperceptibly with a blast from the engine's hooter we were off. We had, as the enginemen say "13 on", one of these a 12 wheeler, and a tare weight of the train was 408 tons; probably 435 tons with passengers and luggage. With three nozzles in use 6202 began to move this over on to the up main, and as she did so Robinson started firing. Almost at once began the stern business of the ascent to Edge Hill, and as we moved out the difference between the

working of 6202 and that of a locomotive of normal kind was most striking. I must, I suppose have seen and travelled with scores of engines out of Lime Street, and with heavy loads their mighty exhausts beat when getting away almost threatening to shake the walls of the grim canyon leading up to Edge Hill. Now, however, there was no puffing exhaust, no rhythmic clank of connecting rods; just a humming noise from the gears, and literally a roar from the fire as the continuous purr of the exhaust whipped it into a seething mass of flame.

'I looked back to see the train snake its way over the crossovers behind us; with smoke and steam hanging low between the cutting walls and under the first few bridges we were more or less blanketed in gloom.'

'North Western' then described the journey to London in great detail and his words capture the romance of steam locomotion and the sheer hard work it entailed. But he also caught the professionalism of the crew and their pride in what they did. Driver Worman had become something of a specialist with Turbomotive and was enjoying his second press outing on the footplate. A few years earlier he had driven the engine while a journalist from the *Engineer Magazine*, Edward Livesay, had witnessed his work and wrote a lengthy article for a rather smaller readership. He, like other drivers, found Turbomotive a pleasure to drive and many memoirs make mention of this locomotive.

Perhaps the greatest compliment it received was from one of the LMS's most famous drivers,

Running at speed and adding to the fog.
(Author)

Lawrence Earl of Camden Shed. Renowned as a 'Top Link' man, he had worked on 6202 from her earliest days, even during her three measured trials in 1936/37. The opinions of a man with his reputation, who was trusted with the most glamorous and prestigious trains on the LMS, were worth listening to. In 1948, following his retirement, he wrote:

'We used to get the "Turbo" on this trip (Euston to Liverpool) and what a lovely engine she is! Not so much science about the driving, perhaps – turning the valves on and off one by one instead of the careful adjusting of regulator and cut off to suit every change of the road – but for continuous strength and speed there is not another engine in her class to touch her.'

It is remarkable how Turbomotive stayed in the public eye for so long, but her time was drawing to an end and her unique status would eventually act against her. Gradually she had reached more than 400,000 miles and the wear to her turbines was pulling her closer to a maintenance period where replacement might prove necessary. After four months of relatively trouble-free running she entered Crewe Works on 5 December 1948 for light casual repairs, but remained out of traffic until March the following year. It was an exceptionally long period that her Record Card does not explain in any

Out of steam and waiting for her next turn of duty. (AE/RH)

detail, but is likely to have been caused by the need to overhaul the turbines at Metrovick. Alternatively, she could have remained out of service for so long because senior managers were contemplating her future. But there was a shortage of these powerful engines at the time, as the railway struggled to catch up with long-delayed maintenance work, and 6202 may have had to re-enter service to fill crucial gaps. We will never know why, but when she returned to service her performance was strong, reliable and virtually trouble free.

Between April 1949 and April 1950, 6202 would run more than 62,000 miles and spend seventy-three days out of traffic. Most of the maintenance work undertaken during these absences was declared 'not classified' in the surviving records. By comparison her sisters in the Princess Class ran an average of 43,000 miles and averaged 105 days in the workshop in the same period with none individually exceeding 6202's mileage (with maintenance downtime ranging from 48 days to a high of 249 days). 6206 has not been included because her servicing records for the period are incomplete, but her mileage was approximately 50,000. So in her last year, before entering another period of heavy general repair, 6202 bettered all her sisters.

Although her records do not elude to any breakdowns, an eagle-eyed RCTS observer reported one failure during this period:

'46202 (her new BR number) took the 8.30 am to Euston from Liverpool on 22.11.1949, but lost time all the way to Rugby and was replaced by a Class 5 4-6-0. The train reached Stafford 1 hour late and 46202 was towed away by an LNW 0-8-0.'

In January 1948 British Rail came into existence and created the Railway Executive to manage all areas of its business. This Executive mirrored the Committee of the same name formed in 1939 to manage wartime needs. Riddles, now a Vice President with the LMS, was offered the post of Railway Executive Member for Mechanical and Electrical Engineering. In reality this equated to CME of one of the Big Four companies, but now for the whole of BR. His fellow members on the Executive ranged from ex-general managers of the Southern Railway and the LNER, men of other railway specialisations to General Sir William (later Viscount) Slim. It was hoped that he would bring his vast experience of leadership to BR and help reduce or remove any residual competition still existing between the new organisation's constituent parts.

Riddles's first job was to bring the CMEs of the four pre-nationalisation companies together, to act as one, accept the standards of design and best practice the new BR regime demanded and produce a railway fit for purpose. But Riddles was a realist and knew instinctively that there would be resistance to change and a strong desire to continue with long-established ways of working. His experience of the LMS told him this would not be straightforward. To ease himself into this new role he selected a group of men he felt he could trust and recruited Bond, Cox, plus Ernest Pugson and C. Dennett from the LMS; only Charles Cock came from one of the other companies, in this case the Southern. Choosing such a team had many benefits. They had proved their loyalty to Riddles. They were men of great engineering knowledge and skill. They had extensive experience of the largest of the railway companies, and they were well grounded in the business principles of that company, so carefully fostered by Josiah Stamp.

Riddles realised very early in his career that an organisation or engineering project must evolve using tried and tested techniques, as a base, if they are to be successful. Innovation had its place, but sudden leaps of the imagination, which took a company in a new, novel but untried direction must be managed carefully and quickly discarded when success, measured by cost and performance, came at too high a price. With each of BR's constituent parts adhering to their own development programmes, which seemed to be pulling in many different directions, and with a plethora of designs in service, standardisation became his mantra. Once again, he had learnt much under Stanier and the LMS Board.

To reinforce his view he looked to locomotive experiments of the pre-war years, when the LNER and the LMS wasted time and money on 'Hush Hush' and 'Fury' respectively. Even steam turbine power was included in his assessment, despite

both Stanier and Bond believing in its potential and wider development. And, when he took his new BR post, these experiments continued: Oliver Bulleid on the Southern with his 'Leader' class, gas turbine engines on the Western Region and a plethora of both diesel and electric proposals elsewhere. There was much to weigh up and much to rein in before he could direct

development in what he saw as a practical and sensible direction.

With financial limitations on what he could do, a near bankrupt economy hugely reliant on the UK's massive stocks of coal, the fledgling state of alternative methods of traction, an infrastructure geared to steam engines and the advanced state of their design and reliability, it is little wonder that Riddles gave

priority to steam locomotives. Over time he convinced other Executive members that this was the best way forward, though some had serious misgivings. He was not blind to alternatives, but felt that they needed much more design work, with the speculative support of companies such as English Electric and Metrovick, if they were to succeed. He realised that steam

46202 looking a little dog-eared. She will soon be at Crewe awaiting a decision about her future and then rebuilding. (AE/BR)

would eventually give way to other means of traction, but for the moment he pressed ahead with a standardisation programme, getting the best out of a technology that was understood and worked effectively, by the standards of the time.

To develop this idea, the Railway Executive set up a series of interchange trials in 1948, which saw the best designs from each region running over other regions' tracks. The hope was that the best elements could then be highlighted and brought together in new designs. By 1951 this work was nearing completion and building of a new range of standard-design locomotives had begun, to supplement the best of those engines already running in the regions. By

the end of the programme, in 1960, 999 new engines had been added to BR's stock, seeing service over the entire network. But even as they were being built, with planned lives of thirty years or more, dieselisation and electrification programmes advanced quickly to replace steam engines, which were condemned to scrap yards by 1968.

In 1948 this seemed like an unobtainable future and the investment was deemed sound. In this rush to standardisation, and recognising Riddles' belief that research should be focused primarily on proven, established principles, it is not surprising that anything outside this pattern should be scrutinised. With Turbomotive still in existence, presenting a clear

anomaly to his working principles, it is not surprising that this unique locomotive should feature in his planning. There is no evidence to suggest that her time in workshops, during 1948 and 1949, was part of a review process, especially as she reappeared and ran successfully for another twelve months. But there is a suspicion that this may have been so and only a shortage of engines made her temporary reinstatement possible.

For much of the engine's life Riddles had been a major figure in the LMS and must have been involved in the development programme, or at least briefed on its progress. Yet he made no public utterance on Turbomotive. In fact there is a marked silence on the matter. Even when speaking to his biographer, Colonel H.C.B. Rogers, in the late 1960s, when he could have expressed an opinion, he said nothing. This was most strange, especially when considering that Stanier was his great mentor, and this was his great innovation. Silence, when political, usually denotes a diplomatic disagreement. If so, this view could lead down many interesting paths.

If 46202's demise was planned, just waiting a cause, then the speed of her withdrawal and the argument that she was beyond economic life can be seen in a different light – the end of another 'rogue' development to be written off as a gallant effort. And in May 1950 Turbomotive entered Crewe Works for a heavy general repair that would end Stanier's experiment.

Looking the worse for wear and soon to be withdrawn from traffic for rebuilding. (AE/RH)

CHAPTER 8

REBORN
(1950–1952)

When Turbomotive entered Crewe Works in May 1950 few expected her to reappear quickly, based on the pattern of past maintenance periods. Added to this it seems that she may have failed in the days before her time in works began. But no official records appear to have survived to confirm this and no unofficial sightings have come to light either. However, part of any heavy general repair cycle is to strip down the locomotive, examine all working parts and replace or repair those badly worn. Being a unique engine where there was little or no past history or collective experience to fall back on, no one could predict, with any certainty, what state the turbine system would be in. Repair might not be possible and a costly new build or reconditioning might be the only options available.

The LMS, and later the new British Rail regime, had both reached the conclusion that the turbine experiment, though of interest, had now run its course. Although she ran effectively and equalled the performance of her sisters, there seems to have been little opposition to her remaining in service, but a prolonged period in the workshops gave BR a reason to consider her future: break her down for spares or convert her into a reciprocating engine.

When the LMS had considered ways in which the Princess Class might be improved, in the late 1930s, Derby Drawing Office came up with a series of modifications. The plans were shelved and work began on the Coronation Class instead, but the earlier work had not been forgotten and lay in the archives at Derby, periodically reviewed in case a problem occurred with a member of the class necessitating a major rebuild.

46202 was dismantled and surveyed at Crewe, and the turbine and gears were dispatched to Metrovick for specialist analysis. The survey took a short time, but the results took much longer to be considered before firm proposals for her future were put forward. In summary, the report concluded that repair work for all but the turbine system was routine and manageable. Despite the size of his task in bringing the four railway companies under the BR banner and achieve standardisation of operation and development, Robert Riddles became personally involved in 46202's future. In the limited correspondence that survives, marking the progress of these discussions, his name appears many times – for his comment or simply as an information addressee. His interest in the fate of one locomotive, out of many thousands under his control, is remarkable.

On 20 April 1951 the Chief Regional Officer of the Midland Region, J.W. Watkins, wrote a memo to the Railway Executive, based on internal memos from various less senior officers. In it he summarised the results of 46202's survey and

August 1952 – 46202 emerges from Crewe Works in her new guise, a hybrid – part Princess Royal and part Princess Coronation – painted in BR green. (RH/BR)

Named *Princess Anne* and being made ready for duty. (RH/BR)

financial implications, then recommended a course of action:

'Turbine Geared Driven Locomotive No 46202

'The locomotive renewal programme for 1933, authorised by the LMS Board in July 1932, included the construction of 3 4-cylinder 4-6-2 class passenger engines. In February 1933 the LMS Board gave approval to one of these locomotives being fitted with a Lysholm-Smith Ljungstrom turbine in place of the conventional reciprocating type of driving gear. The purpose of fitting this equipment was to compare the turbine type propulsion with the reciprocating type fitted to the other two engines authorised in the programme

referred to. The three engines have the same wheel base.

'During the time the turbine locomotive has been in service there have been several failures of the turbine and transmission, and last year a further failure occurred affecting the bearings of the transmission [this is the only reference to this failure that appears to have survived]. To make the locomotive suitable for service it will be necessary to incur the costs for the repair of turbine parts which Metropolitan-Vickers, who designed and supplied the turbines, estimate at £460. In addition to this a further expenditure will be necessary of £360, making a total expenditure of £820.

'Metropolitan-Vickers point out that apart from the cost, the turbines on this

locomotive have now reached a stage when after another period of service they will require extensive repairs. The firm are not prepared to give an estimate of the costs of this work, but the Chief Mechanical Engineer considers that this will be very considerable.

'In view of the expense and the fact that it has always been necessary to carry a fitter on the locomotive in addition to the ordinary crew, if trouble is to be avoided, which involves an expenditure of about £500 per annum, it would appear that the time is opportune for the engine to be converted into a normal reciprocating type driven locomotive. It has run 439,931 miles since being built, about 1935, and it is felt that sufficient knowledge of its capabilities has been obtained over the years it has been in service. Furthermore, having regard to its record there does not appear to be any *question of any more locomotives of this type being built.*

'The approximate estimated cost of converting the turbine locomotive to one of a normal reciprocating type is £6,250 as compared with the expenditure of £820 immediately necessary if the locomotive is to continue to operate in its present form. For the net additional outlay of £5430 there would be an assured saving of approximately £500 per annum (or 9.2% of the net outlay) on the wages of the fitter.

'It is, therefore, recommended that turbine locomotive No 46202 should be converted to one of a normal reciprocating type at an estimated outlay of £6250, and it is understood Mr Riddles agrees with this proposal.'

On 17 May 1951 the proposal was discussed at the Railway Executive's Board Meeting and approval given to proceed. The RE gave the project the registered number of WM 1010. In his memo to the Chief Regional Officer of the Midland Region, authorising this work, the Chairman added a specific instruction:

'I should be pleased if you could kindly advise me when the work of conversion is started and, also, when it is completed.'

It seems strange that full RE Board approval for such a small project was thought necessary. With a massive building programme set to deliver 999 new locomotives already underway at a projected cost in excess of £20 million, with ongoing work to support this huge network and its existing rolling stock and with drawing offices and workshops trying to get all this work done, it is

remarkable that the organisation found time to debate and plan the future of one engine. The simple and cheapest course open to Midland Region was to go ahead with fairly low-cost repairs and modify the engine to remove the need for a fitter. The alternative was to withdraw her from service and, if her state was deemed so poor as to make continued running a problem, use her for spares.

The LMS had developed a sound method of economic analysis that underpinned new proposals and projects. It was a system that became imbedded in all they did and Riddles, as the LMS's disciple, brought these processes to British Rail. But in the proposals for

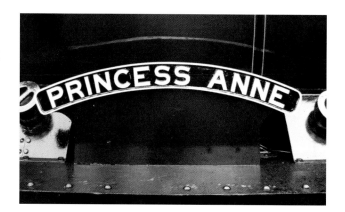

46202, of which he was a part, well-established cost–benefit accounting principles seemed to have been ignored, replaced by something more akin to a 'back of a fag packet' calculation – there is only one option and that is what it will cost. In truth

46202 arrives at Euston for the first time. The LMR's Chief Regional Officer, J.W. Watkins, greets the Driver, Sam Mason, and Fireman, Chris Brereton. (RH/BR)

there were easier and cheaper options, especially as the locomotive seemed to be operating as well as, or better than, her sisters in the twelve months before her latest visit to Crewe.

Against this background Metrovick's own summary of work needed on the turbine makes interesting reading. In his memo to the Board, Watkins painted a gloomy picture of the turbine's condition and potential repair costs suggesting that after 'another period of service they will require extensive repairs'. In reality Metrovick were more upbeat, judging that the fixed turbine blades and rotors might need to be renewed and corrosion to the turbine casings repaired 'in a few years' time'. They did not estimate the value of this work because they felt that 'the requirement is too far in the future, and as yet unclear, to adequately judge the state of machinery and the likely cost'.

In any organisation costings will often be managed to reflect pre-conceived ideas or pre-selected solutions. Turbomotive was no longer needed and, under the guise of a sound management decision, quickly dispatched. The decision to rebuild her at high cost, set to rise to £8,774, seems unjustified in the face of a substantial locomotive building programme already well underway and the heavy workload being borne by the workshops. So, perhaps it was simply a case of Riddles wishing to preserve this lone example of his mentor's innovative work and pulling strings to make sure she survived in this new guise. We shall never know, but it is pleasing to think that Riddles might have felt this way.

The 1936 plans for developing the Princess Class became the basis for 46202's conversion. It soon became apparent that the work recommended would turn her into a Princess

Re-absorbed into Camden's allocation and ready for duty. (ET/RH)

It will soon be autumn as 46202 prepares to leave Euston with the early morning express to Liverpool. (RH/BR)

Royal/Coronation hybrid. She would keep her 6ft 6in wheels, but have main frames modified with a Coronation Class front end. The inside cylinders would be cast steel, the outside ones cast iron, with a set of motion all to the Coronation design. The crank axles, smokebox fittings and superheater header and elements would be built to a new design. The boiler would be an existing Type 1, with sloping throat plate modified with the regulator in the dome. The original cab was reused, suitably modified to take the reversing gear.

With such a heavy workload Derby Drawing Office struggled to get this additional design work done. It was not until February 1952 that they found time to complete the task. By May the drawings were complete, materials ordered and work scheduled to start, but not quick enough for Watkins, who, under pressure from Riddles, sent a number of personal hasteners to John Harrison, then Mechanical and Electrical Engineer for the Midland Region at Derby. On 31 October 1951, for example, he wrote:

'I shall be glad to know whether this work has been started and, if so, on what date, and also when you anticipate it will be finished.'

Harrison responded a month later:

'In reply to your letter of the 31st October, the work of converting locomotive No 46202 to normal

reciprocating type drive has not commenced and I regret I am not in a position to state when it will be taken in hand. It will be some time before it is possible to complete the necessary drawings connected with the conversion and as I have explained to Mr Riddles my Drawing Office Staff are at the present time fully occupied in the completion of drawings for certain of the new BR Standard Locomotives.'

Finally work began and took little more than three months to complete. 46202 was sandwiched on the production line between the first batch of twenty-five new standard

class Pacifics and LMS locomotives in various states of repair at Crewe. On 13 August 1952 she was rolled out of No 10 Erecting Shop, seemingly having been painted in green livery on the production line, not in the Paint Shop. If so, this was unusual, but might reflect the heavy workload that staff at Crewe faced.

After seventeen years of service the locomotive was finally named and followed the pattern set by her twelve sisters. While under construction Royal approval was sought to name her *Princess Anne.* When 46202 re-entered service on

15 August, the young princess's second birthday, a formal but low-key naming ceremony took place. No records seem to have survived describing who attended and there are no photographs either of the event. All we have are a small number of pictures taken of her in ex-works condition, resplendent in her new colour scheme, workmen giving her an additional high-gloss polish ready for service.

A running-in period quickly began and she was noted several times on the main line and at Shrewsbury station, a regular route

No longer the fairly hushed getaway of Turbomotive but the full thrust of a traditional steam locomotive, here leaving Crewe. The few drivers and firemen who had driven 46202 in both forms tended to prefer the turbine version. (RH)

OPPOSITE:
A classic Eric Treacy photo. It almost seems that the crew have deliberately posed the loco for best effect. (ET/RH)

At speed near Tamworth, thundering through the Trent Valley. (RH)

Power and majesty at Hatton. (RP)

for engines just out of the works and under test. Finally, after more than two years away, 46202 returned to her allocated shed at Camden late in August, where she was 'spotted' by an RCTS observer:

'*August 1952..... The outside cylinders are set further forward than the other Princesses and the steam pipes have a distinctive bulbous casing similar to that of the Duchesses. The inside cylinders are of cast steel. No smoke deflectors are fitted. It carries works plates "Rebuilt Crewe 1952" and is back on its old Turbine duty, the 0830 Euston to Liverpool.'*

There was little fanfare or publicity surrounding her return, a

46202 passing Hatton with the Liverpool Euston express in September 1952. (RP)

Waiting to pick up her load. (RR/RH)

far cry from her launch in 1935. On arriving at Euston for the first time, Watkins met the loco and was photographed shaking the hands of her crew, Driver Sam Mason and Fireman Chris Brereton. So she slipped back into service without fuss or particular interest. But those who saw her were impressed by the look of the rebuilt engine, which seemed to combine the best features of the Princess Royal and Coronation Classes. As Turbomotive she had been unique and remained so in this new, more traditional guise. Although largely unannounced by BR and unnoticed by the railway press, footplate crew at Camden and Edge Hill showed great interest and still regarded her as a glamorous locomotive. Bill Starvis, a top link driver at Camden, who had worked on Turbomotive in 1949 and 1950 and been greatly impressed by her, later recalled his thoughts on the new 46202:

'I didn't get to drive her but spent time looking over the engine when she arrived at Camden in '52. If she had survived I would probably have taken

46202 topped off with coal at Edge Hill and ready to back down to Lime Street. (ET/RH)

her out on the road at some stage. She was a good looking loco, more like the non-streamlined Duchesses that appeared pre-war before they were fitted with smoke deflectors, but the Princesses look hadn't gone away. I'm told, by those who did work her, that she performed well, but not as good as the turbo – early days though and she didn't get any time to really prove herself. We all regarded her as something special and all hoped to be given the chance to drive her.'

The Euston to Liverpool route had been specifically chosen for Turbomotive because it suited her

A very grimy 46202 preparing to leave Edgehill with the Red Rose to Euston September 1952. (RP)

performance best – few stops and as much continuous, fast running as possible. With rebuilding, this policy could have ended but the Princesses tended to work this route and so she returned to her old stamping ground. In time, as Motive Power Depots gained experience of this 'new' locomotive with the capabilities of a Duchess, her pattern of work might have changed, but first she had to prove herself in day-to-day service.

If successful, there was a good chance that some or all of the modifications could have been extended to the other members of the Princess Class. There was concern in some quarters that their performance was significantly below the Coronations and rebuilding, when starting a period of major maintenance, was deemed a practical solution. But the cost, if the proposal had ever been more than conjecture, ruled out any change and the Princesses continued as they were, with only minimal modifications, until withdrawn from service in the early 1960s.

There was talk of smoke deflectors being fitted to 46202 soon after arriving at Camden, to correct a drifting smoke problem that obscured the footplate crews's forward view. If completed, it would have increased the resemblance of this hybrid engine to her half-sisters, as well as correcting a problem that often beset steam locomotives. Starvis wondered why they had not been fitted when she was being rebuilt at Crewe and reasoned that it was an oversight due to pressure of other work.

During the few weeks remaining to her, 46202 plied her trade between London and Liverpool making the return trip successfully twenty-eight times, being photographed quite often by line-side spotters. No stronger attention came her way and she slipped into the comparative obscurity of being just another Pacific – wonderful to see in full flow and still unique, but the novelty would soon wear off. Turbomotive had drawn attention throughout her seventeen years of life – railwaymen and lay people continually fascinated by her distinctive looks and her experimental state. She remained an icon to the last, stimulated by the very human need to consider and enjoy novel concepts, then mull over 'what might have been' if only engineers had been braver when new ideas evolved.

Princess Anne would find another sort of fame two months after rebuilding, in a way no one could expect. On 8 October she was again rostered to take the 08.00 train to Liverpool and so began her penultimate journey.

CHAPTER 9

DEATH AT HARROW, BURIED AT CREWE

(1952–1954)

With so many advances in technology we can now see tragedy unfold remotely, live, coldly and uncensored, if we wish. No longer do we have to rely on newspapers or news programmes to prepare us for horrors or edit the worst excesses of tragedy and violence. But this remote voyeurism only plays to our sight, not our other senses. For the victim, who has experienced profound and shocking sights, sounds, smells and the direct touch of violence, the impact is deep rooted and beyond the power of description or explanation.

The internet allows us unrestricted access to today and yesterday's tragedies in a way unthinkable only a few years ago. Images of wars or accidents not shown at the time have remained in archives that have now been opened and can be viewed on YouTube or other sites. In many cases the footage has no commentary, voiceovers only being added to material safe to release at the time.

Many articles and books have been written about the Harrow rail disaster, but the written word or still photographs fail to convey a sense of the time or the awfulness of what took place on that October morning. But view the silent movies on YouTube, containing film held back at the time, and you are transported back to a misty Harrow Station in the immediate aftermath of an appalling accident where death and destruction lurk in every shot. The silence of the film seems to magnify the horror, even though that world is now a 'foreign country where we did things differently', as L.P. Hartley affirmed in his book *The Go Between*. So much of that world is alien to us now and our response to suffering is no longer influenced by the all-encompassing tragedy of two world wars or the misery of abject poverty, making early death or disability common in many households. People were more sturdy and capable then, facing grief, for the most part, with a stoicism borne of experience. But events on 8 October tested even this resolve.

On 7 October Driver Bill Darton and Fireman George Dowler left their homes in Bannerman and Wimpole Streets in Liverpool and made their familiar way to Edge Hill Shed for duty. The 52-year-old Darton had worked on the railways since the First World War and was now a senior driver with experience of many routes. Dowler, at 27, was still fairly new to the railway, but had worked with Darton on many occasions and become friends.

They were rostered to take the 14.00 train from Liverpool to Euston, usually pulled by a Royal Scot Class locomotive in the winter months, when traffic was lighter. The journey passed without incident and they 'clocked off' later that evening having seen their engine safely to Camden. On completing their duty they checked the next day's roster and confirmed they would be working the 08.00 train to Liverpool and Manchester, with 46202 their locomotive, unless it developed a fault. As they left the shed to travel the short distance to their overnight accommodation, they would have seen 46202 come on shed after completing her usual day trip to Lime Street. After only two months of running since re-entering service they

Within an hour the crash site was swarming with rescuers, many having served through bombing attacks on London during the war. (RH)

noticed how jaded she looked and in need of a good clean, her smoke box streaked by leaking steam. Overnight she would be smartened up, but the weather, the smoky conditions and a high speed run north would soon undo this good work.

With dawn getting later as autumn approached, Darton and

Dowler returned to Camden in darkness the next morning. The driver bought his usual *Daily Mirror* from a delivery van 'hoping to snatch a quick read before we got away from Euston at 8'. The paper would remain in his bag, unread, to be retrieved from 46202's cab later in the day and returned to its owner, to

be kept as a souvenir and passed to a friend, still unread, many years later.

The ritual of steam engine preparation had changed little in many decades, although the size and power of locomotives had increased significantly. The tender filled with coal and water, the fire made up and the loco inspected and oiled where necessary. It took time but the crew were experienced and made sure that the engine was fit to run. But today would be slightly different, a second engine having been added to the train; an unnecessary double heading as far as power was concerned, but a useful way of remarshalling locomotives to their home sheds with minimum inconvenience. For Darton, whose engine would run second, it meant an easier, though less interesting journey, the lead crew taking the main responsibility for looking out for lights and hazards ahead. He noted that the other engine was 45637 *Windward Islands*, a Jubilee Class 4-6-0 that he knew well, being based at Edge Hill.

Its crew, Driver Albert Perkins, from Knotty Ash, and Fireman George Cowper, also Edge Hill men, had stayed in the same 'digs' as 46202's crew overnight. Darton and Cowper had joined the railway as engine cleaners more than 30 years before and were old friends, as well as colleagues.

The morning was chilly with only a slight wind to lift the thick fog that had moved down from the north overnight and which now hung heavily over Camden and Euston before dawn. Engine drivers were used to these condition, fog and smog being common in Britain at the time, and would run when visibility could be as little as 50 yards. A story, possibly apocryphal, from the Southern Region at this time related that conditions could be so bad a driver would sometimes stop when they knew a signal was near and the fireman climb up the ladder to see what it was indicating. Perhaps a lighthearted exaggeration, but the reality of life on the London Midland Region in 1952, which for the most part relied on a driver's skill for safe running, was not too far away from this reality. An automatic train control system, to provide aid to engine crews, was long overdue on most railways. The need had long been recognised, but, despite development work, an effective system for the entire network was still awaited on 8 October, though one was soon to be tested and selected. Only on the GWR had development and installation work taken place, beginning before the First World War, with most of its main lines and locomotives equipped by 1939.

Backing down to Euston to pick up their train was a slow process, as Darton recalled when giving evidence to the Accident Investigation Team later. The fog had begun to lift, greatly increasing visibility, but they were stopped for five minutes in the station approaches by signals while other traffic passed by. The fog had delayed many overnight services from the north and it would take some time for station staff to sort out

Considering the violence of the collision, the damage to 46202's tender and the train's first carriage seems mild in comparison to the carnage behind. (RH/BR)

Although on its side, 46202 looks remarkably undamaged considering the severity of the crash. (BR/RH)

Casualty clearance continues. (BR/RH)

much extra power provided by two locomotives the crew expected to make up the lost time fairly quickly. By their own account Darton and Dowler soon settled into their practised routine. A very poor view ahead and the sense that they were pushing the less powerful engine ahead, as well as pulling the load behind, was in their minds. Priding themselves on driving the bigger, stronger engine, it was frustrating to be running second, but they were 'old hands' and quickly dismissed this quirk of the rostering system to get on with the job at hand.

By Willesden the train was running well and accelerated through Harlesden, Wembley and on to Harrow and Wealdstone, picking up lost time in the process.

For Darton and Dowler the collision came without warning, any slight view ahead on either side of their locomotive being completely obscured by the engine ahead, the slight left-hand curve of the track into Harrow and the station buildings. The Liverpool train was travelling at about 50mph and 46202 came to rest, after a brief few moments of extreme violence, 50 yards or so from the point of impact. Neither man could recall the scene on the footplate with any clarity, but as the engine smashed to the left, tilted then rode up the platform they would have been thrown against the side of the cab or against the boiler at great speed, with little time to do anything but raise their arms in a final act of self-preservation. Dowler would later say that everything seemed to move in slow motion and

the problems the weather had caused. The track leading in to Euston was undergoing maintenance and this was also creating delays.

The train waiting for them was a long one – 11 carriages with 4 brake vans at the rear, weighing 444 ¼ tons – but by departure it was far from

full with only 192 passengers on board. Only minutes before leaving, a problem with the steam vacuum system was found at the rear of the last carriage. It took a while to be fixed and the train's departure was delayed by four minutes. But late starts were not unusual and with so

by some miracle he avoided serious injury, the engine ahead having absorbed the biggest blow.

They say that in the seconds, even minutes, after a crash, before shock subsides and movement returns, the silence is intense and unnerving. Then it breaks.

After the silence one witness, safe by only a few yards on the platform, reported whimpering sounds and then the screams of fear and agony. Overcome by the magnitude of what he had seen, he ran for safety, then checked himself and went back to the carnage to help.

The wrecked portions of three trains, one packed with commuters, another with overnight travellers from the north and the Liverpool Express, were compressed by the force of impact into a space 45 yards long, 18 yards wide and nearly 10 yards high. Station buildings were wrecked and carriages behind 46202 had ridden up over one another to demolish the pedestrian bridge linking the platforms. Darton and Dowler were overcome by this scene of devastation as they struggled to extricate themselves from their engine's cab, the driver buried under coal that had slammed forward from the tender. Neither man would ever find the words to describe what they had experienced; like veterans from many wars they remained tight-lipped and circum-spect in what they said, preferring stoicism to unfettered emotion.

Within only a few minutes the first ambulance arrived at the station and an hour later the wreck was being overflown by press and

newsreel-manned aircraft. As they looked down, through clearer, sunnier air, they saw hundreds of tiny figures clambering over the broken trains looking for signs of life. On the ground it was total chaos, with British Rail staff, firemen, ambulance crews, police, a group of American military personnel and members of the public attempting to find the wounded, begin clearance and seek cause. Pandemonium reigned with only the slightest effort being made to co-ordinate all these efforts and control access. Outside the station

entrance a large crowd of onlookers soon gathered, making access and exit difficult and photographers sought the best vantage points to take pictures. Ghoulish elements are always drawn by other people's agony and distress, even after six years of war.

Darton and Dowler scrambled down to the track on which 46202 had come to rest as best they could, the other side of the engine being surrounded by a mountain of debris. Darton's right hand had been badly gashed and blood was flowing freely, but he applied pressure to the

Night falls on 8 October, but rescue work continues unabated and under floodlights. (RH/BR)

46202 is slowly lifted into an upright position. (BR/RH)

wound with a rag in his pocket and eventually found his way to the station entrance where he received first aid. He was then taken to Harrow General Hospital, before transfer to the Royal Orthopaedic Hospital at Stanmore for specialist treatment. Before leaving his engine he asked about his old friend Albert Perkins. He could see how badly damaged *Windward Island*'s cab was, ahead of 46202, and must have realised the chances of his survival were slim. No one could give him any news. His fate would not be known until the following morning. Perkins's fireman, George Cowper, had been thrown or jumped from the cab, he could not recall which, and found himself lying on 46202's right-hand nameplate, with comparatively minor injuries. Shock ran deep and after treatment at Harrow General he was taken to a nursing home in Devon for rest and recuperation.

Dowler, though still in shock, was by some miracle only bruised and grazed. He remained at the scene for several hours helping the emergency services gain access to the carriages immediately around 46202. He would later be taken to Harrow Hospital, but was released and returned home to Liverpool two days later, having given a statement to the police.

Even though it would take many days to clear all the wreckage, extreme care being taken to make sure survivors were extracted as safely as possible, the investigation got underway in the first two hours. By the afternoon specialists were crawling among the wreckage, even before the bodies of the three railway crew, at that stage still deemed dead or missing, had been removed.

It was a gruesome business, but the position of bodies could tell investigators much, especially on the engine deemed, even then, to have caused the accident.

In the early afternoon the Divisional Operating Superintendent at Crewe had already initiated action to call an enquiry into the accident and wrote an internal minute to L.W. Cox at Euston with the details – it was delivered the same day, when many casualties had yet to be found and treated:

'Subject: *8.15 pm Express Passenger train, Perth to Euston, in collision with rear of 7.31 am Tring to Euston and 8.00 am Euston to Liverpool, in collision with* **resultant obstruction at HARROW, 8.10.52.**

'As you have already been advised, the Railway Executive Enquiry into the above will be conducted by Mr Hearn in Room 131 of the General Offices at Euston*

on Friday 10 October, commencing at 10.00 am. At the time of writing I am not able to give you the number of the Waiting Room....*

'It is very difficult indeed at this particular moment to say who will be available as it is assumed that the* following members of the train crew are either dead or in hospital injured, but so far as the injured are concerned, I want you to maintain close contact with Mr Minty and if either of the three men named below are in hospital and in a fit condition to give evidence, transport*

A poor, very grainy press photo, but captures the moment 46202 is lifted, rescuers carefully search underneath for any casualties, sadly they only found body parts. The first collision had thrown some victims in the path of the oncoming express and it is clear that they had little or no chance of survival. (RH)

Lifting work carries on in the background as another body is removed. (RH/BR)

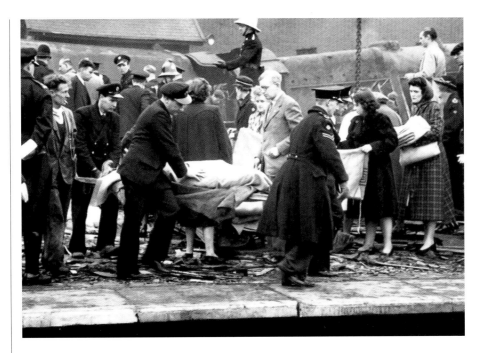

could be laid on for them both to and from the hospital and suitable arrangements made for their welfare while waiting to attend the Enquiry:

'Driver W Darton on engine 46202…. In hospital?

'Fireman G Dowler…. In hospital?

'Fireman G Cowper on engine 45637…. In hospital?

'The information in regard to Driver Perkins of Edge Hill who was on engine 45637 and Driver R S Jones and Fireman C Turncock who were on the 8.15 pm Perth to Euston is such that I have to assume that they have been killed, but if this is not the position and they are in hospital, you will no doubt follow up and arrange as necessary.

'In the course of the next 24 hours it may well be that persons other than those I have named who may be members of the Operating or Motive Power staff will come forward with sound information, and these men should also be asked to make themselves available at the Enquiry.'

This meeting took place as planned but none of the surviving footplate crew were deemed fit enough to give evidence. However, the Ministry of Transport enquiry, led by Lieutenant Colonel Wilson, had already been convened by then and would meet on 15 October for the first time. By this time the 'walking wounded' were available, including Dowler, though he could not add much to the debate, having seen so little.

While the enquiries sat the clear-up continued. Bit by bit the wreckage was checked and removed. Perkins's body was found, as were the crew of 46242, *City of Glasgow*, which pulled the Perth Express, and taken to a mortuary nearby. It took nearly two days for space to be found around 46202 to allow a crane access, but at 02.15 on 10 October she was lifted back onto the track, her front bogie removed and towed away to be held, temporarily, on the electric lines nearby. It would take longer to remove the other two engines, 45637 joining 46202, and 46242 was stabled in the up goods yard at Harrow. With so much to repair and make good at the station, the fate of these engines was of secondary concern, though engineers and investigators continued to examine them hoping to find any new clues. But as the line opened and normal service was resumed they made a melancholy sight beside the main line, even when covered with tarpaulins, and left a constant reminder to the fare-paying public that the railway had failed to protect them. Action had to be taken and two meetings were held on 22 and 24 October to discuss and agree the immediate fate of the engines. The minutes record the discussion:

'It was clear that the remains of engine 45637 and its tender, also the boiler, tender, bissol truck and loading coupled wheels of engine 46202 would require to be loaded up on to rail vehicles for removal from site. Engine 46202 would also require a new bogie fitting to enable the chassis to be taken away on its own wheels. A new tender was required to be provided to couple to the remaining chassis of engine 46202.

'With regard to engine 46242 it was decided that the tender would have to be loaded up and a fresh tender provided to enable this engine to be hauled to crew after certain straightening of frames,

In a matter of seconds 46202 was reduced from a gleaming engine to this sad hulk. (RH/BR)

changing of wheels and possible removal of certain parts.

'As the whole of the removal operations are dependent upon the engines being stripped and ready for loading up by the night of November 9th the Works Superintendent has kindly agreed to undertake the stripping of engine 46202 to enable the boiler to be taken out, also to make it possible for a new bogie to be fitted under this engine and for the main frames at the trailing end of the engine, which are badly out of gauge, to be cut off and pieced up as necessary to bring them within gauge. The Works Superintendent will arrange for the leading engine buffer beam, which is badly damaged, to be built up to enable a guard's brake to be coupled to it. Arrangements will also be made by the Works Supt's staff to liberate as far as possible the locomotive bissol truck. The stripping of fittings etc necessary in conjunction with this will be carried out by his staff.

'An engine and brake to leave Watford on the up electric at about 10.00 am on the 9th November and proceed to the vicinity of the site in readiness for disposing of engine 46202. To perform this, the engine should unhook from the brake and proceed into No 2 siding and couple to the tender attached to the chassis of engine 46202 and haul them out of the sidings and back them on to the guard's brake. Arrangements will subsequently be made for this chassis and tender to be conveyed to Crewe Works by special path. The speed of the train from Harrow and Wealdstone should under no circumstances exceed 8 mph.'

To allow this work to take place the electric lines were closed for part of two days – 8 and 9 November – and a great deal of preparatory work had taken place beforehand. First 46202's tender body was lifted and placed onto a bogie wagon, followed by the frame, and this first load left Harrow at 08.15. Shortly afterwards her boiler was removed on a 40 ton bogie wagon, plus material cut away from her over the previous few days. All that was left were the engine's frames, plus the middle and rear sets of driving wheels, the front set having been removed as their condition was suspect. An undamaged set of bogie and trailing trucks were added to these remains and then, in a more mobile condition, the remains were attached to a tender borrowed from 45257 ready to journey northwards to Crewe. In the early hours of 10 November her last, slow journey began. It would take three days to complete, despite a 'special path' being in place, such was her poor condition. The few pitiful remains of 45637 arrived a day earlier, and 46242 made the journey a week later.

Despite such a large locomotive building programme taking place, which could have easily produced replacements for these three severely damaged engines, it was decided that they should be returned to Crewe for assessment. Some thought that they should have been cut up on site and scrapped – a much easier task than breaking them down and taking them north. But the transfer took place and the remains resided at Crewe while a decision on their future was considered. Most who saw the wrecks thought that 46202

was in a far better condition than the other two.

And so time passed. The Ministry of Transport accident report appeared in June 1953 and sole responsibility for the disaster rested with the crew of the Perth Express. No other conclusion was possible. Only conjecture remained to explain the lapse of attention of this most experienced driver and fireman. Whatever the cause, such mistakes might have been avoided if an automatic train warning system had been installed on all locomotives, so that passing signals on red would have been more difficult. In his report Wilson made a very persuasive argument in favour of this long-delayed modification and few, if any, could object to this investment in the light of what had happened at Harrow.

Assessment of 46202 and 46242 at Crewe was a slow process, unlike 45637 which was written off as being beyond economic repair, and withdrawn in mid-December 1952. Anything of value was salvaged and the rest was scrapped. Meanwhile 46202 and 46242 continued to languish at the works as The Railway Correspondence and Travel Society (RCTS) observers noted:

'January 1953. Of the engines involved in the Harrow accident, 46202 was back in its old resting place in No 9 Shop, minus boiler, and 46242's frame was on the scrap road, having had various parts cut off. It is believed that 46202 had previously visited the scrap road to have damaged parts removed.

'February 1953. The frames of 46202 were in the Erecting Shop North, they

were bent somewhat at the right hand front end. City of Glasgow's frames were a twisted mass in the Scrapping Shed.

'*March 1953. Only a portion of 46202's frame appeared to have been left, whilst those of 46242 had been cut away at the front end just behind the cylinder.*

'*July 1953. The frames of 46202 and 46242 are still in No 9 Shop.*'

There must have been many debates over the fate of these two engines once condition surveys showed them, one assumes, to both be repairable, albeit at some cost. But new build would have been much more expensive. Sadly, no papers seem to have survived in public hands to describe the thought processes behind these deliberations. So one can only guess at the true level of repairs needed to get both engines operational again. However, the rapid withdrawal and scrapping of 45637 suggests that they were not thought to be beyond economic repair.

By all accounts 46202's list of repairs was a long one, but not unmanageable, especially when considering the benefits derived from bringing a virtually new engine back into service. And 46242, although older, was from a class of proven Pacifics, so was still a valuable asset to British Rail, even though more badly damaged than her half-sister. Yet as the months passed BR decided to repair *City of Glasgow* and let her run until her class were withdrawn in the early 1960s, but condemned *Princess Anne*, which to many had just as good prospects, cannibalising her for spares and scrapping what was left.

A few days after the accident 46202 is methodically stripped down near Harrow Station for her last journey to Crewe. (RH)

Robert Riddles in the early 1950s. (RR)

This very puzzling decision raised many eyebrows, particularly among those who had seen for themselves the condition of both engines.

The answer assumed by many was that she was beyond economic repair and the opportunity was taken to build a new Pacific locomotive in her place. This engine, it was argued, would allow BR to take the standardisation programme a step further and develop a Class 8 Pacific, to complement its Class 6 and 7 sisters. However, the operational requirement for this more powerful engine was left hazy. Design work began in February 1953 and in May 1954 the result of this plan, engine number 71000, appeared at Crewe, in time to be towed to a major locomotive and rolling stock exhibition at Willesden, part of that year's high-profile International Railway Congress in London. The locomotive was named *Duke of Gloucester*.

71000's record card reports that the production cost of this engine was £44,655 and history records that she was the only member of her class built, there being no demand for the type. Though impossible to verify now, the likely price of repairing 46202 may have been comparable with her 1952 rebuilding cost of £8,774. To a certain extent this figure is borne out by the fact that her boiler and many other components were in good enough condition to be used, after cannibalisation, on other locomotives of the same class. In addition, *City of Glasgow*, generally considered to be in worse condition than 46202, cost only £6,801 to repair. However, to this can be added £1,155 for additional heavy general repair work carried out concurrently with repairing collision damage and £700 for provision of cast steel inside cylinders; a total cost of £8,656.

It is difficult to understand why this very expensive and unnecessary project went ahead, when BR was already struggling to build all the other standard designs the Railway Executive demanded. Some believe that 46202 was deliberately sacrificed to allow Robert Riddles, who would retire in 1953, a final shot at producing the ultimate steam locomotive, which might place him alongside William Stanier, George Churchward and Nigel Gresley as a truly great engineer. If so, the speed with which the engine was designed and the novel features it incorporated conspired to produce a locomotive of mediocre performance and doubtful need. It would have been better, and cheaper, if he had let 46202 be repaired.

46202's Engine History Card, Form ERO 3666, is one of the few surviving documents to provide any clue to the discussions that took place. In the notes column someone has written 'Involved in Harrow mishap – 8/10/52. Allocated 1953 Prog.' To which has been added, 'W&E Min No 145 16.6.54', then a different person has written 'Withdrawn from stock WE 22.5.54', which has inscribed beneath, but scored out, under 'Special Authority'. Strangely enough 71000's building was only authorised retrospectively in June 1954 while on display at Willesden.

Although ERO 3666 is primarily an accounting form recording work completed, costs, depreciation and general details of the engine, it does provide an unadulterated resumé of actions taken, as well as hinting at underlying cause. In this case the record suggests, in the content and sequence of comments, that BR fully intended repairing 46202, even assigning her a works order number, but this was later withdrawn once 71000 appeared from the workshops at Crewe. A case of 'smoke and mirrors' to hide a development few wanted, or simply management confusion at a time of intense work on many locomotive projects?

The few clues remaining suggest that 46202's progress back to traffic or withdrawal from service was far from clear cut even until the end. Even Riddles's part in the process may have been limited, his retirement in October 1953 effectively removing him from the scene towards the end of 71000's planning stage. So where does the truth lie?

During the development of the standardisation programme in the late 1940s, many alternatives were considered, to supplement the best engines created by the four constituent companies. A Class 8 Pacific was proposed, under the designation Class 75, and preliminary drawings appeared in 1948. It was based on the LMS Coronation Class, with four cylinders, but having many components from the new Britannia Class and shared looks. But after the Railway Executive reviewed the requirement, and found little justification for additional Class 8 locomotives, planning work came to an end. Riddles and Ernest Cox may have found this decision irksome. The desire to develop new ideas is central to a good engineer's psyche, and these men were engineers of the highest quality determined to build the ultimate steam locomotive. And just as Stanier pursued his dream of turbine locomotives to the point of criticism, so Riddles and Cox kept their dream alive, even in the face of

a world determined to embrace change and new, more effective technologies. The Harrow crash gave them the unexpected chance to develop the one major class of engine that seemed likely to elude them in the twilight of their careers. If successful, it would have allowed their work to be compared favourably with the great engineers who had gone before.

When Cox wrote his account of these days in the mid-1960s he only briefly mentioned the demise of 46202 and *Duke of Gloucester*'s creation. He was sparing with his words when he wrote, perhaps a little disingenuously:

'It was the terrible disaster at Harrow in October 1952 which by completely destroying LMS Pacific No 46202 Princess Anne only a few weeks after her conversion from the "Turbomotive", created a vacancy in the BR stock lists. Riddles seized upon this fact to obtain authority for a prototype in the BR standard series.'

Riddles echoed these words when talking to his biographer, Lieutenant Colonel H. Rogers, a few years later. He strongly emphasised how badly damaged 46202 had been at Harrow, adding that this gave him the opportunity to build a new Class 8 Pacific 'with which running experience might be gained for future building of standard Class 8 engines', suggesting that a demand had been identified when clearly one did not exist. By 1970, when this book was published, Riddles's policy in advocating, then building the standard range of steam locomotives, instead of pressing ahead with diesel

or electric developments, had been strongly criticised. As one would expect, Rogers's book contains a strong defence of his actions. His arguments are well stated and persuasive, but in being so robustly defensive it is likely that he might also have been a little self-serving, passing over issues where criticism was justified. I suspect that the demise of 46202 could fall into this category.

By the time BR's finance managers came to close the account for 1954, and balance the books, Riddles had retired, but questions concerning the cost of 71000 were raised. It seems that outlay was likely to exceed estimate by at least 25 per cent. In response, J.F. Harrison, then Chief Mechanical Engineer for the London Midland Region, suggested several measures that could offset *Duke of Gloucester*'s production costs – saving 46202's potential repair costs, her scrap value and the spares her cannibalisation would generate. The book was closed with these savings taken, leaving no option but to action her disposal in late spring 1954. No matter what her actual state she was finally scrapped to offset overspending on 71000. It was a humdrum, inauspicious end to such a dramatic, dynamic existence.

In her last few weeks of life, if that is what it can be called, 46202 still drew the attention of her last and probably most constant advocate, Roland Bond. On Riddles's retirement he had inherited his CME title, though not the role, with changes taking place

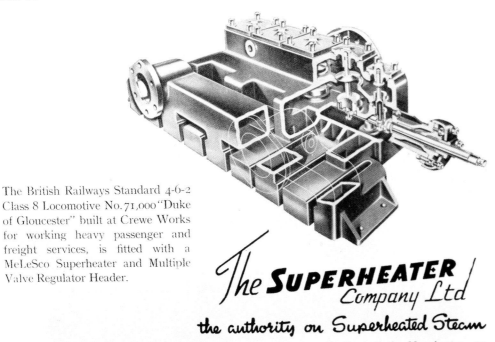
following the demise of the Railway Executive in late 1953 to reflect the Conservative Government's change of direction on railway management. Early in February 1954 he wrote a short memo to Harrison regarding the 'Ex-LMS Turbine Locomotive'. He did not explain his interest, but asked for information and drawings relating to the reversing gear assembly. Harrison forwarded all this material and must have wondered why his new man should show interest in this engine. Perhaps he simply wanted to preserve these items in his archives or enjoy the scientific challenge of finding a solution to the engine's perennial Achilles heel in private. One thing is certain – despite his strong association with the locomotive, it is unlikely that he was contemplating restoring her to turbine condition. But his motive in pursuing this interest will now never be known and the papers he bequeathed to the National Railway Museum give no clue.

As CME he might have been involved in the debate about her future and had the power, if he so wished, to see her repaired and running again. But time had moved on, a replacement had been built and so he allowed LMR managers to make the final decision; to the scrap line her few unserviceable remains were sent.

The phoenix rising from 46202's ashes – 71000 *Duke of Gloucester* is born and her image is soon used for publicity. (Author)

CHAPTER 10

A PLACE IN HISTORY

By the time 46202 was scrapped, anything usable having been stripped away, the Harrow rail crash was slipping into memory. Bill Darton and George Dowler, her last crew, had recovered and returned to duty. Harrow station had been rebuilt, though some scars remained, and press attention had moved to fresher fields. British Rail, 're-organised and re-energised' following the demise of the Railway Executive, continued with its extensive building programme, but with greater emphasis on diesel and electric locomotion. The world moved on repeating mistakes and creating new ones as it lurched forward in the name of progress.

But scars never heal completely. Darton and Dowler, like most victims of an accident, did not forget the events of 8 October and relived them for the rest of their lives. Both visited Crewe in 1953 and saw the remains of their old engine and may have wondered, as survivors do, how they had walked away from the wreck when so many had died or suffered crippling injuries. On their train 7 passengers had died, a mercifully small number considering the 192 on board and the death toll elsewhere, but this was small compensation.

And one by one all those people who had helped create, run and maintain Turbomotive had slipped away, most unnoticed but a few to greater glory. Yet they all seem to have been affected by this one locomotive more than any other and she is often mentioned and fondly remembered in memoirs. Such is the wonder and appeal of steam engines. Clichés describing their appeal abound but their indefinable qualities run counter to reality. They were, after all, only unfeeling metal machines whose 'life' was simply mechanical movement accompanied by great heat, the hissing of steam and clouds of smoke. But the impression they left and continue to leave is profound, even on the minds of professional railwaymen and engineers, who may have been expected to see a machine in a more cold-blooded light. And certain engines continue to be feted for their looks, power and performance, preserved examples still drawing immense crowds. The story of Turbomotive, with its elements of drama, experimentation, individuality, persistence, great promise and tragedy touches the minds of those who sense the allure of steam locomotives. Her achievements may have been slight by comparison to the great Pacifics of the LNER and LMS, but her purpose was more complex. She was a look into the future, with great engineers hoping to find a better, more effective form of locomotion. With hindsight these efforts may seem naive. Developing steam engines, when electric or diesel alternatives would have grasped the future more efficiently, now seems ridiculous, if not unscientific. But the extreme restrictions to which society was exposed by two world wars and our near total reliance on coal, made a continuation of steam engines seem unavoidable.

Sir Nigel Gresley, in his Presidential address to the Institution of Locomotive Engineers in September 1927, caught the mood of these days effectively:

'The idea has been fostered by some, who should have known better, that it is unnecessary to devote more attention to development and improvement of the steam locomotive, as it would be rendered obsolete by the electrification of lines…. I should remind our members that this is an Institution of Locomotive Engineers, not an Institution of Steam Locomotive Engineers; all kinds of locomotives, steam, oil and electric, are our concern.

'It is no part of our policy to perpetuate a kind of locomotive that is not economical…. It is not a case of steam versus electricity, but rather a realisation that the possibilities of steam as a motive power has not yet been fully developed, much less exhausted.

Undoubtedly the extension of the electrified railways has urged steam locomotive engineers to renewed efforts to make the steam locomotive more efficient. This has led to the production of the internal combustion, turbine and high steam pressure locomotives.

.... I venture to think that in the near future such improvements will be made in internal combustion and steam locomotives that they will be able to maintain their position as economical units of transport, even as compared with electric traction, for many services.'

It is hard to give up something that is familiar and steam engines had formed the basis of engineering for such a long time. Even though Gresley recognised the need to change to alternative sources of power, he seems to do so with sadness and regret. William Stanier, George Churchward, Robert Riddles and many others seem to have felt the same way and so steam locomotive design and building in Britain continued long after other developed nations embraced change more effectively. Turbomotive was part of this vanishing world. It was an attempt to push known and trusted technology just one more step and keep its inevitable demise at bay for just a little longer. If designers and their employers had been braver and driven change more effectively then the ludicrous position of steam locomotives being built in huge numbers in the 1950s, only for them to end up in scrap yards a few years later, would have been avoided. We might also have had a more modern railway system much earlier and greatly reduced

our reliance on motor vehicles and the curse of their pollution.

Turbomotive was a worthy experiment in terms of a disappearing technology, but also a distraction. Her 'successor', *Duke of Gloucester*, even more so. Each, in their own way, represented a world in which engineers seemed in denial. Not progress, just a step sideways. But the sideways step towards turbine development was an interesting one and clearly appealed to Stanier and Henry Guy, who leapt at the chance to match it with steam technology. Guy had a broader view, though, and saw its potential beyond the end of steam when powered by different means.

It is harder to assess Stanier's viewpoint, because he was reticent in setting down his thoughts in writing, preferring, if at all possible, to get others to speak for him; as did Roland Bond when presenting 'his' paper on Turbomotive to the Institution of Locomotive Engineers in 1946. But after retirement he scrutinised the development of his engine and other turbine experiments. He was intrigued by GT3 designed by a small team led by John Hughes and built by English Electric, which married a gas turbine power source to a 4-6-0 base. Although ultimately flawed and rejected because it offered nothing that diesel or electric could not produce more efficiently, it was, in many ways, a natural successor to Turbomotive.

At the 1961 railway exhibition at Marylebone, Stanier spent a considerable amount of time looking

over GT3 and, as Hughes later recalled, interrogated him about its design and potential, comparing it to his own work. The older man still felt that turbines should have been fitted to more Pacifics and Class 8 freight locomotives, making them easier and cheaper to maintain than a single specialist engine. Interestingly, he discussed the potential of changing 6202 from coal to oil during the 1940s conversion experiments and wondered whether this might have suited turbine drive better.

Parked ahead of GT3 at Marylebone that May day in1961 was *Duke of Gloucester*, soon to be withdrawn from service having fallen short of the promise Riddles had hoped this engine would fulfil. If 46202 had survived the Harrow crash, and the debates that followed, she would also have been heading for disposal in 1961, like the rest of her sisters. Behind GT3 sat a new 25kV electric locomotive, pointing the way, in sequence of evolution, to the long delayed future.

In summing up Stanier and Guy's turbine locomotive the most commonly used phrase is that she was the most successful experimental locomotive that had ever run in Great Britain. A fitting accolade but one that has to be tempered with caution. The others were not particularly good, none were long lasting and if revenue-earning service was achieved then it did not last long. Turbomotive was different and proved a successful experiment and a relatively successful locomotive in service, though one dogged by

Marylebone, May 1961. Sir William Stanier (second from the right nearest the engine) watches Prince Philip descend from GT3, English Electric's attempt to harness turbine power. (JH)

expensive and time-consuming turbine maintenance.

In pursuing their ideas Stanier and Guy had learnt much from development work carried out by other railway designers over many decades, albeit little of it making a lasting impression and to a condensing form. They also had the successful application of turbines across other industries to learn from and consider. The problem that beset each development was the need to improve upon what was already in place. This proved a stumbling block for railway engineers, but not their

industrial partners, particularly where power stations and ships were concerned. Railways could find equal or better solutions when steam turbines were being developed. So savings from turbine locomotives had to be spectacular if the conventional way of doing business was to be unseated and Turbomotive never established that it could perform more cheaply or more effectively.

Without Stanier's advocacy, determination and reputation the engine would have undoubtedly been rebuilt as a reciprocating locomotive before war broke out in

1939, probably as the Princess/Coronation hybrid she became in 1952. But war changed priorities for everyone and the railways, starved of funds and manpower, could do little but press on with what they had. Under these conditions Turbomotive was given a new lease of life and soldiered on, suffering, as did all rolling stock, under a poor maintenance regime, lack of spares for her turbine and a heavy workload. It says much for her sturdiness that she survived until 1949 and may have gone on longer, and turbines been used in other

Sir William Stanier at Marylebone apparently lost in thought. He toured the exhibition and visited both GT3, where he discussed its potential with the Chief Designer, John Hughes, and 71000 *Duke of Gloucester*, in attendance shortly before withdrawal from service. (Author)

locomotives, if her advocates had still been in place and British Rail had not been created. But change was inevitable and the demise of steam, though delayed too long, was unavoidable.

My experience of engineers is that they find joy in designing machines and only grudgingly see beauty in their mechanical creations, as though an appreciation of aesthetic and artistic values is somehow wrong. My highly qualified engineering father was like this. Art galleries, art programmes and their like were tolerated, but not appreciated. Yet he was moved to silence by a Spitfire in flight, the elegant lines of a Coronation Pacific, a warship scything past at speed and the sophistication of great engineering design. He understood, as engineers seem to, the style and grace of machines, and understood their beauty beyond the purely practical. To him the ultimate praise could only be 'if it looked right, it probably is'. And to his mind, and to many others, Turbomotive met this simple, but almost impossible to achieve, description.

I thought about all the men who had built this locomotive, worked on her footplate and maintained her, when visiting the Doncaster School Railway Museum not long ago. Standing by one of the *Princess Anne* nameplates, mounted above *Windward Island*, her partner in disaster, I was struck by what little remains of those distant days. I also thought about my father and uncle who had witnessed the drama of a time now slipping from firsthand memory, when steam engines were the ultimate form of locomotion. Turbomotive, and all her name conjures up, seems to be such an apt symbol of that time.

I also thought of my late uncle, trapped and solitary in an unhappy marriage finding solace in research and collecting. He made a point of speaking to railwaymen of all sorts, recording their past and the histories of the locomotives central to their lives before it all disappeared. By chance the results of his labours came to me and now some of his work has found a voice and Turbomotive lives once again.

TURBOMOTIVE – KEY BIOGRAPHIES

Richard William Bailey. Born in Romford on 6 January 1885 and died in Leicestershire on 4 September 1957. In 1901 he started an apprenticeship with the Great Eastern Railway Locomotive Works at Stratford. Marked out at an early age as someone with remarkable talents, he was awarded both a Whitworth Exhibition and scholarship to support his continued and advanced education. In 1906, as one of the few technically trained engineers on the railway staff, he became involved with the electrification of commuter lines into Liverpool Street Station and, as an alternative to this, a more advanced steam locomotive (work that resulted in the unique 'Decapod' design – a locomotive with five coupled axles intended to give high and rapid acceleration on suburban services).

With few prospects of promotion on the Great Eastern, Bailey changed direction and became a lecturer at Battersea Polytechnic and then the first Principal of the Crewe Technical Institute. Here he met and befriended Henry Guy. In 1919 it was he who encouraged Bailey to leave the college and join British Westinghouse Company shortly before it became Metropolitan Vickers. He became a senior member of their Research Department, under A.P.M. Fleming, where he remained for the rest of his career, a leading specialist in turbine development (steam and gas) and metallurgy. In these tasks he became closely involved in Turbomotive's design, construction and testing. Later he played a major role in developing jet turbine engines for aircraft.

In 1935, as Turbomotive rolled off the production line in Crewe, Bailey presented a paper to the Institution of Mechanical Engineers that became a landmark in the understanding of creep (the slow deformation of a material with time under load) and the behaviour of materials at high temperature. These were two essential elements in the understanding and development of turbines.

Bailey was elected a Fellow of the Royal Society in 1949 and became President of the Institution of Mechanical Engineers in 1954.

Roland Curling Bond. Born on 5 May 1903 at Ipswich and died in 1980. Educated at Tonbridge School, he became an Engineering Apprentice at Derby Locomotive Works and then a pupil under Sir Henry Fowler, the LMS's CME. Once qualified he specialised in overseeing locomotives built by contractors for his parent company. He so impressed managers at the Vulcan Foundry Locomotive Works that he was 'headhunted' and became their Assistant Works Manager in 1928. A return to the LMS followed in 1931 with a posting to the Horwich Works and then to Crewe as Assistant Works Manager. Despite his comparatively young age he was rapidly promoted and by 1946 had become Deputy Chief Mechanical Engineer for the LMS. Nationalisation of the railways did not hinder his progress and he succeeded Robert Riddles as British Railway's CME Central Staff in 1953. Before retiring in 1968 he held the post of Technical Adviser to the British Transport Commission before becoming General Manager of BR's Workshops Division in 1965. In recognition of his great contribution to engineering he became President of the Institution of Locomotive Engineers (1953/54) and the Institution of Mechanical Engineers (1963/65).

Throughout his career with the LMS he was a strong advocate of the science explored by the building of Turbomotive. Sadly, he was to be CME, BR, when the locomotive, in her modified form, was condemned and scrapped. His 1946 paper to the Institution of Mechanical Engineers remains the primary source of information and analysis of the turbine experiment.

George Jackson Churchward. Born in Stoke Gabriel in Devon on 31 January 1857 and died in Swindon in December 1933. In 1873 engineering skills he had demonstrated as a child were developed when he became a pupil at the South Devon, Cornwall and West Cornwall Railway's Locomotive, Carriage and Wagon Works at Newton Abbot, a short distance from his home. When the Great Western Railway absorbed this company three years later Churchward transferred to Swindon to complete the last year of his education. He remained in Wiltshire for the rest of his life, progressing through the ranks to become the GWR's CME in 1902 (retiring in 1922).

Like his disciple, William Stanier, Churchward was considered an outstanding engineer, but not a great innovator. He understood that all variations on steam locomotive design had probably been discovered and tested by others and that this wealth of experience could inform his own design work. His aim was to establish best practice and absorb this into engine design and take steam development as far as possible. He also understood the need for standardisation, the complexities of engine testing and the streamlining of workshop facilities. In all he did he was ahead of his time and his work gave the GWR a huge advantage, which other companies struggled to match. Some have said that after his retirement the GWR stood still, resting on its laurels. Churchward's impact on railways is undeniable, as was his influence on the great engineers who followed in his footsteps. Stanier, in particular, benefited hugely from his leadership and patronage. Clearly his work for the LMS was sponsored by all he had learnt from Churchward, as was the need to develop all established engineering principles to their absolute limits. The turbine experiment was a natural progression of this design principle.

Herbert Chambers. Born in Derby during 1885 and died in September 1937. On leaving school he became an apprentice at the Midland Railway Works in Derby. Once qualified he found employment in the Locomotive Drawing Office, before being recruited by Beyer Peacock in Manchester in 1911, returning two years later to Derby. In 1923 he was promoted to Chief Locomotive Draughtsman and four years later to Chief Draughtsman of the LMS. In 1935 he became William Stanier's Personal Assistant at Euston, a post he held until his death. As Chief Draughtsman, and then Stanier's technical assistant, he played a leading role in the planning and building of Turbomotive and the standard locomotive designs introduced by the LMS.

Tom Francis Coleman. Born in Gloucestershire during 1885 and died in 1958. After serving his apprenticeship with Kerr, Stuart and Co in Stoke-on-Trent, he was, during 1905, employed by the North Staffordshire Railway Co, rising to become their Works Plant Draughtsman then Chief Draughtsman. The amalgamation saw him move from Stoke to Derby. A move to Horwich Works as Chief Draughtsman followed in 1926, where he remained until 1933 working on a 2F 0-6-0 Dock Tank, followed by a taper-boilered 2-6-0 engine and then the new Stanier Class 5 4-6-0 locomotive. Work on the Class 5 had barely begun when he was transferred to Crewe as Chief Draughtsman, without relinquishing responsibility for Horwich, and so began the most prolific period of his career. When Herbert Chambers became Stanier's Personal Assistant in 1935, Coleman replaced him – a post he held until retirement in 1949. For the work he did in supporting Stanier many consider him to be one of the finest locomotive designers of the twentieth century.

When Stanier wished to develop the Princess Pacifics it was Coleman who led the design work. He wanted to improve their performance and ease of maintenance. Preliminary work was completed but when building additional, streamlined engines were authorised, Coleman took the opportunity to create a completely new class of engine, the Coronations. But the design work for an improved Princess was not lost and eventually formed the basis of Turbomotive's hybrid conversion in 1952.

William Henry Darton. Born in Liverpool in 1900 and died there in 1981. He became a locomotive cleaner at

Edge Hill post the First World War and by gradual steps a driver in the 1930s, remaining at Edge Hill until his retirement in the early 1960s as steam came to an end. He was 46202's last driver.

George Dowler. Born in Liverpool in 1925 and died there in 1994. After service in the Second World War he became an engine cleaner at Edge Hill and by 1952 a fireman, regularly partnering William Darton. Information about his later career is hazy but it seems that he became a driver in the late 1950s and ended his career in the 1980s working on diesel and electric locomotives. He was 46202's last fireman.

Henry Lewis Guy. Born at Penarth, near Cardiff on 15 June 1887, the second son of a local meat supplier. From an early age he demonstrated his engineering skills and, with his father's help, gained an apprenticeship under T. Hurry Riches, the CME, on the Taff Valley Railway. Later he gained a scholarship to the University College of South Wales to study mechanical, civil and electrical engineering, being awarded diplomas in all three subjects in 1909 and winning the Bayliss Prize (awarded by the Institution of Civil Engineers) and a Whitworth Exhibition.

On leaving university he became a lecturer at Crewe Technical College, before finding employment with the British Westinghouse Company in Manchester, where he specialised in the development of turbines. By 1918 he had risen to become Chief Engineer of the Mechanical Department of its successor company, Metropolitan-Vickers, a post he held until his retirement in 1941.

He had a glittering career marked by many prestigious awards and scientific advances. His influence spread and he became the driving force behind the development of Turbomotive, enlisting William Stanier's support and assistance in creating and then sustaining this experimental locomotive. Behind the scenes at Metrovick he enlisted the help of Richard Bailey, another turbine specialist, in designing, then monitoring 6202's drive system.

In recognition of his contribution to science he was elected a Fellow of the Royal Society in 1936 and in 1939 was seconded to the Scientific Advisory Council of the Ministry of Supply. He later chaired many wartime committees dealing with, among other things, the development of guns, ammunition, aircraft weapons and the technical organisation of the Army. In recognition of his work he received a CBE in 1945 and was created a Knight Bachelor in 1949. Ill health forced his retirement in 1951 and he died, at his home in Dorset, in July 1956. William Stanier, not someone who happily 'put pen to paper', felt so moved by Henry Guy's death that he wrote a detailed obituary for the Royal Society, which appeared in Volume 4 of their Biographical Memoirs.

Harold Brewer Hartley. Born in London on 3 September 1878 and died on 9 September 1972. Hartley was educated at Mortimer College, then Dulwich College. He graduated from Balliol College Oxford with first class honours in natural sciences in 1900. He remained at the College as tutor and lecturer and married the Master of Balliol's eldest daughter. During the First World War, he rose from Junior Officer with the 7th Leicestershire Regiment to Brigadier General, Controller of the Chemical Warfare Department. He was awarded the Military Cross for gallantry and was Mentioned in Despatches three times. He advised different governments on the development of chemical weapons until 1950.

Although returning, part time, to the academic world in 1919, he combined this role with work in different industries. But in 1930 he resigned his tutorial fellowship at Oxford to become the LMS's Vice President for Works and Ancillary Undertakings and Director of Research – a move encouraged and sponsored by Josiah Stamp. His influence on many areas of railway work was immense, not least in the design of locomotives. But a man of his drive and ability would be frustrated by the poor business sense and hidebound tradition of the LMS in the early 1930s. He and Stamp saw in William Stanier a man who could move things forward and set out to recruit him. His arrival in 1933 provided the long sought for catalyst for change and they gave 'their man' complete support and huge freedom to develop effective locomotives.

As a scientist he was intrigued by new ideas and the need for effective and novel research. Developing a turbine engine fell naturally into this field and he gave his wholehearted support to the project. There seems little doubt that this made sure that 'trials' with Turbomotive continued far longer than would have been allowed by a hard-pressed Operating Department if left to their own devices – 6202's record of availability being poor, in comparison to her sisters.

Hartley also took the lead in developing streamlined engines for the LMS, having been impressed by Nigel Gresley's work on the LNER and the research by Frederick Johansen on principles of aerodynamics. He recruited Johansen and gave him free reign to develop these ideas still further, even approving construction of a wind tunnel at Derby to test different designs and concepts. Many LMS engineers frowned at these developments and saw them as wasteful of time and resources, but Hartley was a visionary and saw the benefit and long-term potential of this research for railways and aviation. As a test bed for a new drive system he saw Turbomotive as a natural mount to trial streamlining as well, an experiment overtaken by the rapid development and appearance of the new Coronation Class.

For the remainder of his life he involved himself in many industries and retained an interest in scientific discovery, chairing many eminent bodies that advised government. He was elected a Fellow of the Royal Society in 1926 and was knighted two years later. In 1944 he was awarded a Knight Commander of the Royal Victorian Order (KCVO) and a Knight Grand Cross of the Royal Victorian Order (GCVO) in 1957.

Following William Stanier's death in 1965, he wrote a very detailed biography of his late CME, which was published by the Royal Society. His assessment of Stanier was incisive and reflected the deep respect he felt.

Frederick Charles Johansen. Born in1897 and died at his home in Surrey in 1966. He gained his B.Sc and M.Sc at Kings College, London, in the years following the First World War. After working for the Yorkshire Electric Power Co he was appointed to a research post at the National Physical Laboratory (NPL) in Teddington, Middlesex, to study aspects of fluid motion, which led to experiments on air and liquid flow around solid, but moving, objects; this work was relevant to many branches of engineering, including ship and train design. In the late 1920s he produced a series of papers outlining the results of this work (flow around circular cylinders, flow of air behind flat plates, aerodynamic influences on stability, the screw propeller, flow through pipe orifices and more). By using the wind tunnel at Teddington his research was throwing up interesting ideas. These advances were not lost on his fellow scientists and engineers in the railway industry where the drive for greater efficiency, economy and speed were constant needs.

By the 1930s his work resulted in two publications of great significance. In 1934 the Royal Aeronautical Society published their *Handbook of Aeronautics* with Johansen as a major contributor. He also produced a paper entitled *The Air Resistance of Passenger Trains* for the Institution of Mechanical Engineers. Though published in 1936, it contained research going back to the late 1920s, some of which had informed the development of Gresley's 4-6-4 experimental engine 'Hush Hush', the P2 and the A4 class and its associated carriages for the LNER. Johansen was sponsored by Gresley from 1929, on an ad hoc consultancy basis, to test various shapes at the NPL and final designs were heavily influenced by the scientist. As early as 1932 Hartley identified the value of his work and recruited him to the LMS (based nominally at Euston to remain close to the NPL, to take advantage of its research facilities). Concurrent employment by two rival companies seeking advantages over each other was an interesting development.

Turbomotive was to be included in this project work, but was not advanced beyond drawing and model stage because of the rapid development of the streamlined Coronation Class.

Johansen rose to become Deputy Scientific Research Manager for the LMS, but left in 1949, following nationalisation, to become Director of Research at W.T. Avery. His work on air flow, though largely rejected by steam locomotive designers, now has great relevance and is seen as groundbreaking.

Eric Arthur Langridge. Born on 20 May 1896 in London and died in Polegate, East Sussex, on 18 May 1999. Langridge was educated at St Olave's School. He began an engineering apprenticeship at Eastleigh Locomotive Works in 1912, with part of his training being undertaken at Hartley College, Southampton. Subsequently he worked in the Drawing Office at Eastleigh, but it seems that the London and South Western Railway could not offer him longer-term employment and he was recruited by the Midland Railway at Derby. He began work in 1920 and remained in the Drawing Office there for thirty-nine years.

In the years that followed he worked on the design of many locomotives, but eventually specialised in boilers and in this role worked on Turbomotive. Two years later he worked on proposals for an improved Princess Pacific – plans that were then shelved when the Coronation Class came into being. This work was resurrected in 1952 when Turbomotive was converted to a conventional, reciprocating engine.

He holds a unique place in railway history having served for so long in one of the most important centres of locomotive development. In so doing, his work encompassed some of the major steam engine developments of the twentieth century and embraced the future beyond steam traction. In retirement he wrote numerous articles about his work, which were, in time, made into two books, entitled *Under 10 CMEs*.

Ernest John Hutchings Lemon.
Born in Okeford Fitzpaine, Dorset, on 10 December 1884, the youngest of six children, and died in Epsom, Surrey, on 15 December 1954. He was apprenticed to the North British Railway Company in Glasgow, and completed his training in 1905, before spending two years at the Heriot-Watt College, further developing his engineering skills. A brief period of employment with the Highland Railway at Inverness followed and then three years with Hurst, Nelson and Co at Motherwell (wagon builders).

In 1911 he became Chief Wagon Inspector for the Midland Railway, then, in 1917, Carriage Works Manager at Derby, followed, in 1923, by promotion to Divisional Carriage and Wagon Superintendent.

When Sir Henry Fowler retired in 1931, Lemon became the LMS's CME, despite the fact that he had little or no experience of locomotive engineering. But it proved to be a stopgap measure only, the post being filled by William Stanier in early 1932. Lemon became Vice President in charge of the Railway Traffic, Operating and Commercial Section. While CME he had not been idle though, having completed a major review of locomotive stock, identifying and recommending future engine policy and needs. He also oversaw major changes in the way locomotives were maintained and repaired. In so doing he laid valuable groundwork on which Stanier could build the loco modernisation programme.

He fully supported the development of Turbomotive and made sure that his department followed suit during the trials, including the permanent assignment of a fitter to the engine. However, his support waned when expected savings did not materialise. Stanier was critical of the way 6202 was run, believing that more could have been achieved if the number of engine crews had been kept to a minimum, allowing greater expertise to be fostered.

In 1938 Lemon was seconded to the Air Ministry, in recognition of his considerable skills of management and industrial manufacturing. He was appointed Director General of Aircraft Production, his primary responsibility to sort out the many problems that beset aircraft construction. He remained with the Air Ministry until April 1940, when his secondment came to an end. A knighthood was his reward.

Three more years of service with the LMS followed before retirement in August 1943, during which he and Hartley oversaw the reactivation of Turbomotive in 1941. Although retired, he continued to be involved in various scientific and engineering studies, the last as Chairman of the Committee for the Standardisation of Engineering Products for the Ministry of Supply. Their report, published in 1949, was Lemon's final project. After this his health declined and he died five years later.

Robert Riddles. Born 23 May 1892. Died 18 June 1983. His engineering education began in 1909 when he was taken on as a premium apprentice by the London and North Western Railway at Crewe works and then found work as a fitter in the Erecting Shop at Rugby. When war came he volunteered for service and saw action on the Western Front with the Royal Engineers, becoming an officer in the process. Post war he rose rapidly through the ranks and specialised in streamlining and improvement of production processes. His first major success in this field was as part of the team that reorganised Crewe Works between 1925 and 1928, now part of the recently created LMS. He then moved to Derby where he undertook a similar exercise.

Such success did not escape Stanier and a year after his arrival, having carefully assessed his staff, promoted Riddles to be his Locomotive Assistant and then Principal Assistant in 1935. In this supporting role he played a significant part in the development and testing of new engine designs, including Turbomotive. But as a 'rising star' he had to gain wider experience and in 1937 was transferred to St Rollox to become Mechanical and Electrical Engineer, Scotland, though for such an ambitious man this move felt more like demotion. He had hoped to be promoted to Deputy CME, a post that went to his rival, C.E. Fairburn. He need not have worried unduly because shortly afterwards he was selected to go on a high-profile visit to the US, with a new Coronation Class engine and her rake of coaches.

The coming of war changed the course of his life, as it did for the whole population. His skills in production techniques were sorely needed and, under Harold Hartley's guidance, he found himself seconded to the recently formed Ministry of Supply to become Director of Transportation Equipment. To meet wartime needs his principal responsibility was to produce new engines suited to military needs. As a result the LMS's 8F 2-8-0 was selected and 240 were ordered. Later he led on the design of two simplified austerity engines – a 2-8-0 and a 2-10-0 – and the building of 935 of them.

He was awarded a CBE in1943 and then returned to the LMS as Chief Stores Assistant, by which time Stanier had retired and been replaced by Fairburn. On his death in 1944 George Ivatt became CME and a year later Riddles was promoted to Vice President to replace Harold Hartley, so becoming Ivatt's boss.

With nationalisation of the railways in 1948 Riddles became BR's first CME, though initially this post went by other names. He took Roland Bond and Ernest Cox, from the LMS, with him as assistants. Before his retirement in 1953 he led the major programme of steam engine design and production and attempted to bring together the diverse groups that had run the Big Four companies. It is said by some that his primary focus on producing more steam locomotives diverted attention from the development of diesel and electric alternatives, hindering BR's progress by many years.

In the years that followed he became a Director of Stothert and Pitt in Bath, finally retiring aged 75.

His role in Turbomotive's life was an important one – through design, to construction then testing. He even resided over her rebuilding in 1952 and her demise, following the Harrow Disaster.

Josiah Charles Stamp. Born in London on 21 June 1880 and died on 16 April 1941. Following education at Bethany House School at Goudhurst, Kent he joined the Inland Revenue in 1906 and, by 1916, had risen to Assistant Secretary level. An avid scholar, he studied economics as an external student at London University, obtaining a 1st Class Degree in 1911. His thesis on incomes and property became a standard work on the subject and made his reputation as a leading economist.

In 1919 he left the Civil Service to pursue a more ambitious career in industry, first with Nobel Industries then as Chairman of the LMS, in 1926. At the same time he served on many public bodies and became a Director of the Bank of England. His career was one of the highest office and immense achievement.

He was appointed a CBE in 1918, a KBE in 1920 and raised to the peerage in 1938, becoming Baron Stamp. He was also a prolific writer on many economic issues and rose to become Colonel commanding the Royal Engineers Railway and Transport Corps.

A man of drive and huge talent, his role in the development of the LMS and guiding it to success from a group of uncoordinated and conflicting companies was immense. Though not an engineer, he understood the needs of business and set out to recruit a team of specialists from many spheres who could take the company forward successfully. Stanier's appointment was a key part of this process. He backed his CME and gave him free reign to create some of the most potent steam locomotives ever built. Turbomotive was a natural evolution of his positive patronage and leadership.

Sadly, Stamp, his wife and son, Wilfred, died when their bomb shelter took a direct hit during a nighttime attack in April 1941. His passing was a significant loss for the LMS and his country.

William Arthur Stanier. Born on 27 May 1876 at 10 Wellington Street, Swindon. Died at Newburn, Chorleywood Road, Rickmansworth on 27 September 1965. Stanier was the first child of William Henry Stanier, an employee of the GWR, and was educated at Wycliffe College, Stonehouse, Gloucestershire before becoming an office boy at Swindon in 1892, then taking up a five-year apprenticeship in the Works there. On qualifying he then spent three years in the Drawing Office before becoming Inspector of Materials. Under the guiding hand of George Churchward, then C.B, Collett, rapid promotion followed from Acting Divisional Locomotive, Carriage and Wagon Superintendent to Principal Assistant to the CME in 1923. In this role he led the way in the design and construction of two of the GWR's finest classes of locomotives: the Castles and Kings.

By 1931 it was apparent to Stanier that he was unlikely to become the GWR's CME and when an offer from the LMS was made by Josiah Stamp, later that year, to become their CME he jumped at the chance, being appointed in January 1932. And so the greatest challenge of his career began.

The LMS was a colossal business (created at Grouping from many often competing companies) greatly in need of modernisation if it were to meet the challenging business targets set by its Board. Throughout the late 1920s great advances had been made, but when Stanier arrived its locomotives left much to be desired, reflecting as they did the outdated and often limited requirements of the LMS's constituent companies. Stanier's target was to establish standardised design and construction methods and to provide a fleet of new, more powerful and efficient locomotives. And this he did, with the aid of some very able assistants.

Such was his success that two of his designs – the Class 5 and Class 8F – were still in service when the last steam locomotives were withdrawn from traffic in 1968. His work also greatly influenced British Rail's standardisation work in the 1950s. But it is for his high-profile Pacific locomotives and Turbomotive for which he is best remembered. His ability to persuade often sceptical colleagues of 6202's worth allowed the project to reach fruition and continue for such a long time. Success was achieved but he always felt that more had

been possible, if there had been more effective support from the running department, some modifications to the design and a relatively small investment in additional turbine locomotives. Lack of support, the war, then his retirement in 1944, made these developments impossible.

The coming of the Second World War led to a great increase in his duties on the LMS, but also in the wider service of his country. In the early years he oversaw the building of weapons in LMS factories and in 1942 was seconded to the Ministry of Production, as one of three full-time scientific advisors. Later he became a member of the Aeronautical Research Council, then Chairman of Power Jets Limited, a Government-owned concern developing jet propulsion, principally gas turbines, and became a Director of several companies, including H.W. Kearns of Altringham and Courtaulds.

He gathered many awards during his career (including a Knighthood in 1943 and a Fellowship of the Royal Society in 1944, only the second locomotive engineer to do so – the other being Robert Stephenson). Other forms of recognition included President of the Institution of Loco-motive Engineers on two occasions and President of the Institution of Mechanical Engineers, being awarded medals by both bodies.

Lieutenant Colonel George Wilson. Born in Devizes in 1896 and died in London on 20 March 1958. Wilson was educated at Marlborough College and the Royal Military Academy at Woolwich. He served with the Royal Engineers in the First World War. In 1919 he became an instructor at the military establishment at Longmoor, where the Army trained its specialists in railway matters. Following service in the Second World War, he retired from the Army and was appointed to the Railway Inspectorate of the newly formed British Rail. He became BR's chief accident investigator and analysis of the Harrow railway disaster was one of his key tasks in the years that followed. At the time of his death he was working on the investigation of the Lewisham rail crash (4 December 1957), which claimed ninety lives. Following the Harrow crash, he spent considerable time advising the Ministry of Transport on the development of an automatic warning system to aid train drivers. His was a significant and very worthy legacy.

THE SCIENCE OF STEAM TURBINES

Gustaf de Laval's impulse turbine 1888 Deutsches Museum Munich. (BG)

Turbomotive embraced a technology that had intrigued scientists for centuries, but had only been fully understood and applied in a practical way as the nineteenth century came to an end. As is frequently the case, such a development is dependent on the dynamics of different ideas, often spaced over long periods of time, coming together to produce a single advance of great significance – scientific dominoes falling to create a pattern often unseen by each individual participant.

Definition of a turbine
A machine for producing continuous power in which a wheel or rotor, typically fitted with vanes, is made to revolve by a fast-moving flow of steam, air, gas, water or other fluid. The wheel or rotor extracts kinetic energy from this flow and converts it into mechanical energy.

The simplest form of turbine is a windmill, which captures energy from the wind through its sails, which rotate and drive the mill stones.

The primary parts of a turbine are a set of blades that catch the moving fluid, then a shaft or axle that rotates as the blades turn and finally a machine that is driven by the axle and produces an output.

Steam turbines
In thermodynamics an adiabatic process is an idealised concept in which the working movements of a system are frictionless, without transfer of heat or matter from input to output; energy is only transferred as work. But no steam turbine can match this ideal and will only achieve isentropic efficiencies up to a maximum of 90 per cent.

Turbines driven by steam work in two different ways: impulse and reaction:

- **Impulse turbine:** Steam is forced at high speed through a narrow, fixed nozzle at bucket/cup-shaped turbine blades, which 'catch' the fluid and direct it off at an angle, making sure constant energy impulses. This method increases the efficiency and strength of energy transfer.
- **Reaction turbine:** The blades sit in a much larger volume of fluid and turn smoothly and evenly as the fluid flows past them. The blades simply spin and any change of direction is small in comparison to that of blades in an impulse turbine. The rotor blades themselves are arranged and shaped to form convergent nozzles. To make sure that a steam turbine

achieves its maximum efficiency it was discovered that a mix of both impulse and reaction designs would attain this goal – the higher-pressure elements typically being reaction types, and lower-pressure stages would use impulse techniques.

Condensing/non-condensing steam turbines

Steam turbines are often divided into two types: condensing and non-condensing.

In the former, steam is condensed at below atmospheric pressure so as to gain a maximum amount of energy from the process. To achieve this, large quantities of cooling water are needed to carry away the heat released during condensation. As condensing turbines condense below atmospheric pressure, this allows for larger expansion of the steam resulting in higher, more efficient work output and efficiency. This makes them ideally suited for work in power stations.

In non-condensing turbines, steam leaves the unit at above atmospheric pressure and this is then used for heating, for example, before being returned as water to the boiler. One of the primary benefits of a non-condensing turbine is that it requires relatively little additional fuel to increase the steam generator exit pressure and the temperature needed to produce the superheated steam necessary to drive the turbine. Consequently, this is a more economical way of producing power when substantial amounts of heating or process steam are required, such as within a locomotive. It also saves on the weight of providing a condensing unit, a critical factor in engine design.

Operational problems

During the operation of a steam turbine, high rotation velocities are achieved. If there is an imbalance in the rotor, this can lead to vibration, which can cause blades to break away and damage the turbine and its casing.

Steam turbines run on superheated or saturated steam with a high dryness factor. This is necessary to reduce or eliminate erosion to blades. Liquid water may also seep into the mechanism damaging the blades and thrust bearings in the turbine shaft.

Turbines need to be run up slowly to prevent damage. Without controlled acceleration the nozzle valves,

Charles Parsons. (BG)

Gustaf de Laval. (BG)

Aurel Stodola. (BG)

controlling the flow of steam to the turbine, close. If this happens, the turbine can continue accelerating until there is a catastrophic failure.

Steam turbines – design history

Turbines driven by steam had their origins in the first century when the Greek mathematician, Hero of Alexandria, designed and built an aeolipile, a simple bladeless radial steam turbine, which began spinning when water in a central container was heated and steam was forced through external, angled nozzles. Thereafter there were periodic attempts to develop the concept further, but it was not until 1884 that Anglo-Irish inventor Charles Parsons created a reaction steam turbine of real potential, which found wide use in the production of electricity in power stations and the development of high-performance ships's engines.

At the same time, Swedish inventor Gustaf de Laval was building an effective impulse turbine and led the field in this alternative technology, in the process developing a nozzle that increased the steam jet to supersonic speeds (now named after him and still used in rockets today). Both his and Parsons's work was greatly influenced by the research and development work undertaken by the Slovakian scientist Aurel Stodola, who published two seminal works on steam and gas turbines, in 1903 and 1922.

The collective results of these three scientists's work was profound in the extreme and revolutionised the way machines were powered and their effectiveness.

The Application of steam turbines

Power generation: Most electrical power stations around the world now use steam turbines to drive the generators that produce electricity. These facilities were driven by steam-powered reciprocating engines, but their size and slow speed made them increasingly uneconomic and steam turbines became a very effective alternative. The world's first turbine power station was commissioned in 1890 by the Newcastle and District Lighting Company, formed by Charles Parsons a year earlier (the Forth Banks Power Station).

Ship design: Steam turbines also had a profound effect on marine propulsion and replaced larger, less efficient reciprocating engines in the twentieth century. However, their advent was largely driven by the development of robust reduction gears, which could balance the RPM of turbines measured in thousands to propeller/shaft speeds of less than 300 RPM, though some ships did manage with direct drive from the turbines to the propeller shafts (by directing the steam flow only). The biggest and most dramatic impact of this new technology on ship design came with the launch of a turbine-driven 'yacht' laid down in 1894. This boat was the product of another Charles Parsons enterprise, the Parsons Steam Turbine Company of Newcastle. Designed by Parsons, largely working in isolation, the boat made a dramatic appearance at the 1897 Diamond Anniversary Fleet Review, at Spithead, with the intention of achieving maximum publicity. The crew manoeuvred the boat at speeds up to 34.5 knots in the limited space between the assembled ships, in what the Times later called 'a brilliant but unauthorised' display. The boat had been named Turbinia, in recognition of its source of power but also with an eye to headlines.

By 1906 the Royal Navy was well advanced in using steam turbines, with other navies following suit, and this concept held sway in ship design through the two world wars until replaced by gas turbines, turbo electric drive and nuclear power.

Locomotive design: Turbines, for a time, became the 'Holy Grail' for some locomotive designers, with variable success and ultimately little acceptance by railway companies. On paper the benefits seemed substantial, but in practice projected savings, over reciprocating engines, proved insufficient to justify mass production or continuation. Even when gas turbines were developed, in place of steam, the benefits could not compete with those derived from dieselisation or electrification.

However, a suspicion remains among turbine advocates that given greater support in the 1930s, leading to the building of more turbine-driven locomotives, they would have proved a sound and valuable investment.

LEFT:
Battersea Power station. A Metrovick turbine installed in 1935 working in ideal conditions for maximum efficiency and output. (BG)

RIGHT:
Turbinia at full speed. (BG)

THE EVOLUTION OF STEAM TURBINE LOCOMOTIVES

The active development of steam turbine locomotives covered a comparatively short period. Performance potential and scientific curiosity sponsored many projects in many countries, but rarely did the engines manufactured produce something better than already existed in conventional form. With diesel and electric designs waiting in the wings, progressing steam turbine projects seemed even less attractive. But for a few decades there was sufficient impetus to push forward with turbine experiments, in many ways a 'last hoorah' for steam traction. Yet some of the key developments, in this doomed attempt to ring just a little bit more from coal-powered locomotives, are worth recording.

GUISEPPE BELLUZZO'S TURBINE (1908)

Belluzzo designed and built a turbine system to match the outline of an old 0-4-0 shunting engine (built by Swiss Locomotive Works, Winterthur).
(RH/Author)

Belluzo's concept. His experimental work continued for some years and proved relatively successful. His 0-4-0 conversion was still working, in Milan, until the late 1920s. (RH/Author)

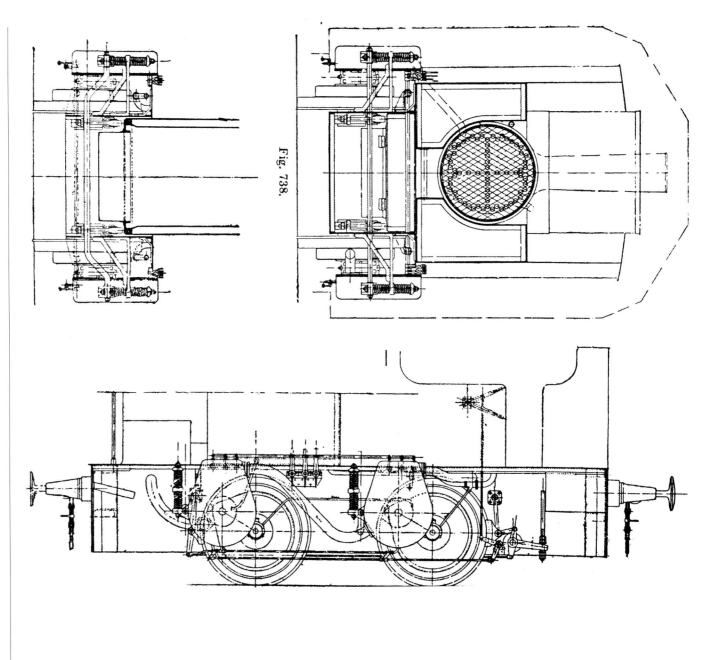

Fig. 738.

THE REID-RAMSEY TURBO-ELECTRIC CONDENSING LOCOMOTIVE (1910)

A strange, ungainly design. A conventional boiler fed superheated steam into an impulse turbine. This was coupled to a dynamo, which powered four 275hp traction motors. (RH/Author)

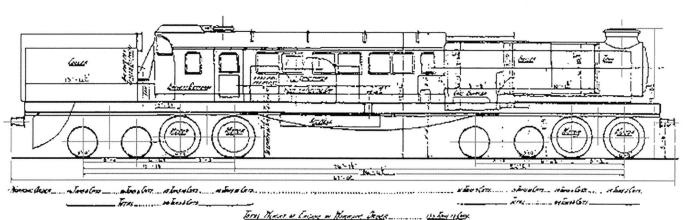

NORTH BRITISH LOCOMOTIVE CO. LTD.
110 FLEMINGTON ST SPRINGBURN.
GLASGOW.

The locomotive's layout. It was an exceptionally heavy engine, with a total weight of 129 tons, and its performance was unspectacular. (RH/Author)

THE REID-MCLEOD TURBINE CONDENSING LOCOMOTIVE (1921)

After his 1910 development, Hugh Reid felt that turbines were still an important area to explore and with James Macleod produced a direct drive type turbine locomotive. It was a rebuild of his earlier engine – frames, bogies and boiler being reused. Trials ran until 1927, but, by all accounts, did not prove successful. The engine languished in the North British Locomotive Company's Works until the early 1940s when it was scrapped.

(RH/Author)

THE ARMSTRONG-WHITWORTH TURBINE-ELECTRIC CONDENSING LOCOMOTIVE (1921)

D.M. Ramsey, who had been involved in the 1910 turbine-electric development, revisited this concept with Armstrong-Whitworth's support a decade later. Its weight was excessive at 156 tons and its performance poor. Trials carried on until 1923 but no significant improvements were achieved and the engine was later written off by the company. (RH/Author)

THE BEYER-LJUNGSTROM CONDENSING LOCOMOTIVE (1924 –1926)

Frederick Ljungstrom had been developing condensing turbines for a number of years in Sweden and this work came to the attention of Beyer-Peacock of Manchester. They built a similar machine to Ljungstrom using much of the technology he had designed. Trials began in 1926 and continued until 1928, but despite this prolonged period of testing no discernible advantage over reciprocating engines could be proved and the experiment ended.

(RH/Author)

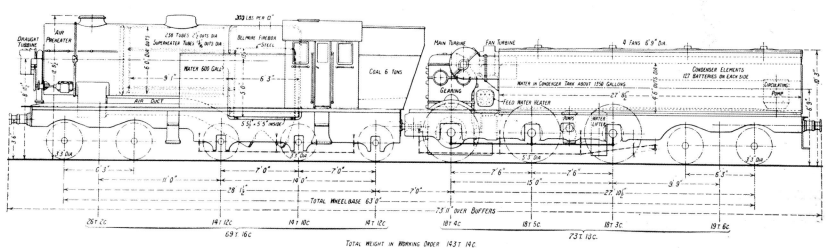

Diagram and Leading Dimensions of Ljungström Locomotive.

TURBINE DEVELOPMENTS IN GERMANY (1927–1939)

Having witnessed turbine development in other countries, three German companies committed themselves to design and build their own versions: Henschel, Krupp-Zoelly and Maffei.

The Henschel Condensing Turbine Locomotive (T38-3255). The company converted an existing Class 38 4-6-0 engine by fitting a booster tender containing a condenser, a three-stage forward turbine and a single-stage reverse turbine, all mounted on coupled driving wheels. Tests began in 1927 but the engine's performance fell far short of expectations. Despite this it stayed in service for ten years and was then returned to conventional form with a new tender, serving through the war before being scrapped in 1961. (RH/Author)

The Krupp-Zoelly Condensing Turbine Locomotive (T18-1001). A more successful design than T38-3255, but did not lead to more engines being built. It was configured as a 4-6-2 engine, with forward and reverse turbines supplied by Escher Weiss and Co of Switzerland. The locomotive remained in existence until 1940 when written off during an air raid. When built she was streamlined, but this was removed to allow easier access for maintenance. Photo on the left shows the turbine drive. (RH/Author)

The Maffei Condensing Turbine Locomotive (T18-1002). Slightly more expensive to run than T18-1001, but proved effective in service. Configured as a 4-6-2 engine, with a main turbine over the leading bogie, a high-pressure boiler and a maximum speed of 75mph. In 1943 the engine was damaged during an air raid. Only the boiler was salvaged, being used to test safety valves until 1961. (RH/Author)

THE LJUNGSTROM NON-CONDENSING TURBINE LOCOMOTIVE (1931)

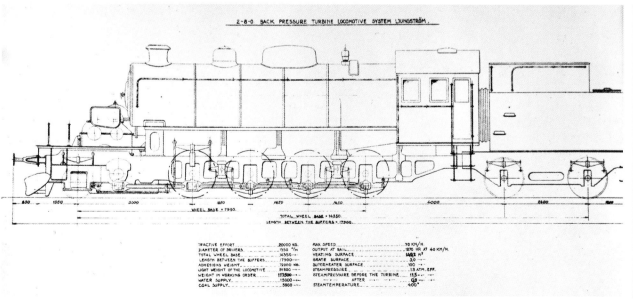

2-8-0 BACK PRESSURE TURBINE LOCOMOTIVE SYSTEM LJUNGSTRÖM.

TRACTIVE EFFORT	20000 KG.
DIAMETER OF DRIVERS	1550 ᵐ/ᴹ
TOTAL WHEEL BASE	14350 ᵐᵐ
LENGTH BETWEEN THE BUFFERS	17900 ᵐᵐ
ADHESION,S WEIGHT	72000 KG.
LIGHT WEIGHT OF THE LOCOMOTIVE	91500 ᵐᵐ
WEIGHT IN WORKING ORDER	117500 ᵐᵐ
WATER SUPPLY	15000 ᵐᵐ
COAL SUPPLY	5000 ᵐᵐ

MAX. SPEED	70 KM/H.
OUTPUT AT RAIL	1270 HP AT 40 KM/H.
HEATING SURFACE	140,? ᴹ²
GRATE SURFACE	3,0 ᵐᵐ
SUPERHEATER SURFACE	100 ᵐᵐ
STEAMPRESSURE	13 ATM. EFF.
STEAMPRESSURE BEFORE THE TURBINE	11,5 ᵐᵐ
″ ″ AFTER ″	0,3 ᵐᵐ
STEAMTEMPERATURE	400°

In conjunction with Nydquist and Holm of Trollhattan, Fredrik Ljungstrom discarded the condensing concept and designed a non-condensing turbine locomotive, based on an existing 2-8-0 design. Its turbine transmitted power through reduction gearing to a jack staff drive to the coupled wheels. Three were built and greatly influenced William Stanier and Henry Guy in developing their own Turbomotive. All have been preserved in Sweden. (RH/Author)

TURBINE DEVELOPMENTS IN FRANCE (1937–1940)

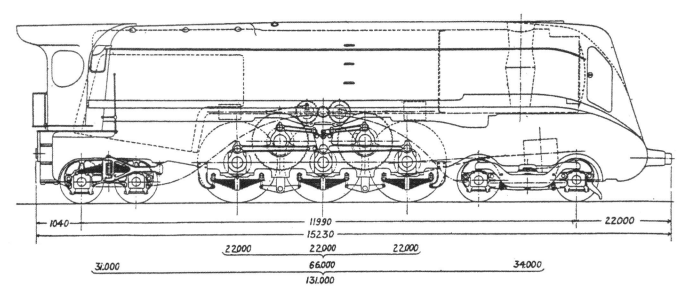

The Nord Turbine Project. Inspired by work on Turbomotive and streamlining experiments, the company decided to modify a locomotive originally intended as a conventional three cylinder 4-6-4 reciprocating engine. It would have employed a non-condensing triple expansion system, using steam superheated in two stages. (RH/Author)

For reasons that are not clear the project did not go ahead and the locomotive was eventually built as a conventional four cylinder compound. The turbine was to have been mounted over the leading driving wheels. Six nozzle control valves appear to have been planned, with an exhaust duct directed towards the blast pipe. It seems likely that this engine would have followed Turbomotive in having a separate reverse turbine, but this cannot be confirmed. (RH/Author)

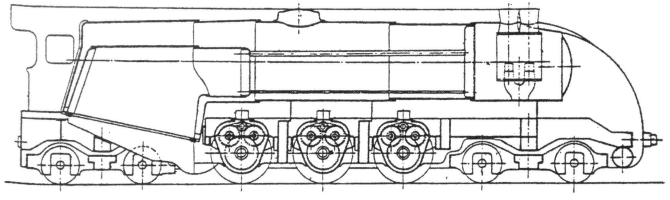

232Q1 saw service on the Creusot – Montchanin line and was tested at Vitry in 1941. Three years later it was badly damaged by retreating German forces and presumably scrapped. (RH/Author)

The SNCF Non-Condensing Turbine Locomotive (232Q1). Design work began on this 4-6-4 engine in 1937 and one locomotive was built by Schneider & Co at Creusot by 1940. This complex, streamlined engine had three turbine units fitted (one source has them designed by Curtis, another assigns them to Schneider-Westinghouse, which seems more likely), with each placed above a pair of driving wheels, so eliminating the need for connecting rods. (RH/Author)

Each turbine unit contained six row forward and two row reverse elements. These were connected to the driving wheels through two-stage gearing. Each turbine could be controlled independently or in parallel. The drive system was described as 'Quillcupdrive' and the engine was given the name 'Locatu' (short for 'Locomotive a turbines'). (RH/Author)

TURBINE DEVELOPMENTS IN THE US (1944–1949)

American locomotive designers experimented with steam turbines, but this work was largely overshadowed by diesel developments that forged ahead in the post-war years, sponsored by a wealthy and booming economy. But a small number of steam turbine locomotives did appear, the most famous being one built by Baldwins in 1944. (RH/Author)

The S2, number 6200, was of 6-8-6 configuration and had separate forward and reverse Westinghouse turbines. With a power output of 6900hp the S2 was capable of pulling 1,000 ton trains at more than 100mph, an achievement witnessed by E.S. Cox, of the LMS, when travelling on its footplate during his 1945 tour of the US. It is remarkable that in the thirty-plus years since Belluzzo's turbine experiments that the design should progress so far. (RH/Author)

TURBOMOTIVE'S DESIGN

Once Turbomotive's construction had been approved the LMS's Drawing Office at Derby and Metrovick's Drawing Office in Manchester worked closely together to prepare detailed plans and specifications. Only some of these items have survived the blitz on records, in both organisations, that took place in the 1950s and 1960s as steam gave way to other forms of motive power. In the words of instructions issued on record regarding preservation they are 'to be retained for the life of the asset'. Luckily some far-sighted people intervened at the time and a number of items have been preserved, in institutions and in private collections. For this reason we can now follow the design process and see how these two technologies were married together and Turbomotive was created.

Boiler.

MODIFICATIONS TO THE PRINCESS

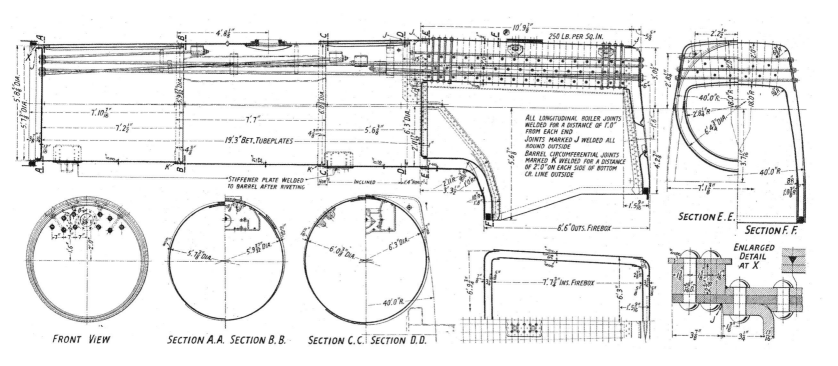

Boiler number 9100 being fitted to 6202's frames. (RH)

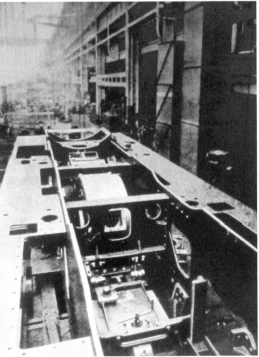

The frames before the boiler was fitted – gear unit in place. (RH)

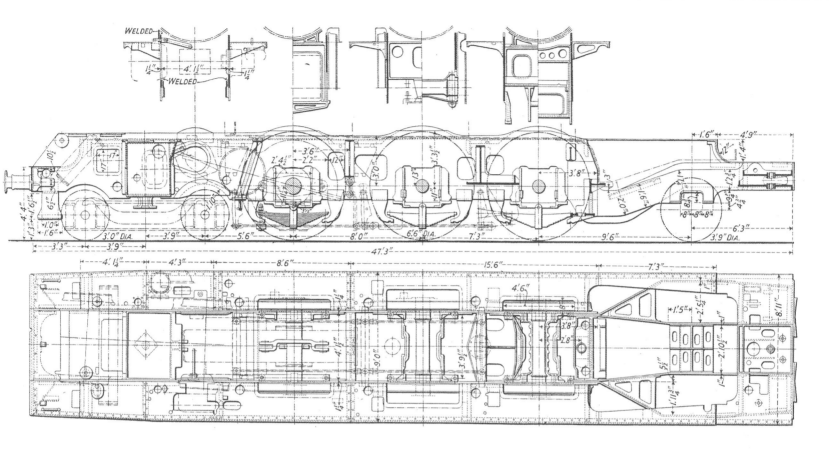

Altered Frame Arrangement.

The turbine units and gear box in place. (RH)

6202's boiler ready to lifted into her frames. (RH)

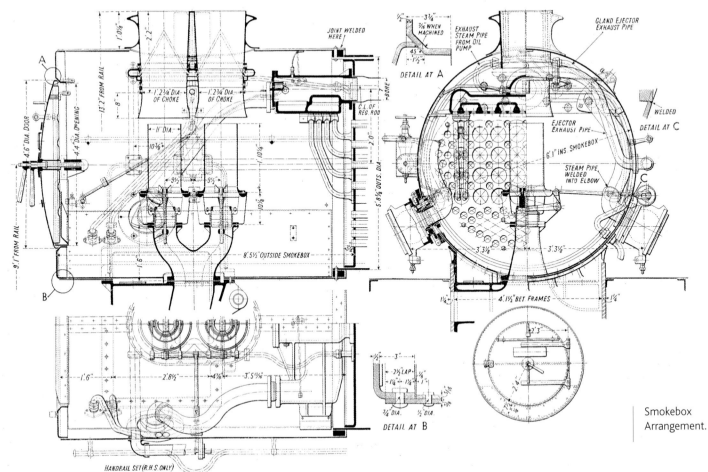

Smokebox Arrangement.

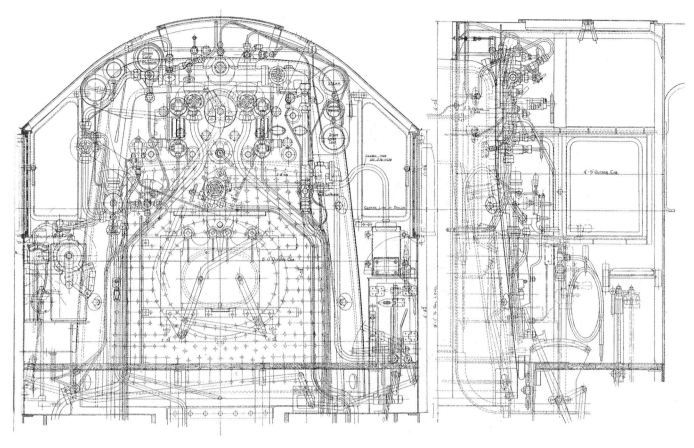

Arrangement of Cab, Fittings and Controls.

LEFT:
6202's cab waiting to be fitted. (RH)

RIGHT:
6202's backhead and cab completed. (RH)

THE TURBINES, GEAR BOX AND ANCILLARY EQUIPMENT

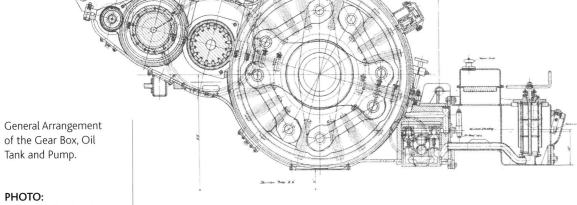

General Arrangement of the Gear Box, Oil Tank and Pump.

PHOTO:
Timken Roller Bearings were fitted to all wheels on Turbomotive. This picture shows how they appeared with covers removed.

Cross Section - Gear Box, Oil Tank and Pump in place, showing the Timken Roller Bearings in place.

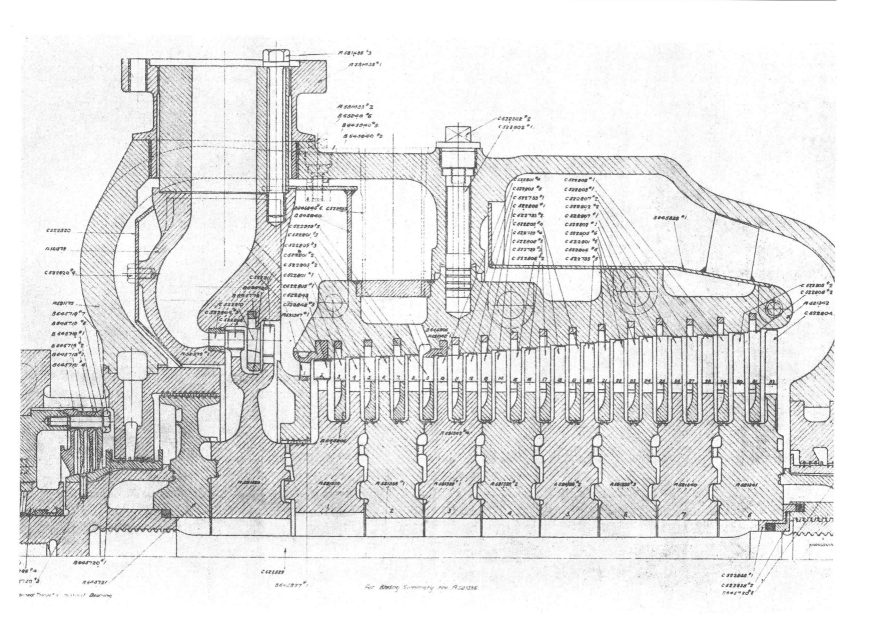

The Forward
Turbine Unit.

LEFT:
Working on the turbines (forward turbine nearest the camera). (RH)

ABOVE:
The double helical triple reduction gear and transmission unit (covers removed). (MP)
(Taken at Metrovick's Trafford Park factory)

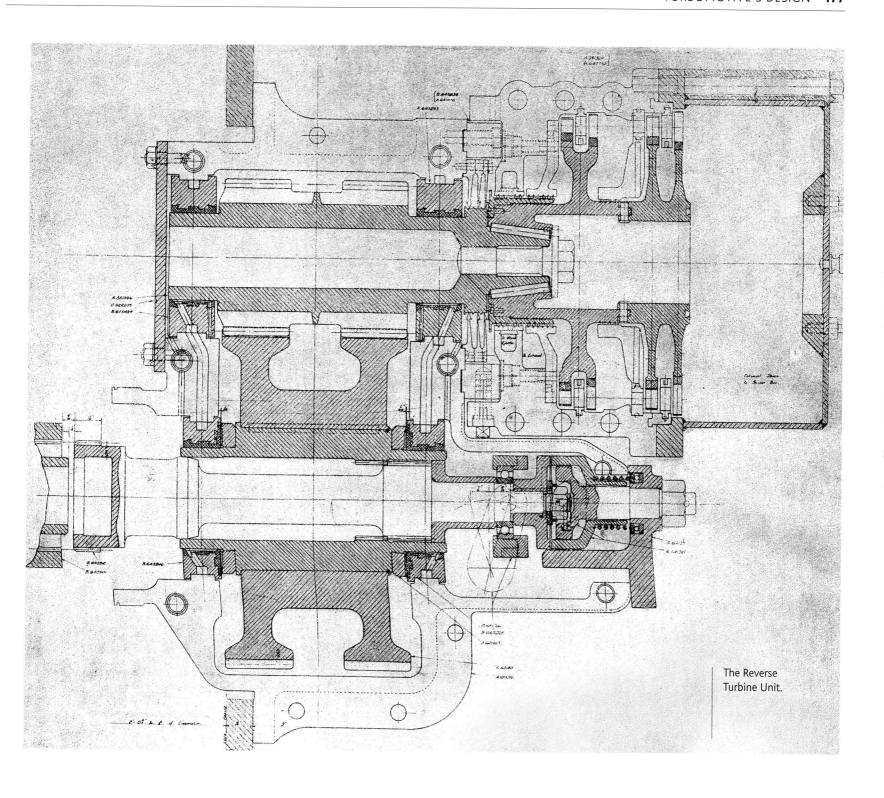

The Reverse
Turbine Unit.

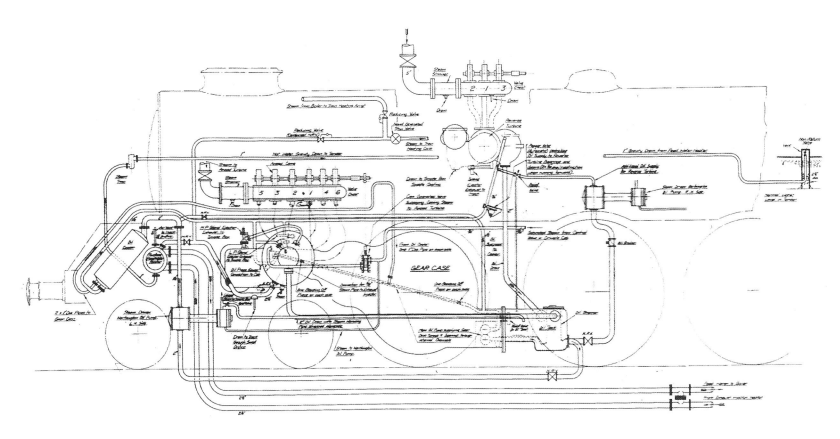

GEAR CASE

Diagram of Pipe
Connections.

The unit fitted to the
leading coupled axle
before installation in
the frames. (RH)

Turbomotive – an early
publicity photo. (RH)

6202's leading
bogie. (AE)

6202' s trailing
bogie. (AE)

6202 – EVOLUTION OF A LOCOMOTIVE
(1933–1952)

It is a basic tenet of engineering that no machine will go through life without undergoing modification or refinement, particularly if it is experimental. From outline design, through detailed specification to construction, then in service, a machine undergoes change as problems are discovered, the requirement changes or new ideas are proposed. Turbomotive's life was a constant process of modification and refinement and this appendix sets out how this engine evolved from the first tentative drawings, prepared following William Stanier and Henry Guy's visit to the Ljungstrom Works in Sweden, to its 1952 reconstruction. No detailed workshop files or records seem to have survived for 6202, as is the case for most other steam locomotives, so what follows will be incomplete.

An Evolution Captured in Drawings

6202 closely followed the design of her two experimental sisters, 6200 and 6201. The drawing offices at Derby and Metrovick in Manchester took the initial Princess plans and modified the shape and structure to allow the turbines, gears and ancillary equipment to be fitted. In seeking LMS Board approval to construct this third, radically different engine, an outline specification and drawing were produced as part of the justification paper.

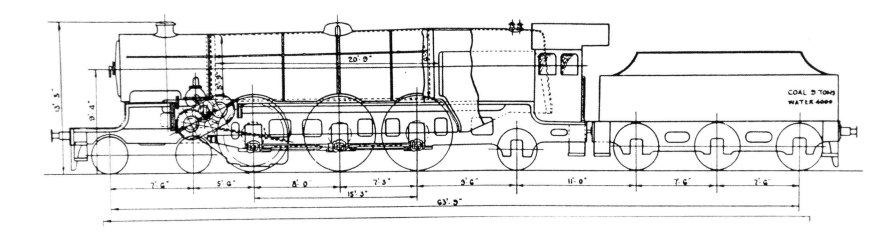

1933 – DRAWING AND SPECIFICATION

Specification for Proposed 2600hp Turbine Locomotive System Ljungstrom

Diameter of wheels – 6′ 9″
Grate area – 45sq ft
Steam pressure – 250lbs
Steam supply to prime mover – 30,000Ibs
Total temp – 850F
Heating surface total – 2,100 sq ft
Weight on drivers – 68 metric tons
Max speed – 90mph
Overall length over buffers – 74′3″
Wheel base length – 63′ 10″

Turbine performance
- at starting to produce tractive effort of 40,000Ibs plus
- at 70mph 12,000Ibs plus
- the turbine will be designed for max efficiency at 60mph (at which the turbine will rotate at 760rpm)
- at 90mph the max speed of the turbine will be 10,220rpm (sub-note in Ljungstrom's brief: 'the turbine will be capable of an rpm higher than this with speeds in excess of 90mph. Road and static tests will identify the locomotive's potential').

Turbine construction
- the turbine will drive through a double reduction gear, a gear wheel coupled to the driving axle (of the front driving wheels). A separate reversing turbine will be provided that drives the main turbine high-speed pinion through a wheel clutch and an additional reducing gear.

1935 – 6202 AS CONSTRUCTED

Supplementary Information

Diameter of wheels – 6' 6"
Boiler – Type 1 Belpaire taper (No 9100)
Total temp – 750F
Chimney fitted – double blast-pipe
Max speed – 90mph
Tractive power at 85% – 40,300Ibs
Tender fitted – No 9003

- **Forward turbine** – this power unit comprises a multi-stage turbine and treble reduction gear, bolted to the left-hand side of the frames. Steam from the boiler is fed to a steam chest, which contains six control valves operated by the footplate crew in the cab. The speed of the turbine is controlled by opening these control valves progressively, steam exhaust exiting through the smoke box. The final drive ratio for the forward turbine was 34.4 to 1.
- **Reverse turbine** – this unit is of the impulse type with an additional single reduction gear, the wheel shaft of which is in line with the high-speed pinion of the main gear. For reverse running, this wheel shaft is coupled to the main gear by a mechanical clutch operated from the cab. This turbine is bolted to the loco's right-hand frame and had a final drive ratio of 77 to 1.

- **Wheel bearings** – Timken roller bearings and axle boxes fitted to all the locomotive and tender wheels – four different designs incorporated to meet the individual conditions imposed on each axle/wheel by their position and purpose on the loco and tender.

Suppliers of Components and Material for 6202

- Turbines, transmission gear, control valves and so on – Metropolitan Vickers of Manchester.
- Exhaust steam injector (right-hand side) – Davies & Metcalfe Ltd of Stockport.
- Live steam injector (left-hand side) – Gresham & Craven Ltd of Salford & Manchester.
- Axlebox roller bearings (engine and tender) – British Timken Ltd of Birmingham.
- Steam pump for oil cooling circulation – Worthington-Simpson Ltd of London.
- Steel boiler plates for barrel and firebox wrapper (2 per cent nickel steel) – Colvilles Ltd of Motherwell.
- Superheater apparatus – The Superheater Company Ltd of Manchester.
- Monel metal firebox stays – Henry Wiggins Ltd of Birmingham.
- Buffers – Geo. Turton, Platts & Co Ltd of Sheffield.
- Insulating materials for boiler, firebox, turbines, control valves and piping – Alfol Insulation Co Ltd of London.

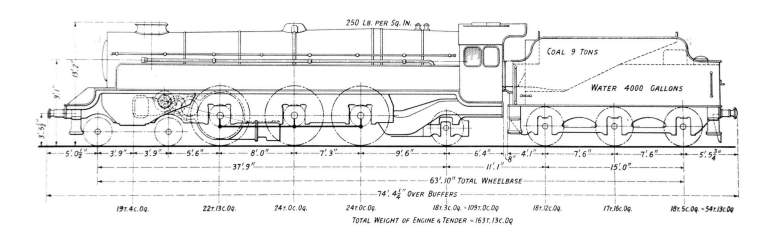

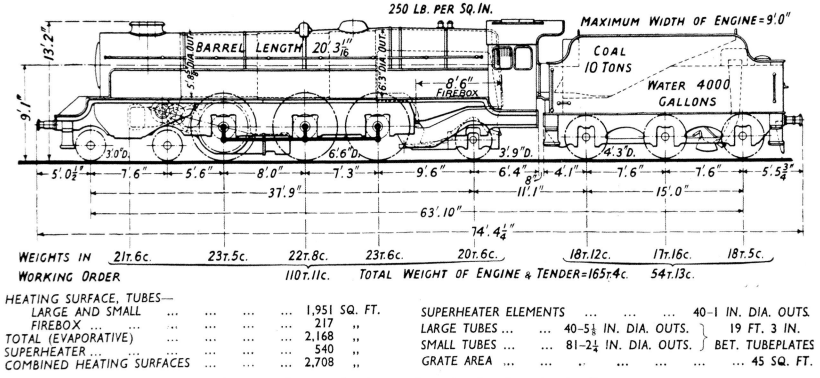

Recent change not shown on drawing : coal capacity of tender reduced to 9 tons

HEATING SURFACE, TUBES—		
LARGE AND SMALL	1,951 SQ. FT.
FIREBOX	217 ,,
TOTAL (EVAPORATIVE)	2,168 ,,
SUPERHEATER	540 ,,
COMBINED HEATING SURFACES	2,708 ,,

SUPERHEATER ELEMENTS ... ... 40–1 IN. DIA. OUTS.
LARGE TUBES ... ... 40–5⅛ IN. DIA. OUTS. ⎫ 19 FT. 3 IN.
SMALL TUBES ... ... 81–2¼ IN. DIA. OUTS. ⎬ BET. TUBEPLATES
GRATE AREA ... ... ·· ... ... 45 SQ. FT.

1936 – MODIFICATIONS

Major Modifications Carried Out in 1936

- **Boiler** – the original boiler only produced a steam temperature of approximately 620 F, against a specification of 750 F, and this was not deemed sufficient for truly effective running. So in July 1936 a new 40 element domed boiler (No 9236) was fitted. This change pushed the steam temperature up to approximately 685 F.

- **Reverse turbine** – during the first few months of operation, the reverse turbine performed poorly. To improve performance, it was redesigned to increase its power and efficiency. Other modifications were

undertaken at the same time to eliminate the causes of breakdowns:
- The clutch and turbine steam valves were interlocked to prevent the valves being opened until the clutch was fully engaged.
- The steam reversing cylinder was replaced by a hand-operated screw arrangement on the control box in the engine's cab.
- The turbine thrust bearing surfaces were increased in area and the lubricating arrangements improved.
- A visual indicator was attached to the clutch so that its operation could be checked.

1936 – STREAMLINING PROPOSAL

The success of Nigel Gresley's streamlined A4s, supported by similar developments elsewhere in the world and F.C. Johansen's experimental work at the National Physical Laboratory and the Research Department at Derby, proved an attraction to the LMS Board. This work would eventually have the biggest impact on the building of the new Coronation Class, but proposals were floated to include all the Princesses as well. Derby Drawing Office produced a series of plans showing how this need might be met. Subsequently wooden models were produced so that wind tunnel tests could be undertaken to establish the most effective streamlined shape. Nothing came of this work, but in this drawing we are left with a tantalising glimpse of the way 6202 and her sisters might have looked if the work had gone ahead.

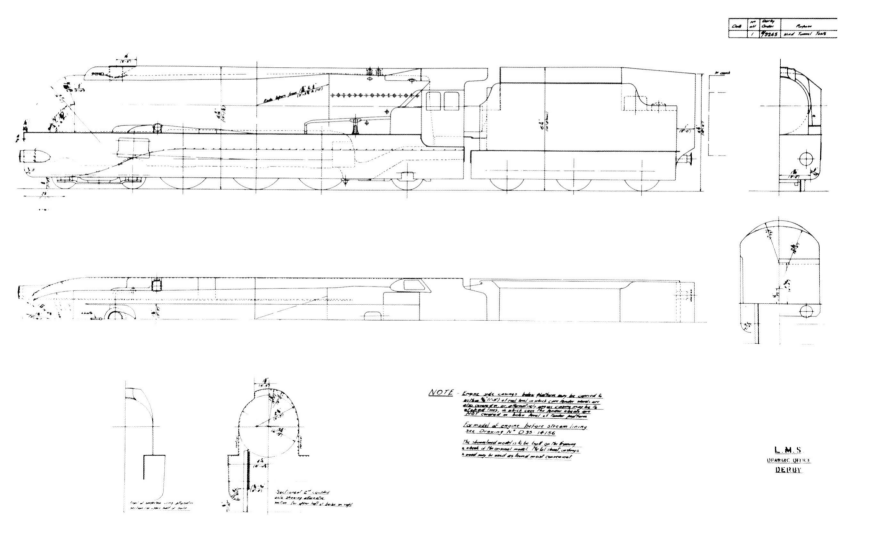

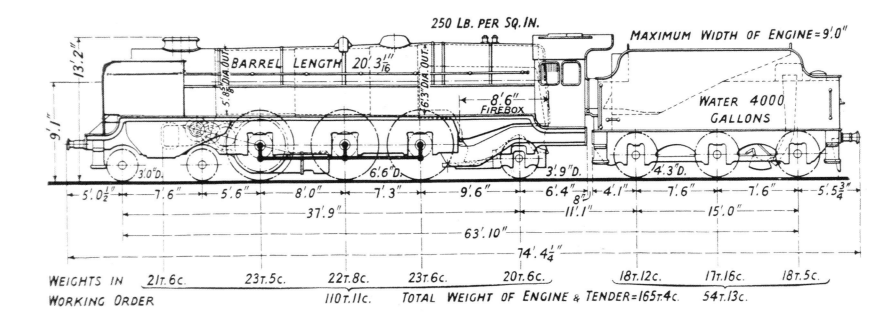

1937-1950 – MODIFICATIONS

- **Smoke deflectors** – drifting smoke obscuring the forward view from the cab was a constant problem. To improve visibility smoke deflectors were fitted in July 1939, shaped around the casing containing the steam supply, nozzles, piping and controls.

- **Reverse turbine** – an additional Worthington pump fitted to improve oil supply to this turbine unit (1941), following failure. At the same time the left-hand side casing was extended towards the cab (but did not mirror the full-length casing on the right-hand side).

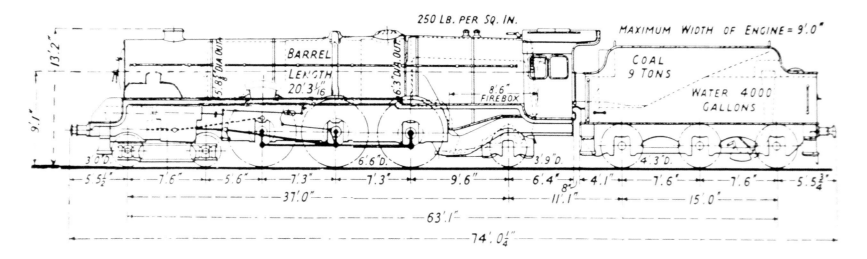

1952 – RECONSTRUCTION

Major reconstruction was authorised under Job No 5621, with all drawings for the 'new' engine undertaken at Derby. Work was completed at Crewe in August 1952. The major elements of this task were:

- **Frames** – Turbomotive's frames were built differently to her sister engines, so that turbines and gears could be accommodated. Reconstruction necessitated major changes to the frames to allow four cylinders, of the Coronation type, and other equipment to be fitted. Front sections were cut away and new sections welded to the remains, with spacing between leading and intermediate coupled wheels reduced to 7' 3''. The frame stretchers, boiler carrier, steam pipes, smoke box saddle, outside motion plate, sandbox and extension pipes, sand shields and buffer beam were all redesigned and modified.

- **Boiler** – boiler number 9236 was refitted to the engine (having been attached to 46204 from 1950 to 1952 while 46202's future was under consideration). Its internal layout was altered with 101 small tubes and 9swg trifurcated elements being fitted, giving a tube heating surface of 2,232sq ft and a superheated surface of 720sq ft. A new smoke box and single chimney were also fitted. Coronation-style outside steam pipes to all four cylinders were installed, sheathed in bulbous casings either side of the smoke box.

- **Cylinders/Valves/Motion** – layout of the cylinders and Walschaerts valve gear to the Coronation design, with the outside cylinders between the bogie wheels. Only the outside valve gear was used, the inside sets being driven by rocking levers behind the cylinders. The eccentric rods were fitted with ball bearing ends to the return cranks.

- **Cab/Wheels/Tender** – the cab underwent minor modifications to allow it to house the control layout of a reciprocating engine. The 6' 6'' size driving wheels were retained and refurbished. The original tender, number 9003, was reattached to the engine when reconstruction was completed.

THE DYNAMICS OF AN ACCIDENT AND ITS CONSEQUENCES

46202 AFTER HARROW

In considering the future of the three locomotives damaged at Harrow the focus of attention for engineers at Crewe should have been on one single issue – are the engines repairable and is it cost effective to do so. Rightly or wrongly Riddles's design team, in their desire to continue development of their own Class 8 Pacific, took the opportunity offered by the 46202's damaged state to justify developing 71000, *Duke of Gloucester*, at great cost and with hardly any benefits accruing. Sadly, few papers have survived in public hands that map the debates that took place and describe the decision-making process that led to 46202 and 45637 being scrapped, whereas 46242 was repaired. And later biographies steer clear of the

issue, simply conveying the message that two engines were beyond economic repair. This lack of transparency gave rise to speculation that the process was seriously flawed and 46202 should not have been scrapped.

In his report on the accident Lieutenant Colonel Wilson concluded that:

' *…engine No 46202 did not suffer so severely as the other two (engines) which had taken the main shock.'*

This was a view shared by many witnesses at the time, including engineers and locomen at Camden, Crewe and Edge Hill, who were surprised that 46202 was not restored to working order. If detailed survey reports had survived, things might be clearer, but in their absence Wilson's cursory summary is all that remains:

'The structural and other damage to engine No 46202 was also severe and extensive and included the buckling of the main frames and the fracture of the bogie centre pivot casting; the frame of the rear carrying truck was also broken. The tender, which was still coupled to the overturned engine was more or less upright on its wheels on the remains of the platform; it was heavily damaged at the rear presumably as the leading coach was driven against it, and its frames were buckled.'

In the accident 46242 suffered three major collisions: hitting the back of the commuter train where the main force of impact was absorbed by carriages that buckled, so offering some protection for the engine, then being hit

by a 740 ton load travelling at about 50mph. Finally, some carriages from the Liverpool train careered past their prone locomotives, piling upwards then bringing a pedestrian bridge down before burying *City of Glasgow* in debris. The first impact would have been the lesser of the two head-on collisions, but it drove the engine downwards and to the right, into the path of the Liverpool Express. 45637 hit 46242 nearly head on, but the lower profile of 46242 lifted the northbound train up and away to its left and through the platform onto her side, dragging 46202 with her. The second engine was saved from a head-on collision by this motion, but 45637 took the brunt of the impact, fore and aft, as a result, her tender providing some cushioning effect to protect 46202, whose tender in turn gave the locomotive some protection from the carriages piling up behind, their lighter structures collapsing and compressing in concertina style, absorbing even more energy. So it is understandable that Wilson believed 46202 had received the lightest damage of the three engines. His professional skills, his knowledge of the dynamics of this accident and his assessment of each locomotive's condition meant that no other conclusion seemed possible.

Despite the extreme damage caused by the two collisions, 46202 was the best placed of the three engines involved to 'survive' such an appalling accident. This fact was borne out by the survival of her driver and fireman, with only minor injuries, and the death of three out of four footplate crew on 46242 and 45637, such was the extent of the damage their engines sustained.

To underline this Wilson provided a detailed assessment of 46242 and 45637's condition:

'Except for the boiler, engine No 45637 was practically reduced to scrap. The bogie was wrecked and its component parts scattered, and the buffer beam and the frames folded back as far as the leading coupled wheels. All three cylinder castings were smashed, and the tyre was broken off the right hand leading coupled wheel centre, which was itself fractured in several places. There was also heavy damage at the rear end as the tender was driven into it…. The tender tank was torn

Having been pulled clear of the debris and set upright in a nearby siding, the full extent of the damage to 46202 could be assessed. Considering the force absorbed by the engine, the damage does not appear severe. (BR/RH)

46202 is slowly dismantled ready for transfer to Crewe. The impression that the damage was repairable is given support by the apparent condition of the component parts gradually being uncovered. (BR/RH)

from the main framing and turned upside down, and one of the distorted side frame plates was found underneath engine No 46202 as it lay on its side.'

The damage sustained was so severe that 45637 was quickly condemned as beyond economic repair and scrapped at Crewe.

There was never any intention of rebuilding her, but she was not offered up as a compensating saving against the construction of Riddles's new Pacific either.

'No 46242 must have dealt a severe vertical blow to the track as it plunged into the local train. It was derailed to the right on the Down Fast line and came to rest more or less upright. The tender was overturned to the left, and had crushed the left hand side of the engine cab as it was slewed at right angles to the track. From the heavy damage which the engine sustained at the front, particularly at the right hand side, it was clear that it had been struck directly by the leading engine of the Liverpool train.

'…twisted rods and other motion were cut away. The main frames were severely buckled, and the front end of the right hand frame plate was torn away from the inside cylinder casting and that the right hand outside cylinder and steam chest were smashed. The crushing of the comparatively light smoke box plating had saved the boiler from serious structural damage, though the front tube plate was bent.

'The main damage (to the boiler) was concentrated at the smoke box end. The header casting was fractured at the tube plate flange and had been forced upward. The header flange for the right steam pipe had also been smashed off and the pipe was

46202 stripped and ready to be towed north. (BR/RH)

badly flattened and twisted and the smoke box side was folded tightly round it. The left smoke box steam-pipe had snapped off at the weld adjacent to the top flange. The twin outlet snub for the tube cleaner and atomiser steam pipes had snapped off and the cleaner pipe was broken off behind the cone.

'The upper section of the blower pipe was fractured behind the cone adjacent to the header connection and had also been wrenched out of the bottom flange. The lower section had been wrenched from the "Tee" connection to the twin blast pipes.'

In addition, the tender, cab, the remaining cylinders and motion were badly damaged, but the sideways and upwards movement of the two engines pulling the Liverpool train, following the second collision, saved 46242 from more severe damage and left her driving wheels largely intact. Even so, photographs reveal that she was in a very sorry state when re-railed after the accident.

Any debate about the engine's future lasted until early summer 1953 when repairs were finally authorised, by which time her boiler had been refurbished and, during February, attached to 46254, following a period of 'Light Casual' repair. Her tender, No 9816, had also been repaired in advance of a decision being made about

46242's future and sat in sidings at Crewe until needed. In late 1953 it was reattached to the now restored *City of Glasgow* and remained with her until both were scrapped in November 1963.

It seems that managers at Crewe were far from certain whether 46242 should be repaired and stripped of anything repairable for re-use, in expectation of an instruction to scrap the remains. 46202 was held in limbo in the same way. Her boiler and tender were repaired and eventually reallocated: the former to 46212 in 1954 and the latter to 8F number 48134, sometime later. But this was much slower than 46242, suggesting that *Princess Anne* was considered to be a better option for repair, once the two wrecks had been assessed.

Apart from Wilson's superficial statement little now remains to confirm how badly damaged 46202 was, except the briefly stated opinions of witnesses to the process, an analysis of photographic records and the modelling of damage likely to be inflicted during high-speed collisions of this nature. But Wilson's opinion is clear: 46202 was not subject to the same violent collision as the other two engines and was not damaged as severely. Other witnesses confirm this and believe she was repairable, or a more manageable project than 46242. The survival of her crew, with only slight injuries, the rapid repair of two of her major components – boiler and tender – and the apparent lack of terminal damage to other major components suggest that she could have been returned to traffic quickly and cost effectively if so desired.

Photographs can only act as a guide and do not reveal the depth of damage to metal components. Ultrasound, close inspection and testing or simply the skills of experienced engineers are required for this to be exposed. Nevertheless, the photographs of 46202 at Harrow and later at Crewe do reveal many details. It seems that the following work may have been required to bring the engine back to operational condition:

- **Boiler** – as a result of the collision the smoke box plating was badly distorted. This would probably have caused some damage to the internal fittings (for example, the petticoat, blast pipe and saddle, steam pipe, tube plate, superheater elements and so on). The smokebox door and ring were ripped away, but the rest of the boiler – casing, tubes and fittings back to the firebox – seem to have survived the crash well. The complete boiler was salvaged, a new smoke box fitted and the rest repaired without any significant difficulty or excessive cost being incurred (the primary calculation being, is it cheaper to repair or replace with a new unit).
- **Frames and components** – these are designed to not only withstand the severe stresses and strains of normal operational running but also to absorb some of the excessive amounts of energy generated by collisions – fore, aft, above and below and from each side – and provide protection. Basically they are designed to be strong, but flex and cushion when necessary. In 46202's case the frames seem to have sustained most damage under the cab and around the front bogie where the impact was most severe. In his report Wilson describes the main frames as 'buckling'. However, the engine's chassis, stripped of the boiler and other parts, was capable of running, under tow and at low speed, from Harrow to Crewe, with two sets of driving wheels and a replacement front bogie in place. This suggests that Wilson's

cursory survey may have overstated the extent of the buckling of the main frames and the damage caused to the bogie centre pivot casting. In reality the basic integrity of the structure may not have been unduly compromised (it is hard to imagine that the operations department or engineers from Crewe would have allowed the loco to run if there was any risk and with public scrutiny at its height). Major repairs to frames (cutting off sections and welding or bolting on new ones) were not unusual and 46202 may have needed some such work; at most to replace the obviously damaged rear and forward sections around the leading and trailing trucks. In fact, the Princess Class had, in 1952, just begun a repair programme that saw the front 16 ft of their frames being cut away and replaced with new sections, butt-welded onto the remaining pieces.

- **Cylinders/Valves/Motion** Impact damage appears slight, considering the ferocity of the collision, but as

Windward Islands, in comparison to the other locomotives, was reduced to so much scrap metal and the cutter's torch was the only viable option. (BR/RH)

City of Glasgow emerges from under a huge pile of debris to be set on her wheels and made ready for survey. These photographs provide an interesting comparison with those of 46202. From a cursory view the damage appears more severe. Like the other Pacific, 46242 was broken down to component parts for transport to Crewe. (BR/RH)

the moving parts were brought to a very violent stop they would have suffered accordingly: distortions, hairline cracks and breakages. All parts connected to the driving wheels had to be isolated or removed to allow 46202 to be towed to Crewe. In the absence of a survey report it is safe to assume that complete replacement or major rebuilding of these components would have been required.

- **Leading and trailing trucks** The leading truck was torn away during the accident and a temporary unit was fitted to allow 46202 to move northwards to Crewe. The trailing truck was removed before this journey. As both units had taken the brunt of the collision they would both have required replacement or major repair.
- **Wheels/Axles/Axle boxes/Horn gaps/Springs** All subject to excessive shock and some impact damage (principally on the left-hand side as the engine drove through the platform, demolishing it). But as the chassis was capable of being towed, the level of damage may have been lighter than expected and repair relatively straightforward.

- **Brakes/Sanding gear/Other engine controls** All damaged to some extent and repairs necessary.
- **Tender** The damage proved to be fairly limited and the tender was repaired and attached to another locomotive once 46202 had been condemned.
- **Cab** Buckled by the collision and repair necessary.

- **Buffer/Boiler cladding/Running plates** All damaged and requiring repair.

This list is not exhaustive and other minor items would have required repair or replacement as well, but their cost would have been slight in comparison to the major components likely to have been damaged: boiler, frames, tender, cylinders, trucks, driving wheels and motion.

   The list of repairs would have been extensive, but probably no greater than 46242's would have been, possibly less, and cost a similar amount. So scrapping her does seem unnecessary, unless the frames were more severely damaged than expected, but this is unlikely considering the engine's chassis was capable of being towed from Harrow to Crewe. One can only conclude that repair was possible and cost effective, but she became a victim of Riddles' plan to develop a new Pacific engine at a cost more than five times greater than 46202's estimated repairs (£44,000 as compared to a possible £8,000) or nearly twice as much to build another Coronation Class engine (the last one built in1948 costing £21,400). So a simple 'write-off' to allow accountants a compensating value to offset 71000's exorbitant development and construction costs proved to be 46202's fate.

6202/46202 – SERVICE HISTORY 1935–52

Summary of Repairs and Modifications

Date taken out of traffic	Date to traffic	Weekdays out of traffic	Class of repair (Note 1)	Mileage since new	Boiler (Note 2)	Work carried out by:	Cost of repairs (£.s.d) (Note 3)	Cause/summary of work (New construction: total cost = £18,765)
25 June 1935	29 June 1935	4	LO			LMS Crewe/ Metrovick	230.0.0	Repairs/adjustments to turbines.
6 August 1935	Not recorded		LO			LMS Crewe	Not recorded	Oil leakage from turbine bearings and ingress of water in roller bearing axle boxes. Oil seals modified.
24 September 1935	21 December 1935	77	LO	9,164		LMS Crewe/ Metrovick	546.0.0	Reversing mechanism failed. Complete overhaul of reverse turbine and reversing mechanism. Forward turbine and gears examined. The cost of £546 includes £242 for work by Metrovick.
15 January 1936	4 February 1936	18	LO	12,644		LMS Crewe/ Metrovick	92.0.0	Reverse turbine failed. Turbine and clutch repaired. Main and reverse steam valves examined.
15 March 1936	24 June 1936	35	LO	40,653		LMS Crewe/ Metrovick	602.0.0	Reverse turbine failed. Complete overhaul of reverse turbine. Forward turbine, main gear and control gear examined.
14 July 1936	31 July 1936	16	HO	45,668	1	LMS Crewe/ Metrovick	813.0.0 (LMS) 1,301.0.0 (LMS) 242.0.0 (Met)	Leakage of oil from turbine bearings. Repaired at the same time as the engine was given a heavy overhaul, including a new boiler with a 40 element superheater (cost £1,301).
28 January 1937	13 April 1937	64	LO	78,812	4	LMS Crewe/ Metrovick	990.0.0 (LMS) 514.0.0 (Met)	Failure of forward turbine. Complete overhaul at Metrovick's factory in Manchester. Reverse turbine, main gear train and oil system examined. All wheels taken out for tyres to be turned. Spring, brake gear and coupling rods repaired.

Date taken out of traffic	Date to traffic	Weekdays out of traffic	Class of repair (Note 1)	Mileage since new	Boiler (Note 2)	Work carried out by:	Cost of repairs (£.s.d) (Note 3)	Cause/summary of work (New construction: total cost = £18,765)
18 October 1937	11 November 1937	21	LO	122,127		LMS Crewe/ Metrovick	505.0.0	Routine repairs and attention. Alterations to control gear, flexible coupling and control box. Ventilation louvre added to the turbine casing. Tender wheels turned.
29 November 1937	16 December 1937	15	LO	125,791		LMS Crewe/ Metrovick		Failure of reverse turbine. Complete overhaul and repair.
2 June 1938	24 October 1938	123	LO	158,502	4	LMS Crewe/ Metrovick	Not costed against 6202 schedule	Routine repair and inspection programme of work. Both turbines overhauled. Larger oil drain pipes fitted to forward turbine thrust bearings. Distant reading indicator fitted to main oil tank. All engine and tender tyres turned. Forty small tubes changed. All superheater flue tubes re-expanded and beaded. 532 steel stay nuts changed. Firebox seams fullered.
8 February 1939	31 July 1939	147	LO	177,413	4	LMS Crewe/ Metrovick	279.0.0 (LMS)	Failure of forward turbine. Complete repair undertaken at Metrovick's Manchester factory. Also gears examined and reverse turbine bearings renewed. New design control box fitted and control rods overhauled. New top frame bars fitted to leading bogie and springs changed. Smoke deflectors fitted.
21 September 1939	24 July 1941					LMS Crewe/ Metrovick	Not costed	Withdrawn from traffic for storage due to war conditions. Reactivation preceded by condition survey and a maintenance period to make the engine ready for operational use. Work completed not listed or costed against 6202's schedule.
17 September 1941	14 July 1942	257	LO	195,370	4	LMS Crewe/ Metrovick	287.0.0 (LMS) 68.0.0 (Met)	Reverse turbine failed. Reverse turbine completely overhauled by Metrovick at their Manchester factory. Additional Worthington pump fitted to augment the oil supply to the reverse turbine unit.
1 August 1943	8 August 1943	7	LO	198,237	4	LMS Crewe	62.0.0 (LMS)	Light casual repair – no further details available.
21 November 1942	9 January 1943	42	LO	219,261	4	LMS Crewe/ Metrovick	133.0.0 (LMS)	Oil leakage from both turbines. Repaired following examination.

Date taken out of traffic	Date to traffic	Weekdays out of traffic	Class of repair (Note 1)	Mileage since new	Boiler (Note 2)	Work carried out by:	Cost of repairs (£.s.d) (Note 3)	Cause/summary of work (New construction: total cost = £18,765)
11 June 1943	22 September 1944	402	HG	249,261	2	LMS Crewe/ Metrovick	3,023.0.0 (LMS) 753.0.0 (Met)	Failure to flexible drive between slow speed gear wheel and driving axle. Following examination, heavy general repair programme authorised. This work included overhaul of both turbines, gears and drive.
18 December 1944	18 January 1945	27	LO	252,473	4	LMS Crewe/ Metrovick	65.0.0 (LMS)	Reverse turbine failure. Blockage to oil passage caused during heavy general repair.
12 April 1945	1 June 1945	43	LO	270,233	4	LMS Crewe/ Metrovick	334.0.0 (LMS)	Oil leakage from turbine bearings. Both turbines removed from the frames for examination and repair.
12 July 1945	25 July 1945	12	LO	296,903	4	LMS Crewe	377.0.0	Light casual repair – no details exist of work carried out.
9 March 1946	8 April 1947	337	HG	306,683	2	LMS Crewe/ Metrovick	4,343.0.0	Heavy general repair – no details exist of work carried out (Metrovick's costs are included in £4,343).
16 August 1947	9 September 1947	21	NC	333,984	4	LMS Crewe	109.0.0 (LMS)	Work carried out marked 'Not classified'.
23 September 1947	15 October 1947	20	NC	334,444		LMS Crewe	78.0.0	Work carried out marked 'Not classified'. During the repair period, an additional oil tank was fitted.
5 December 1947	3 January 1948	25	LO	345,913	4	BR Crewe	172.0.0	Light casual repair during which an additional oil tank was fitted.
16 April 1948	10 March 1949	280	LC	369,014		BR Crewe/ Metrovick	2,059.0.0	No record remains to confirm the extent of work carried out during this expensive and prolonged period in the Works. It is assumed that the turbines needed work and spent a considerable time at Metrovick's factory, possibly waiting for spare parts to be manufactured. The locomotive was painted in black livery at the end of this maintenance period.
13 June 1949	22 June 1949	9	LC	382,286	4	BR Crewe or shed	134.0.0	Light casual repair. No further details available.
27 September 1949	14 October 1949	16	NC	402,988	4	BR Crewe or shed	106.0.0	Work carried out marked 'Not classified'.
21 December 1949	17 January 1950	22	LC	414,577	4	BR Crewe or shed	183.0.0	Light casual repair. No further details available.

Date taken out of traffic	Date to traffic	Weekdays out of traffic	Class of repair (Note 1)	Mileage since new	Boiler (Note 2)	Work carried out by:	Cost of repairs (£.s.d) (Note 3)	Cause/summary of work (New construction: total cost = £18,765)
18 February 1950	23 February 1950	4	NC	421,624	4	BR Crewe or shed	37.0.0	Work carried out marked 'Not classified'.
17 March 1950	13 March 1950	4	NC	436,902	4	BR Crewe or shed	103.0.0	Work carried out marked 'Not classified'.
6 May 1950	15 August 1952	708	HG	442,320 (Note 4)	2	BR Crewe	6250.0.0 (estimated)	Heavy general repair and conversion from turbine to reciprocating engine.
8 October 1952	22 May 1954			453,736		BR Crewe		Locomotive seriously damaged at Harrow on 8 October 1952 and scrapped on 22 May 1954 (tender and boiler salvaged and repaired).

Notes

1. Class of repair – definitions:
LO – Light
HO – Heavy
NC – Not classified
HG – Heavy General

2. Action with boiler when engine in the workshop:
1. New boiler fitted
2. Boiler changed
3. Boiler lifted and put back after maintenance completed
4. Boiler repaired on frames

3. Cost of repairs:
The costing information contained on the surviving Engine History Cards is incomplete, so cannot be regarded as a wholly accurate account. For example, only some of Metrovick's costs have been recorded on these documents (of course, Metrovick may not have charged for some work, particularly when Turbomotive was under test and the project was regarded as a joint exercise. The phrases 'let the costs fall where they may' and 'loss leader' spring to mind). In addition, most costs incurred at sheds in correcting defects are not covered in detail, although the cost of the fitter who was a permanent part of the footplate crew can be calculated. Undoubtedly a very detailed maintenance record, containing all approvals for work and costing information, would have been kept at Crewe or Euston, but these files do not seem to have survived.

4. Turbomotive's mileage:
There is some difficulty in assessing the locomotive's mileage from the Engine History Cards. The method of recording mileages, linked to periods in works, presents a confused picture. At the end of the engine's life someone has written: 'Miles run as a turbine locomotive = 458,772.' From all the individual figures collated from the maintenance record the total figure would seem to be 442,320. If this is the case, the engine as a turbine and then a reciprocating locomotive ran a total of 453,763 miles.

TURBOMOTIVE – A USER'S GUIDE

Each railway company issued generic instructions and guidance to their footplate crews on managing, driving and firing locomotives. For obvious reasons it had to be a rigorous process, especially at a time when there were so few external aids to assist each crew. A great deal rested on the level of skill and fitness of these men, who have been described as the largest group of independent, unregulated, specialist workers in Britain. Turbomotive being a non-standard type warranted additional instructions for the driver and fireman, but also the fitter who always rode on the footplate.

In April 1935, using a draft provided by Ljungstrom for footplate crew operating the Swedish turbine 2-8-0, the LMS issued their first set of instruction to 6202's crew. In time, as experience developed, they would be refined and improved:

'TURBOMOTIVE FOR LMS RAILWAY
'E.R.O. 62011 (April 1935)
'Operating Instructions

'Notes on General Care and Operation
'Care should be taken that drains work effectively at all times

'It is important that the hand operated drains should be operated according to the prescribed routine.

'Lubricating System
'The efficient lubrication of the turbine bearings and of the gears is of the utmost importance, and care must be taken that it is, at all times, in satisfactory order.

'Special care must be taken that the oil is kept clean and particularly that make-up oil is clean'Lubrication is effected by a closed forced oiling system in which two oil pumps draw oil from a sump tank and pass it, under pressure, through all the bearings and through sprayers on to the gear teeth.

'One pump is situated in the gear casing. This is a reversible gear wheel pump, driven by the main slow speed gear wheel through a small increasing gear. This pump consequently, only works when the engine is moving, and the pressure and quality of the oil delivery will vary with the speed of the engine. A second pump supplements the gear pump oil supply at all times, and particularly at starting and when run slowly. This is a steam driven reciprocating pump and is supported on a bracket below the footplate at the front of the engine on the left-hand side.

'The oil from this pump, together with a small proportion of the oil from the gear pump, is passed through a cooler (air radiator type) before reaching the bearings. A strainer in the oil sump tank at the suction branch to the pumps ensures continuous straining from the oil. The strainer is of the "auto clean" type, and can be cleaned at any time by turning the handle on the top through one revolution. It should be periodically removed completely from the tank and thoroughly cleaned.

'A dirty oil strainer may be indicated by a fall in oil pressure, although this might also indicate an air leak on the suction side of the pump.

'An oil pressure gauge is provided in the driver's cab, and this should be watched by the Enginemen.

'The oil in the system should occasionally be drained from the tank and filtered, after which it can be used again for "topping up".

'GENERAL

'Careful attention should be given to the routine procedure which is outlined below:-

'Before leaving shed

'1. Inspect oil level in tank and "top up", if necessary, to level of overflow cock. Occasionally drain off water by partially unscrewing drain plug.

'2. Give auto-clean strainer a turn.

'3. Open all drain cocks by means of lever in cab.

'4. Inspect control box in cab to check the following:

'(a). All turbine control valves are shut.

'(b). Safety handle is in running position.

'(c). Reverse level is in the required position.

'5. Frequently oil the reversing shaft and links of the reverse turbine bearing engine.

'6. Frequently oil universal couplings on the control rods from the driver's side.

'7. Periodic attention:

'(a). Oil the oil ways in the steam chest cam housing with cylinder oil.

'(b). Use grease gun to nipples on control rod bracket bearings and control rod bevel gear boxes.

'8. Fill up the sight feed lubrication box of the reciprocating oil pump.

'9. Immediately before starting, open reciprocating pump drain cocks, start up the reciprocating oil pump (42 double strokes per minute, 7 drops lubricant per minute). Check oil pressure gauge in cab. Close oil pump steam cylinder drain cocks when all the water has been cleared.

'To start

'1. Open main steam regulator (this does not start engine).

'2. Admit steam to turbines by starting handle on the control box.

'3. Close drain cocks.

'During running

'1. Check oil pressure on pressure gauge in cab.

'2. For method of controlling speed, see separate notes on driving.

'To stop

'1. Close all control valves and apply brake in the usual way. Main regulator must **not** be closed.

'2. Open all drain cocks.

'3. Check oil level in the tank as opportunity occurs.

'The reciprocating pump should only be shut down if the stop is of lengthy duration. If it has been shut down it is necessary to:-

'4. Open reciprocating pump steam cylinder drain cocks.

'5. When standing for any length of time, or when engine is put away, close main regulator.

'NOTES ON DRIVING

'The Control Box has 3 controls, namely:

'(a). Driving handle.

'(b). Reversing lever.

'(c). Safety handle.

'Driving Forward

'The position of the controls should be as follows:

'(a). Driving handle in zero position on indicator.

'(b). Reversing handle in "forward running" position.

'(c). Safety handle in "running" position.

'Then operate as follows:-

'1. Open the main regulator.

'2. Open the turbine control valves by turning the starting handle clockwise notch by notch until the engine moves.

'Speed Control

'The speed is regulated by opening or closing a control valve by turning the driving handle one notch forward or back, as required.

'The main steam regulator should be fully open all the time the engine is running.

'Stopping

'(a). Shut all turbine control valves (driving handle back to zero).

'(b). Apply brakes.

'(c). Close main steam regulator if stop is of some duration.

'Coupling the reverse turbine for reversing

'(a). Close all control valves (driving handle back to zero).

'(b). Raise safety handle from "running" to "locking" position.

'(c). Pull reverse lever from "forward gear" to "reverse

gear" position. This engages the coupling between reversing turbine and gear pinion. If the teeth of the two portions of the coupling are opposite one another, the coupling may not fully engage first time, but will do so at the second or third attempt.

'(d). Lower safety handle to the "running" position.

'Reversing

'The position of the controls should be as follows:

'(a). Drive handle in the zero position.

'(b). Reverse lever in the "reversing gear" position.

'(c). Safety handle in the "running" position.

'Then operate as follows:

'Open reverse turbine control valves by turning the driving handle anti-clockwise, notch by notch, until the engine moves. Further procedure as for forward driving.

'Slipping of Wheels

'If slipping occurs, close the turbine control valves, and apply sand as necessary. When slipping has ceased, re-open turbine control valves as required.'

Initially a separate instruction for the 'footplate' fitter was not considered necessary, suggesting that this post was only thought necessary when 6202 entered service. There is no evidence to suggest that this was at the suggestion of the Running Department or the CME:

'EXAMINATION OF, AND ATTENTION TO, 4-6-2 TURBINE ENGINE 6202, TO BE CARRIED OUT BY THE FITTER

'Handle on top or oil strainer to be turned daily.

'After the engine has been standing, without pumps working, for the maximum possible period, draw off all water which has separated out from the oil, by means of the cock provided at the bottom of the oil tank, **daily before the auxiliary oil pumps are started up.**

'Inspect the oil level in the sump daily removing all water and top up, if necessary.

'Leather bags on driving axle to be drained of water daily.

'See that the following Drain Cocks are open:

'Forward turbine cylinder high-pressure end.

'Forward turbine cylinder low-pressure end.

'Steam chests for forward and reverse turbine.

'Drain sump in base of smoke box saddle casting.

'To Test Oil Pumps

'Open the L-H auxiliary oil drain cocks and start up the pumps at a rate of about:

'L-H pump 20 double strokes per minute.

'R-H pump 10 double strokes per minute.

'The pressure on the oil gauges, which should be registered while the engine is standing and the auxiliary pump working, is about 7lbs per sq inch.

'When the water has been cleared from the pipes and cylinder, partially close the pump drain cocks of L-H auxiliary pump.

'Attention to Turbines, Gears, Auxiliary Pumps etc with Boiler Full

'Open all drain cocks.

'Shut down auxiliary oil pumps after engine has been standing for about half an hour.

'Open drain cocks on pumps.

'Check forward turbine thrust bearing indicator.

'Examination at Wash Out and Firebox Examination with Boiler Full

'Oil strainer and magnets to be removed and cleaned.

'Oil ways in steam chest cam housing to be oiled with cylinder oil.

'Nipples on control rod bracket bearings and control rod bevel gear boxes to be greased.

'Nipple on control rods between driver's cab and turbine to be oiled.

'Examination at 6,000 Miles

'Oil in sump to be drained off and oil system cleaned and refilled with clean oil, every 6,000 miles.

'Feed water tubes to be cleaned.

'Inspection plates over reverse turbine rotor bearing and cover plate on reverse turbine exhaust casting to be taken off to inspect turbine bearings and blades. "Timken" roller bearings to be checked for oil and refilled where necessary.'

REFERENCE SOURCES

The primary sources of information for this book are the R.A. Hillier Collection and the A. Ewer Collection. These archives have been supplemented by material from a number of institutions and online sites. Various books, magazines and journals have also been consulted. These are:

Institutions

1. National Railway Museum (York)
    Records Consulted –
        Loco/Expt/1.
        Test/LMS/21.
        Test/Expt/1.
        The E.A. Langridge Collection.
        The E.S. Cox Collection.
        The Robert Riddles Collection.

2. The Institution of Mechanical Engineers (London)
    Records Consulted –
        Record of Proceedings (1935–1952).
        Sir William Stanier's personal copy of the 1933 concept document he and Sir Henry Guy prepared and presented to the boards of the LMS and Metrovick.

3. National Archives Online Discovery Site
    Records Consulted –
        File AN 172/261.

Online Research Facilities Consulted

- **Steam Index –** An excellent website that contains the extensive results of many areas of railway research.
An invaluable, and growing, source of information.
- **The Railway Archive –** Of equal status to Steam Index, especially in its coverage of railway accidents.
- **Rail Online –** An excellent source for steam locomotive photographs.
- **Rail Photo Prints –** Also an excellent source of photographs.

Books and Other Publications Consulted

LMS Locomotive Profiles produced jointly by Wild Swan Publications and the National Railway Museum:
    Number 4 – *The Princess Royal Pacifics* (ISBN 1 874103 86 0).
    Number 11 – *The Coronation Class Pacifics* (ISBN 978 1 905184 46 0).
O.S. Nock – *Sir William Stanier – An Engineering Biography* (1964). *LMS Steam* (ISBN 07153 5240 7).
H.C.B. Rogers – *The Last Steam Locomotive Engineer – R A Riddles* (ISBN 0 04 385053 7).
I. Sixsmith – *The Book of the Princess Royals* (ISBN 1 903266 01 7).
A.C. Baker – *The Book of the Coronation Pacifics* (ISBN 978 1 906919 17 7).
H.A.V. Bulleid – *Master Builders of Steam* (1965).
J.E. Chacksfield – *Sir William Stanier. A New Biography* (ISBN 0 85361 576 4).
E.S. Cox – *Locomotive Panorama* (two volumes) (1965/66).
R. Bond – *A Lifetime With Locomotives* (ISBN 0 900404 30 2). 'Paper 458 presented to the Institution of Locomotive Engineers in 1946'.
E.A. Langridge – *Under 10 CMEs* (two volumes) (ISBN 978 0 85361 7013).
The LMS Journal – Volumes 10 and 11.
The Railway Gazette (1933–1940).
The Meccano Magazine (1935–1940).
The Engineer (1935–1940).

INDEX